1, murder

2 Gonzalo

3, Saliar

4, song

5, Gonzalo

6, forgiveness

7, Miranda

8, Ariel

9, Ariel.

ESSAYS ON SHAKESPEARE

ESSAYS ON SHAKESPEARE

Edited by *GORDON ROSS SMITH*

THE PENNSYLVANIA STATE
UNIVERSITY PRESS

UNIVERSITY PARK   LONDON

1965

Library of Congress Catalog Card Number 65-18461
Copyright © 1965 by The Pennsylvania State University
All rights reserved

Printed in the United States of America by The Colonial Press Inc.

Designed by Glenn Ruby

PREFACE

Gentle Will seems to have been one of the most tolerant of men; so his friends once testified, and we can believe it from his works. It therefore seemed appropriate that a volume of essays to honor his memory should not be assembled around some arbitrary theme, but rather that every person invited to contribute should be free to write upon whatever aspect of Shakespeare he pleased. If economic man and political man work best when they are free of arbitrary pressure and direction, so must scholarly and intellectual men, and though no one need contribute against his will to a theme-oriented *Festschrift,* many men will in good faith try something which their hearts are not in. The result is like the architecture of an army camp: uniform but squalid. *Carte blanche,* of course, is no guarantee of merit, but the committee charged with assembling these papers were agreed that the best chance of getting worthwhile papers lay in allowing authors full freedom of subject and treatment. By sheer accident the papers have fallen into a limited group of subjects, and they have been grouped accordingly, but the authors differ among themselves on many points, and the merit of each writer's argument is for the reader to decide.

I am much indebted to the other members of the Pennsylvania State University English Department committee, Professors Wilfred Jewkes, Harrison T. Meserole, and Paul West, for assistance in reading these papers and for giving me the benefit of their judgments.

G. R. S.

8 September 1964

CONTENTS

ESSAYS ON SHAKESPEARE

MERCUTIO, MINE OWN SON THE DENTIST

NORMAN N. HOLLAND

> *Yet sit and see,*
> *Minding true things by what their mock'ries be.*
> *Henry V*

"He has long outlived his century, the term commonly fixed as the test of literary merit"—so Dr. Johnson in 1765. Now he has outlived four centuries, and we pay tribute to him for having done so. When we pay tribute to him, we celebrate an imagination with a magnificent capacity for uniting things: the two traditions of his own day, popular and courtly; the most primitive functions of the human mind and the most intellectual—though every poet does that. More important for crossing centuries, he was able to span realism and nonrealism, "true things" and "their mock'ries." That is, Shakespeare could transmute his own realistic experience localized in space and time, by somehow informing it with a nonrealistic, unlocalized significance. So informed, his characters from the sixteenth century can become part of the realistic experience of others four centuries later in states unborn and accents yet unknown. But how? How, despite the appalling weight of respectability and three centuries of criticism, indeed, an entire industry, can Shakespeare still appeal to an audience that has never seen or heard Shakespeare before? The Central Park Shakespeares are the obvious case in point.

Nowadays, they are a form of middle-class and middlebrow entertainment in midtown Manhattan, but, in 1957, when Mr. Papp first began the series, the company traveled around the city playing in the small parks of Queens or the Bronx or, even, I suspect, Staten Island. They were playing to audiences many of whom had never seen a live actor before, most of whom had never seen Shakespeare before, and all of whom must have found such matters as doublet, rapier, and the Elizabethan world picture as foreign as armadillos. They were, nevertheless, excited, pleased, identifying audiences who unabashedly rooted for the characters they liked. Especially enthusiastic, according to the *New Yorker*,[1] were the grandmothers on their campstools. Quite delighted by Mercutio at a moment when he was playfully slapping the Nurse's backside, one elderly lady leaned to her neighbor and stage-whispered, "Like mine own son the dentist. A real chektah!"

Shakespeare, I think, would have been pleased, but most of his twentieth-century critics would not. The lady shows the same bridging quality we admire in Shakespeare himself—in her phrase, "a real character," she has managed to put back together something our century of critics has pulled apart, namely, the Shakespearean character. She can see Mercutio both as real ("like mine own son the dentist") and as a character (if you will pardon her pun). As for today's critics, most insist that Shakespeare's plays are mythic, thematic, stylized, in short, antirealistic, and so are the people in them. Few today hold the older view—that his plays realistically portray realistic people in realistic situations.

Throughout the neoclassical period, though, most critics held that Shakespeare's characters were like, or, for all practical purposes, the same as, real people. A minor, but earliest example is Margaret Cavendish describing in 1664 how "he Presents Passions so Naturally, and Misfortunes so Probably, as he Peirces the Souls of his Readers with such a True Sense and Feeling thereof, that it Forces Tears through their Eyes, and almost Perswades them, they are Really Actors, or at least Present at those Tragedies." Dennis and Rymer and Voltaire took the contrary view, but the main line of English critics came out resoundingly for the realism of Shakespeare's characters: Dryden, Pope, Lord Kames, and that most devious of critics, Dr. Johnson—"*Shakespeare* has no heroes: his scenes are occupied only by men, who act and speak as the reader thinks that he should himself have spoken or acted on the same occasion."

When, however, we turn from Johnson to Morgann, a dozen years later, we make a decisive shift into truly Romantic criticism of Shakespeare. That is, neoclassic critics like Johnson stressed our identification with the character, but Morgann saw the

4

Shakespearean character as an historical being outside ourselves:

> He boldly makes a character act and speak from those parts
> of the composition, which are *inferred* only, and not dis-
> tinctly shewn. This produces a wonderful effect: it seems
> to carry us beyond the poet to nature itself. . . . It may be
> fit [therefore] to consider them [the characters] rather as His-
> toric than Dramatic beings; and, when occasion requires, to
> account for their conduct from the whole of character, from
> general principles, from latent motives, and from policies
> not avowed.

This historical externalization, looking at the events described
by the text rather than the text itself, became the Romantic approach to Shakespeare. We see it in Goethe's remarks on *Hamlet*
in 1795, in almost all of Coleridge's Shakespeare criticism, much
of Hazlitt's, and on through the century in the effusions of Mrs.
Jameson, Victor Hugo, Pushkin, or Swinburne. The culminating
figure is, of course, Bradley. In our own time, this approach to
character has fallen into desuetude. Mostly, it survives only in
high-school teaching, the *New York Times Book Review,* and
the writings of Miss Mary McCarthy who, in this context, keeps
strange company indeed.

With one important exception (the psychoanalytic critics),
twentieth-century criticism has turned its back on Bradley and
all his works. Though, oddly enough, Edgar Allan Poe was the
first to rebel against the nineteenth-century view and insist that
Shakespeare's characters should not be treated as real people, the
locus classicus for this point of view is L. C. Knight's 1933 essay,
"How Many Children Had Lady Macbeth?" He took the basic
twentieth-century position: the main business of the critic is to
examine the words on the page and " 'character'—like 'plot,'
'rhythm,' 'construction,' and all our other critical counters—is
merely an abstraction from the total response in the mind of the
reader or spectator, brought into being by written or spoken
words" and entitled to no separate validity. Although Kenneth
Burke, Kenneth Muir, Edmund Wilson, C. S. Lewis, F. R. Leavis,
and many others take roughly the same view of Shakespeare, the
most explicit anti-character Shakespearean is, of course, G. Wil-

son Knight: "The persons, ultimately, are not human at all, but purely symbols of a poetic vision." Furthermore, in a rare instance of critical and scholarly congeniality, the critics have received aid and comfort from those of the persuasion of Professor E. E. Stoll who have shown how unrealistic Shakespeare's theater and conventions were—as a matter of historical fact. Essentially, the new and neo-new critics are insisting on the formal nature of a work of art, and they deny the reality of character not just in Shakespeare's plays but in all kinds of fictions, notably the naturalistic novel—the examples are legion: Leavis, Mark Schorer, Harry Levin, Virginia Woolf, E. M. Forster, T. S. Eliot. And not New Critics only—from the quite alien point of view of Marxist criticism, one could cite Lukács, or, in the visual arts, E. H. Gombrich. Even Freud, in his introduction to the "Dora" case, distinguishes between fictional editings of psychological reality and psychological reality as the psychiatrist sees it (though later psychoanalytic critics by and large have not followed Freud's dictum).

We have come, then, to an impasse. The old critics say we must think of Shakespeare's characters as real people; the new critics say we must not. Logically, we cannot have it both ways, and logic comes down squarely against treating the characters as real.

Literary characters exist in the contrived, shaped world of a work of art. Real people live in the unshaped world of everyday reality. It makes little sense to apply psychological concepts (Morgann's "general principles" of human nature) taken from the disorderly everyday world to a quite different world shaped by theme and form. In fact, literary characters are so shaped by the world in which they exist they cannot even be moved from book to book or play to play. One could not, for a crude example, move the characters from *Peanuts* to *Pogo,* nor would an Homeric hero fit in a tragedy of Euripides, nor one of Dostoevsky's possessed into the saner world of Tolstoy. Even similar characters created by the same author face trouble moving from one work to another. Falstaff would bulk too large in the romantic and pastoral world of *The Winter's Tale,* while Autolycus with his ribbons and laces could hardly parade on the field at Shrewsbury or masquerade as Mother Prat of Brainford. If even such adaptable con men as Falstaff and Autolycus cannot move from one

6

Shakespearean play to another, it seems to make still less sense to apply to both of them concepts of human nature from still a third world in which neither of them could be, namely, the real world.

Logically, it simply does not make sense to treat literary characters as real people. But does logic govern here? Or experience? H. L. Mencken had the answer. Because he was famous as an atheist, people liked to badger him on the subject, and one day a reporter asked him if he believed in infant baptism. Replied Mencken, "Believe in it? Hell, I've *seen* it!" And much the same thing is true of character analysis. Logically it is unsupportable, but I have seen, by the dozens, psychoanalytic studies which diagnose Shakespeare's characters as though they were real people on couch or in clinic; and these studies, even when they are contradictory, give ample, more than ample, evidence from the plays themselves. The psychoanalytic critics are indeed applying psychological concepts from the world of everyday reality to characters who exist in a wholly different kind of world—it should not work, but it does. I have even done it myself by analyzing Romeo's little three-line dream as though it had been dreamed by a real young man who had lost his virginity the night before. In fact, some of the elements in the dream led me beyond the sacrosanct words-on-the-page to infer in the discredited manner of Morgann certain things about the wedding night, though Shakespeare himself had tactfully drawn across them the curtain of the upper stage.

We have traveled a long way from that park in the Bronx where the grandmotherly lady on her campstool found Mercutio "like mine own son the dentist," and we need to travel further yet: to Smith College, where in 1944 two psychologists performed a quite remarkable experiment. To a group of undergraduates, they showed an animated cartoon which detailed the adventures of a large black triangle, a small black triangle, and a circle, the three of them moving in various ways in and out of a rectangle.[2] After the short came the main feature: the psychologists asked for comments, and the Smith girls, "with great uniformity," described the big triangle as "aggressive," "pugnacious," "mean," "temperamental," "irritable," "power-loving," "possessive," "quick to take offense," and "taking advantage of his size" (it was, after

all, the larger triangle). Eight percent even went so far as to conclude that this triangle had a low I.Q. Now, if Smith girls can see
that much in a triangle, how much more they—or a grandmother
—are likely to see in Mercutio!

In effect, the psychologists were finding experimental confirma-
tion for something Dr. Johnson with fine intuition had said about
tragedies long before:

> The reflection that strikes the heart is not, that the evils
> before us are real evils, but that they are evils to which we
> ourselves may be exposed. If there be any fallacy, it is not
> that we fancy the players, but that we fancy ourselves un-
> happy for a moment; but we rather lament the possibility
> than suppose the presence of misery, as a mother weeps over
> her babe, when she remembers that death may take it from
> her. . . . Imitations produce pain or pleasure, not because
> they are mistaken for realities, but because they bring reali-
> ties to mind.

From the somewhat different point of view of the Romantic
critic: "His plays have the force of things upon the mind," said
Hazlitt. "What he represents is brought home to the bosom as
a part of our experience, implanted in the memory as if we had
known the places, persons, and things of which he treats." And
we might put beside Hazlitt and Johnson, Proust:

> In reality, each reader reads only what is already within him-
> self. The book is only a sort of optical instrument which the
> writer offers to the reader to enable the latter to discover in
> himself what he would not have found but for the aid of the
> book. It is this reading within himself what is also in the
> book which constitutes the proof of the accuracy of the
> latter. . . .

Realism, like beauty, is in the eye of the beholder.

We can see this fact all too plainly as the realism of one age
becomes the academicism of the next. We can see it in ourselves
as, comparing notes with a friend with whom we have gone to the
movies, something seems "real" to us that he found "contrived."
And we see it with the grandmotherly lady in the park for whom
Mercutio, foreign as he must have seemed, was yet, "like mine

own son." She, like the author she was admiring, indeed, like her son the dentist, was a maker of bridges. But we are all such bridgemakers—we make the characters within ourselves, and we make them real or not real as we choose.

The wise man chooses to make them real, for how else could he experience the play, except by relating himself to the characters on the stage as people that he has known or been? From the lines we are hearing, we re-create the characters, the words on the page controlling and shaping the characters we create. Then, as in that writers' cliché, the characters "take on a life of their own," and they in turn shape and inform the words on the page. In short, we are not quasi-scientific observers of a phenomenon outside ourselves, historical as the Romantic critics would have it, or the words-on-the-page as the New Critic would have it. Rather, we are involved with the text and it with us in a way that demands the description of a harshly scientific word: feedback. We and the words-on-the page bind ourselves in the literary transaction, a process as mutual as any bargain. Once we accept this bridge, namely, that we in the audience make the characters real, we are in a position to see how a character like Mercutio can be both realistic and, as Wilson Knight would have him, "purely symbol[ic] of a poetic vision."

At first glance, Mercutio is outrageously unrealistic. I have known a lot of witty and literary people, and never have I known anyone who was as fluent in blank verse as Mercutio or who could while away the hours of an adolescent evening by coming up *ad lib* with something like the Queen Mab speech. But I have known many people like Mercutio in other ways. He is the classic joker: he pours out a perfect stream of puns, rhymes, and cheerful obscenities. I have known people like that, and so I suspect have you—and so has Romeo, for he recognizes Mercutio as a type: "He jests at scars that never felt a wound." But what type?

We can tell from the kind of joke he makes. He aims his wit at Tybalt's Italianate duello, a "new form," like the pose of courtly love, Romeo's initial "groaning" toward Rosaline which also draws Mercutio's fire. He can speak of "my gossip Venus" and "young Abraham Cupid"; he can accuse Romeo of thinking Laura a kitchen-wench, "Dido a dowdy, Cleopatra a gypsy, Helen and Hero hildings and harlots, Thisbe a grey eye or so, but not

9

to the purpose." Mercutio, in short, attacks idolatries. It is no coincidence (if we can believe the current chronology of the plays) that it is this one character who cut down the whole tradition of English fairy-lore from the Celtic fays of medieval romance, adult- or child-sized, to Queen Mab: no glamorous Titania or Oberon she, but, so prosaically, "No bigger than an agate stone on the forefinger of an alderman."

And yet, even as he tears down the gods and goddesses of others, he wishes himself to soar. In the very first words we hear him speak, he urges Romeo, who says he is feeling heavy, "Nay, gentle Romeo, we must have you dance," and he urges him to "borrow Cupid's wings and soar with them above a common bound," to "beat love down" as he himself does. The epitaph Benvolio gives him is all too fitting:

> That gallant spirit hath aspired the clouds
> Which too untimely here did scorn the earth.

And it is fitting, too, that Romeo should attack Tybalt shouting,

> Mercutio's soul
> Is but a little way above our heads,
> Staying for thine to keep him company.

Mercutio's jokes, then, do two things. First, they attack the high and formal. For example, though he is invited to the Capulets' ball, he chooses instead to crash. Yet, even as he puts aside the formal invitation, he dons a mask to disguise himself, another kind of formality. The pattern of Mercutio's wit, then, is that he pulls down the imposing forms and idols of others but, second, he sets up in their high place his own artificial gestures—puns, rhymes, jokes, set speeches, and other masks. He attacks in others his own chief trait, and we can guess his reason—a sense of his own insufficiency. He calls his mask,

> A visor for a visor! What care I
> What curious eye shall quote deformities?
> Here are the beetle brows shall blush for me.

Mercutio's wit follows the school of Hobbes or Kenneth Burke: "sudden glory arising from some sudden conception of some eminency in ourselves, by comparison with the infirmity of others or with our own formerly" or Burke's reversal, "not so much a glorifying of the self as a minimizing of the distresses menacing the self." Laughter, Hobbes goes on, "is incident most to them that are conscious of the fewest abilities in themselves; who are forced to keep themselves in their own favour by observing the imperfections of other men."

As for Mercutio's sense of his own insufficiency, we can guess—again, from a heavily realistic point of view—its roots in child-hood. They show in the speech where Mercutio conjures up the spirit of the absent Romeo, in the process making some grandly obscene remarks about Rosaline. The peaceful Benvolio remonstrates, "Thou wilt anger him." Not so, says Mercutio.

> This cannot anger him. 'Twould anger him
> To raise a spirit in his mistress' circle
> Of some strange nature, letting it there stand
> Till she had laid it and conjured it down.
> That were some spite; my invocation
> Is fair and honest: in his mistress' name,
> I conjure only but to raise up him.

It was Romeo's "calm, dishonourable, vile submission," literally, his 'putting himself under' that so infuriated Mercutio; and there is a grim irony in his being killed "under" Romeo's arm. Raising up seems to represent for Mercutio a child's ithyphallic notion of virility; being laid—down—its opposite, and so his defense is:

> If love be rough with you, be rough with love.
> Prick love for pricking, and you beat love down.

The best defense is a good offense. Romeo says, "He jests at scars that never felt a wound," but we could with a more sophisticated psychology paraphrase him: He jests at scars that fears to feel a wound—a certain kind of wound, the kind that comes from real love that would lay him low, make him undergo a submission like

11

Romeo's. Mercutio's bawdry serves to keep him a noncombatant in the wars of love; it enables him to make allies of his companions, notably Romeo, against his own emotions—as he says, after a wit-sally, "Why, is this not better now than groaning for love?" Not for Mercutio is that entrance into the tomb or womb or maw which is Romeo's dark, sexual fate.

Whether we re-create Mercutio psychoanalytically or in the simpler and more loving way of the grandmotherly lady in the park, he can become the most realistic of real characters. He is a bit "thin"—that is, he does not have the great variety of traits a real person has, but what traits he does have are real enough. I have known him, I have even been him, warding off the dangers of emotion with a smokescreen of words—and not just as a literary critic. Once upon a time I attended parties where the girls lined up on one wall and the boys on the other, giggling and making jokes in their newly-deep voices. And, no doubt, from the point of view of the adolescent I once was, my present world of monogamy, diapers, and the P.T.A. must indeed seem a "calm, dishonourable, vile submission." Yet I find this man I have known or been in the most formal, artificial, and stylized of Shakespeare's plays: truly an imaginary garden with a real toad in it. I find in my own response the paradox or impasse between, on the one hand, Shakespeare's seventeenth-, eighteenth-, and nineteenth-century critics and, on the other, his twentieth-century critics with their antirealistic view of character.

Shakespeare's modern critics turned away from character to imagery, and if we take off our nineteenth-century spectacles, the set of images that first strikes the eye consists of what Professor Harry Levin has called "formality": the ceremonies, such as the Capulets' ball, the marriage of Romeo and Juliet, the Prince's decrees, or Juliet's funeral; the images of books, reading and writing, or words ("A rose by any other name would smell as sweet") and even letters of the alphabet—the two the play toys with are "R" and "I" which, by some strange coincidence, happen to be (in Elizabethan orthography) the initials of the two lovers. It is a pretty device, entirely too pretty and artificial. One senses in the tragedy as a whole a tension between this formality and the raw emotions of love and hate seething beneath its surfaces.

In other words, the whole work of art uses the same defense that the individual character does. Just as Mercutio puts up words as a screen against emotions that might wound, so the tragedy as a whole poises against the love of Romeo and Juliet the names Montague and Capulet or that other word that has "no end, no limit, measure, bound," the Prince's word "banished." As always in tragedy, the defense fails. There is a return of the repressed, love bursts through, and the tragic catastrophe follows. Romeo and Juliet's love undermines the words "Montague," "Capulet," "banished," just as Mercutio's jokes do not keep him from being laid low by Tybalt's "envious thrust."

This tension between verbal formality and raw emotion, however, makes but one in a whole series of formalized opposites into which the images of the tragedy divide: love-hate, old-young, male-female, water-fire, night-day, long-short, sweet-sour, vice-virtue, and even dog-cat. In the movement of the play as a whole, the tragic catastrophe comes when these opposites engulf each other, when the hate of the old Montagues and Capulets entombs the love of Romeo and Juliet, and when their love breaks down the families' hate:

> These violent delights have violent ends
> And in their triumph die, like fire and powder,
> Which, as they kiss, consume.

What is true of the play as a whole holds true for Mercutio in particular. He tries to pull down to earth the idolatries of others and set his own formalities on high. But just the opposite happens to him in this play of opposites. He is brought low by "a braggart, a rogue, a villain that fights by the book of arithmetic" and a friend who "kiss[es] by th' book." And even as he is made "a grave man," "worms' meat," his spirit "has aspired the clouds." So in the tragedy as a whole: as the Prince tells old Montague at the end:

> Come, Montague; for thou art early up
> To see thy son and heir more early down.

As the lovers sink down into the tomb, so old Montague and Capulet promise to "raise" their statues in gold.

Pulling down the formalities of others to set up one's own, the two key elements in Mercutio's realistic character pervade the nonrealistic play. Or perhaps we should put it the other way around: the key themes of the play, the collapse of opposites, particularly verbal formality as against emotion, have shaped the naturalistic character of Mercutio. Each informs and creates the other. In short, we have found our bridge between the seventeenth, eighteenth, and nineteenth centuries' realistic view of Shakespeare's characters and our own view of the play as a "poetic construct."

From the words on the page so important in modern objective or formalist criticism, we have managed to cross by way of our subjective re-creation of the play to the Romantic sense of the tragedy as an external quasi-historical reality. In effect, we have found a bridge, but we never lost one. All we needed to do was to look not just at what the play brings to us, but also at what we bring to the play. The bridge was always there, in the human psyche, our own, but more to the point, Shakespeare's. He could create a thing of formal beauty that would nevertheless evoke from all of us, groundlings at the Globe or grandmothers in the Bronx, our deepest selves. This is the creative gift, the heart of the mystery. The poet informs realism with nonrealism and nonrealism with realism and so moves from his own unique and local experience to ours equally unique and local. Both are "solely singular for the singleness," but the poet can bridge from himself to us by finding in his own realistic experience timeless and universal form—or, if not timeless, at least a form for the celebration of which, four hundred years is all too short a date.

Massachusetts Institute of Technology

NOTES

[1] J. M. Flagler, "Gentles All," *New Yorker*, 31 August 1957. I have taken poetic (or critical) license with the incident actually reported on p. 63.

[2] Fritz Heider and Marianne Simmel, "An Experimental Study of Apparent Behavior," *American Journal of Psychology*, LVII (1944), pp. 243-259.

14

THE BALANCE OF THEMES IN *ROMEO AND JULIET*

GORDON ROSS SMITH

> *The fault, dear Brutus, is not in our stars,*
> *But in ourselves, that we are underlings.*
> *Caes.,* I.ii.140-141.

In the last few years modern paperback anthologies of Shake-spearian criticism have included occasional selections from critics before 1910, but such critics, if one may judge by citations from them in modern criticism, are either not much discussed or not much read. Perhaps one reason is the assumption that what is good in them has been winnowed out and preserved among the standard interpretations, and that what was left is best left lying. Another reason may be the fact that so many people think that the style is the man, and that those writers with romantically heightened and fatuous sensibilities, or with the acrid aroma of obtuse moralism about them, cannot have anything to say to us, especially about Shakespeare. But while style may be the man if he's a buffoon, in other kinds of writers an execrable style may nevertheless embody ideas worth considering—as in Dreiser and Veblen, two masters of foreigner's English whom everyone reads. A third but dubious reason—rather, inconvenience—is the inaccessibility of older writers in newer libraries. The fourth reason is a certain understandable but uncommended irresponsibility before the continuously rising mountains of Shakespearian criticism. Attempts to deal with it all in the form of such histories of Shakespearian criticism as Augustus Ralli's, Alfred Westfall's, and Paul Conklin's have tended to be more surveys than critiques. Compilations of abstracts or excerpts, of course, are useful guides, but again if one may judge by footnote citation, they seem not so much to replace as to displace the originals. The originals deserve to be reexamined now and then, in spite of their dated

15

styles, because critical sensibility, whether Dowden's or T. S. Eliot's, is never pure, unfettered objectivity. The critic himself may feel that he is riding the bowsprit on a voyage through strange seas of thought alone, and he may be right in that he returns with some new seaweed or a purple pearl; nevertheless the rudder on the other end of that ship is an amalgam of his own tastes and personality, the tastes and outlook of his times and social class, and of the cultural patterns which molded them and him. As times change further, he too becomes dated, and the elements in himself that date him may be more alien to Shakespeare than the elements that molded the earlier critics whom he rejected. The further we get from Shakespeare's times and the greater the number of intellectual, social and political revolutions that intervene between his times and ours, the more we need to study his times, and the more relevant may be those old critics not so removed by revolutions of thought and taste from his times as we are ourselves.

In the history of *Romeo and Juliet* criticism over the last century and a half we can see these principles in operation several times. A widely accepted interpretation of the earlier nineteenth century was quite overturned by a critic of a subsequent generation without his offering an alternative interpretation of any comparable cogency. Twenty years later a new interpretation was offered that accorded better with what was then the climate of critical opinion. That view has held with some critics until our own times. Now modern historical criticism has heavily eroded that interpretation also. The interpretations I am chiefly referring to are those of Gervinus (1850), Dowden (1875), Boas (1896), and Franklin Dickey (1957). The purposes of this paper are to show how historical findings have impaired the interpretation of Boas, have partially rehabilitated that of Gervinus, and have provided new evidence which suggests a conflict of themes lying beneath the obvious conflicts of characters, but far from identical with them. Finally, I wish to offer some suggestions as to how these conflicting themes operate to insure the appeal of the play.

GERVINUS' INTERPRETATION

Gervinus asserted that Friar Laurence was a choral character and that the central principle animating the action and justifying the catastrophe was that "excess in any enjoyment, however pure in itself, transforms its sweet into bitterness." [1] In support of his interpretation, which was shared to one degree or another by Horn (1823), Tieck (1826), Ulrici (1839), and Kreyszig (1859), Gervinus cited a number of specific passages given Friar Laurence. The first was that in the herb-gathering scene:

> For naught so vile that on the earth doth live,
> But to the earth some special good doth give;
> Nor aught so good but, strained from that fair use,
> Revolts from true birth, stumbling on abuse.
> Virtue itself turns vice, being misapplied,
> And vice sometime's by action dignified.
> Within the infant rind of this small flower
> Poison hath residence, and medicine power.
> For this, being smelt, with that part cheers each part,
> Being tasted slays all senses with the heart.
> Two such opposed kings encamp them still
> In man as well as herbs, grace and rude will;
> And where the worser is predominant,
> Full soon the canker death eats up that plant.
>
> (II.iii.17-30) [2]

These ideas are by no means unique in Shakespeare. The first two lines, asserting that evil contains good, remind one of a similar statement in *Henry V*:

> There is some soul of goodness in things evil,
> Would men observingly distil it out.
>
> (IV.i.4-5)

The reverse of this idea, that good contains evil, is fully and calmly developed here in the remainder of this passage, developed more pointedly later on, and then illustrated in the action. Gervinus next quoted Friar Laurence's intense reproach to Romeo:

17

> These violent delights have violent ends,
> And in their triumph die; like fire and powder,
> Which as they kiss, consume.
>
> (II.vi.9-11)

As Caroline Spurgeon, among others, has pointed out,[3] a more concise figurative description of the whole action of the play could hardly be made: violence, triumph, death; suddenness, love, and death again; all are there. Shakespeare then gives Friar Laurence the pointed moral: "Therefore, love moderately, love long doth so" (II.vi.14). This line may out of context sound dull and stodgy, but in a play so old its very strangeness should be a signal to consider it, not to disregard it. It should be contrasted with the remark given Romeo which ostensibly provokes it:

> Do thou but close our hands with holy words,
> Then love-devouring death do what he dare,
> It is enough I may but call her mine.
>
> (II.vi.6-8)

That's romantic beyond words. The very phrase "love-devouring death" states the love-defeating contradiction in Romeo's attitude. The gunpowder image is repeated by Friar Laurence in his later, stronger admonitions:

> Thy noble shape is but a form of wax,
> Digressing from the valor of a man;
> Thy dear love sworn, but hollow perjury,
> Killing that love which thou hast vowed to cherish;
> Thy wit, that ornament to shape and love,
> Misshapen in the conduct of them both,
> Like powder in a skill-less soldier's flask
> Is set afire by thine own ignorance,
> And thou dismembered with thine own defense.
>
> (III.iii.126-134)

This is vigorous admonition, as is the whole passage of which it is part. If it is delivered on the stage with the strength of indignation which informs the lines, I do not see how anyone with ears could fail to get the message.

18

Gervinus next cited the outraged reproaches that Shakespeare supplied Friar Laurence against Romeo after the death of Tybalt (III.iii.122-134), and finally the third appearance of the gunpowder image in the apothecary scene (V.i.60-65). Gervinus might have added more from Friar Laurence (III.iii.109-121 and 135-145), and some further evidence from Juliet:

> Although I joy in thee,
> I have no joy of this contract tonight.
> It is too rash, too unadvised, too sudden,
> Too like the lightning, which doth cease to be
> Ere one can say "It lightens."
>
> (II.ii.116-120)

All these ideas which amount in general to the notion that too much is not enough are all variants of the classical and Renaissance motto, *festina lente,* "make haste slowly." Edgar Wind has pointed out that it was "the most widely cherished Renaissance maxim." [4] Gellius and Erasmus expounded on it; Ficino and Machiavelli approved; the woodcuts of Colonna's *Hypnerotomachia Poliphili,* printed by Aldus in 1499, show over eighty variations of it; the Aldine anchor and dolphin are themselves emblematic of it; the benign or useful union of contraries of which it was the chief form was symbolized (and incidentally given the proper classical authorization), by the crab and butterfly of the Emperor Augustus. Wind shows that Shakespeare used the idea comically in *Love's Labour's Lost,* in some tomfoolery between Moth and Armado (III.i.57-65), and that the gunpowder simile used there often accompanied the *festina lente* idea in other Renaissance writers; Wind has titled his chapter on this subject with a phrase from *King Lear* which expresses its essential idea: Ripeness is All.

Shakespeare provides two versions of *festina lente* in *Romeo and Juliet*:

> Wisely and slow. They stumble that run fast.
>
> (II.iii.94)

> Too swift arrives as tardy as too slow.
>
> (II.vi.15)

The typical association of gunpowder images has already been cited, as has their appearance in this play. Other forms of this Renaissance attitude, often with fire images, are scattered through plays that chronologically both precede and follow the writing of *Romeo and Juliet*. In *Love's Labour's Lost* Berowne says to Rosaline,

> Your wit's too hot, it speeds too fast, 'twill tire.
> (II.i.120)

In *The Taming of the Shrew* Petruchio says,

> Though little fire grows great with little wind,
> Yet extreme gusts will blow out fire and all.
> (II.i.135-136)

In the *Two Gentlemen of Verona* Lucetta says to Julia,

> I do not seek to quench your love's hot fire,
> But qualify the fire's extreme rage,
> Lest it should burn above the bounds of reason.
> (II.vii.21-23)

In *Richard II*, nearly contemporaneous with *Romeo and Juliet*, Old John of Gaunt says of Richard,

> His rash fierce blaze of riot cannot last,
> For violent fires soon burn out themselves;
> Small showers last long, but sudden storms are short.
> He tires betimes that spurs too fast betimes,
> With eager feeding food doth choke the feeder.
> (II.i.33-37)

It sounds as though Shakespeare were ringing the changes upon a familiar theme. Two years later, in *1 Henry IV*, the king is supplied with a lecture to Hal containing the same idea:

> The skipping king, he ambled up and down
> With shallow jesters and rash bavin wits,
> Soon kindled and soon burnt.
> (III.ii.60-62)

20

The same idea appears three times in *Hamlet*:

> This is the very ecstasy of love,
> Whose violent property fordoes itself.
>
> (II.i.102-103)
>
> The violence of either grief or joy
> Their own enactures with themselves destroy.
>
> (III.ii.206-207)
>
> . . . Goodness, growing to a pleurisy,
> Dies in his own too much.
>
> (IV.vii.118-119)

As though never tired of what he thought were obvious truths, Shakespeare supplied Troilus with the same idea at the climax of that play:

> What will it be
> When that the watery palates taste indeed
> Love's thrice repurèd nectar? Death, I fear me,
> Swounding destruction, or some joy too fine,
> Too subtle-potent, tuned too sharp in sweetness,
> For the capacity of my ruder powers.
>
> (III.ii.19-26)

These passages from other plays do not of course establish the centrality of the idea in *Romeo and Juliet*. They do establish, however, that that idea was something of a Shakespearian commonplace, and not merely one of the erring aspects of Friar Laurence as a faulty minor character (Dowden's overconfident assertion).

It seems to me self-evident that part of Romeo's behaviour is extravagant and disgraceful. He rolls about the floor, blubbers and weeps, and threatens to kill himself (III.iii.65-108). Upon first learning of his banishment, his laments and protests are relatively temperate, although he answers Friar Laurence with "Hang up philosophy!" and "Thou canst not speak of that thou dost not feel" (III.iii.56,64). This much appears to be Shakespeare's elaboration of a short expository passage in Brooke (1311-20).[5] In Brooke, Romeus had fallen upon the ground at

21

once, "his golden lockes he tare . . . and with his brest doth beate the troden grounde" (1291-94). Shakespeare's Romeo works himself into a frenzy gradually, describes himself as "doting" (III.iii.67), and then announces that he falls upon the ground, taking the measure of an unmade grave (III.iii.70-71). The absurdity of this self-conscious frenzy is not mitigated by any explanation via primitive dramatic technique. How wrong it is the Nurse and the Friar declare:

> Stand up, stand up, stand, an you be a man.
> (III.iii.88)

> Art thou a man? Thy form cries out thou art.
> Thy tears are womanish, thy wild acts denote
> The unreasonable fury of a beast.
> (III.iii.109-111)

As in Brooke, Friar Laurence excoriates such behaviour at length, assures Romeo of the amount of *good* fortune he can still enjoy, and tells him they will arrange for him to visit Juliet after dark. Romeo's answers are very brief, e.g., "How well my comfort is revived by this." His mute satisfaction is like that of a child who has thrown a wild tantrum and got what he wanted thereby. In this Shakespeare is deviating from Brooke, for there Romeus is properly contrite after the lecture:

> For very shame, the blood doth flashe in both his
> cheekes,
> He thankes the father for his lore, and farther
> ayde he seekes.
> He sayth, that skilles youth, for counsell is unfitte,
> And anger oft with hastines are joind to want of witte;
> But sound advise aboundes in heddes with ho[a]rishe
> haires,
> For wisdom is by practise wonne, and perfect made by
> yeares.
> But aye from this time forth, his ready bending will
> Shalbe in awe and governed by fryer Lawrence skill.
> (1488-96)

In reversing his source, Shakespeare has sharply decreased the hero's self-control. Yet even in Brooke, the rightness of reason and the danger of passion is as stressed as with Shakespeare's Friar. Brooke's prologue is direct and unequivocal:

> The glorious triumphe of the continent man upon the lustes of wanton fleshe, incourageth men to honest restraynt of wyld affections, the shamefull and wretched endes of such, as have yelded their libertie thrall to fowle desires, teache men to witholde them selves from the hedlong fall of loose dishonestie. . . . And to this ende (good Reader) is this tragicall matter written, to describe unto thee a coople of unfortunate lovers, thralling themselves to unhonest desire, neglecting the authoritie and advise of parents and frendes, conferring their principall counsels with dronken gossyppes, and superstitious friers (the naturally fitte instrumentes of unchastitie) attemptying all adventures of peryll, for thattaynyng of their wished lust, usyng auriculer confession (the kay of whoredome, and treason) for furtheraunce of theyr purpose; abusyng the honorable name of lawefull mariage, the cloke the shame of stolne contractes, finallye, by all meanes of unhonest lyfe, hastyng to most unhappye deathe.

The tone of this would make one think it by Stephen Gosson, who was only eight years old when it was published; it is signed by Brooke himself. Although the lovers are called "unfortunate," their culpability seems plain, and although the aggressively abusive tone is repugnant, it must be admitted that the substantives do denote the events of the play. The "dronken gossyppe" is Nurse Angelica. Her name is Shakespeare's addition (IV.iv.5 only), and by the principles of primitive dramatic technique should be descriptive, not ironic. Angelica twice calls for aqua vitae (III.ii.88;IV.v.16). The parallel in Brooke to the first of these occasions is one line only, "A warmed and holesome juyce she [Angelica] powreth downe her [Juliet's] throte" (1180); hot broth, obviously. Brooke is often comically prosaic. The second occasion in the play has no parallel in Brooke at all. We may conclude that Shakespeare's aqua vitae is derived from Brooke's dronken gossyppe, and that Shakespeare read the preface. The

23

body of Brooke's poem is by no means so moralistic as the preface, but elements of Shakespeare's Friar Laurence are there. Fryer Lawrence says to Romeus, "proove not thy selfe a foole" (1381), along with much else of like tenor, and Brooke in his own person speaks of "seely Romeus" (1061), i.e., fond, foolish, irresponsible.

If we turn to William Painter's version (1567), translated from Boiastuau, we find the opening paragraph declares that many men and women have died of excessive passions, and that

> amongs the same, Loue is not the least, whych when it seazeth uppon any kynde and gentle Subject, and findeth no resistaunce to serue for a rampart to stay the violence of his course, by little, & little vndermineth, melteth and consumeth the vertues of naturall powers, in sutch wyse as the spyrite yealdinge to the burden, abandoneth the place of lyfe.[6]

Whether Shakespeare used Painter's translation has been doubted; in effect, however, the play reverses an important detail in Painter, for after his banishment Rhomeo does not display the abandonment to passion that Romeus and Romeo do. When Julietta offers to accompany him to Mantua, Rhomeo answers her that among other things she should "recline thy self to reason, (the ryght rule of humane Lyfe)" (p. 119).

Of these three extant sixteenth century English versions, Shakespeare's Romeo is the most given over to unreasonable and uncontrolled passion. How far we could suppose an Elizabethan audience would stretch its real-life mores for these harlotry players we do not know. Most likely there was considerable variation: the graver and the wiser sorts would view with alarm, while giddier heads would wear out the pages, like the students at Oxford, as soon as they could lay hands on a printed copy. Modern critics might do well to note that a "Romeo" in modern tabloid headlines is a term of patronage or mild contempt, that for a man to abandon himself to passion to this degree is ridiculous in someone we're indifferent to, disgraceful in someone we like, or in a relative from whom we cannot be detached. The Nurse's exhortation is one we all might make:

> Stand up, stand up, stand an you be a man.
> (III.iii.88)

But for generations who had joyed in the sorrows of Werther, or who had been educated to admire such lines as, "Oh lift me from the grass! / I die! I faint! I fail!" Romeo's behavior might seem nothing untoward. Gervinus recognized that the view he had shared with some contemporaneous German critics had been rejected by some others, including Schlegel, because of their involvement with the Romantic Movement. According to Schlegel, the play was a picture of love and its pitiable fate in a world too sharp for this tenderest blossom of human life, and "The echo it leaves in the mind resembles a single but endless sigh." His attitude is much like that of Goethe toward the character of Hamlet, and to have so nearly equated two such different plays must be considered a pyrrhic victory for *Weltschmerz*.

DOWDEN'S DEAF INDIGNATION

The English translation of Gervinus' *Commentaries* appeared in 1863, and about twelve years later the analysis Gervinus had made of *Romeo and Juliet* was attacked with such ferocity by Edward Dowden that it seems never to have recovered. To espouse Gervinus is to provoke such responses as one gets for praising Shadwell, and indeed, although Dowden's attack lacked the wit of Dryden's, it resembled Dryden's in that both attacks ignored the substance of the disagreement and resorted to abuse and ridicule instead. Prof. Elmer Stoll wrote in 1937, "Dowden . . . has admirably refuted the critics' dour morality, particularly that of Gervinus." [7] Because the influence of Dowden's attack has continued to our own day, I think it is worth examining in some detail.

Dowden began as follows:

It is impossible to agree with those critics, among others Gervinus, who represent the friar as a kind of chorus expressing Shakspere's own ethical ideas, and his opinions respecting the characters and action. It is not Shakspere's practice to expound the moralities of his artistic creations;[8]

I am afraid I cannot avoid the necessity of heckling across the decades. This part of Dowden's argument is begging the question. Whether Shakespeare expounds moralities is the very question under debate, and it can be answered only by references to the text—whether the lines given to Friar Laurence are borne out by the action—not by categorical assertions of the truth or falsity of the proposition. And if in *Richard III* Shakespeare doesn't expound the morality of his creation,[9] no writer ever did, not even Aesop.

> nor does he ever, by means of chorus, stand above and outside the men and women of his plays, who are bone of his bone and flesh of his flesh.

That bone-flesh analogy seems to mean Dowden thinks Shakespeare uncritically identified with all of his character creations. If not that, I don't know what, for Dowden was resorting to a figurative cliché of Biblical origin (Genesis 2:23), when he might better have been concisely analytical. Having said that Shakespeare has no choruses, Dowden then went on to cite some:

> The nearest approach, perhaps, to a chorus is to be found in the person of Enobarbus in *Antony and Cleopatra*. Hamlet commissions Horatio to report him and his cause aright to the unsatisfied; and Horatio, placing the bodies of the dead upon a stage, is about, in judicial manner, to declare the causes of things; but Shakspere declines to put on record for us the explanations made by Horatio. No! Friar Laurence also is moving in the cloud, and misled by error as well as the rest.

If Horatio is short of being a chorus because he doesn't review the action of the play, then by that principle Friar Laurence must really be a chorus, for he reviews the action quite fully (V.iii.229-269). Queen Margaret in *Richard III* has often been called a chorus.[10] She is more of a chorus than Enobarbus, for he has a part in the action, but she is purely—shall we say?—lyrical. Shakespeare departed still further from "naturalism" than choral characters by using formal choruses in *2 Henry IV* and *Henry V*. I think Dowden assumed a degree of naturalism in Shakespeare's method that we can no longer accept. As George Ian Duthie has remarked, "Shakespeare's plays are liable to be only partly naturalistic."[11] The other parts are conceptual, schematic, traditional, or merely dramaturgical apparatus. Dowden continued as follows:

> Shakspere has never made the moderate, self-possessed, sedate person a final or absolute judge of the impulsive and the passionate. The one sees a side of truth which is unseen by the other; but to neither is the whole truth visible.

These general assertions sound more Shelleyan and Hegelian than Renaissance-like. That counter-renaissance figures like Montaigne were disillusioned with reason is obvious, but then Montaigne substituted faith in religion, empiricism in his daily life, not passion in either. And while some voices were scoffing at reason, or exalting passion, as did Marlowe and Donne, the Christian Humanist voices exalting reason continued to be heard from More past Milton, until the eighteenth-century cult of reason—together with economic and political developments— brought into being the romantic reaction. Shakespeare therefore might have been in either camp, and simply to assert that he was in one, not the other, is to beg the question again.

> The friar had supposed that by virtue of his prudence, his moderation, his sage counsels, his amiable sophistries, he could guide these two young, passionate lives, and do away the old tradition of enmity between the houses. There in the tomb of the Capulets is the return brought in by his investment of kindly scheming. Shakespere did not believe that the highest wisdom of human life was acquirable by mild, monastic meditation, and by gathering of simples in the coolness of the dawn. Friar Laurence too, old man, had his lesson to learn.

What Shakespeare personally believed is not known, and therefore the question is what this play says when the whole of the action and the words are considered. Whether the death of the lovers in the Capulet tomb is because of or in spite of the Friar's kindly scheming is the question in hand—once more. It does seem to me that to put more blame upon Friar Laurence for the outcome than upon the lovers themselves is to indulge in a nineteenth-century transvaluation of the traditional Christian values of Shakespeare's times. Shakespeare's play concludes with a passage containing the ambiguous line, "Some shall be pardon'd, and some punishèd" (V.iii.308). Who is pardoned and who punished we don't know, but if we look into Brooke we find that the Nurse is banished and that "Thapothecary, high is hanged by the throte" (2993), but that "fryer Lawrence" "was discharged quyte, and no marke of defame / Did seem to blot, or touch at all, the honor of his name" (2999-3000). Painter's version disposes of these characters in the same way. Continental versions of the story had sometimes made the Friar an evil man; the sole trace of such a concept in Brooke is that fryer Lawrence had a secret room at his cell, complete with comfortable bed, "Where he was wont in youth, his fayre frendes to bestowe" (1273). Shakespeare ignored this suggestion. He accepted the rest of Brooke's conception of the Friar as a good man, and apparently he considered him pardonable, for when Friar Laurence offers his life in expiation of any fault, Prince Escalus merely answers, "We still have known thee for a holy man" (V.iii.270). In brief, Friar Laurence seems a well-meaning, sensible man, and in blaming the Friar, Dowden erred against the very high probability of Shakespeare's intention.

Dowden argues subsequently that the theme of tragedy is spiritual fulfillment and that "To die . . . may be a higher rapture than to live." It is true that Romeo is depicted as thinking so (II.vi.6-8, already cited), but those lines may be as readily used as evidence for one interpretation as for the other. Friar Laurence's fault lies not in his counsels of moderation, but in his unworldly expectation that so elaborate a scheme could be made to operate properly in all parts. What overthrew his good intentions was heedless passion in someone—Romeo particularly —and mere accident had that passion not been present would not have sufficed. We can readily imagine that if Romeo had not killed Tybalt, all might have been well, and that if Juliet had tempered her passion at Romeo's banishment, she might not have provoked the sudden marriage to Paris. If Romeo had been more patient or temperate either in Mantua or in the Capulet tomb, neither life had been lost. Or earlier, if either had kept his wits about him, she might have followed Romeo down that rope ladder to Mantua. If Romeo and his man could get out of Verona that early morning, so could Juliet dressed as a boy. In Luigi da Porto's early version of the story, Giulietta makes that very proposal, but is overruled by Romeo. The detail comes down through

Boiastuau to Painter, and Brooke. In Brooke, Romeus overrules Juliet by arguing that they could not escape her father's rage, that he would "pursue us both" and that they would both be punished, he as a ravisher, she as a disobedient child (1613-1664). However, Romeus adds, if he cannot get his banishment repealed, then they can consider secret flight (1677-1682). Juliet's readiness to follow Romeus is expressed very early in the poem, where she says she will "Obedience set aside, unto my parentes dewe" (536-540), in order to follow Romeus. The offer reappears in Shakespeare (II.ii.143-148), but without the line upon disobedience, so that she seems merely to be accepting Romeo's offer of marriage, if that it should be. Comparable conversation appears in Painter. A delightfully devoted Julietta declares "who shall let me to chaunge myne apparell? Shall I be the first that haue vsed lyke shiftes, to escape the tryanny of parentes?" (p. 118). Rhomeo's answer is similar to that of Romeus in Brooke, but with the addition of the bit about reason, the ryght of rule of humane Lyfe, already cited. In Brooke the idea of secret flight is revived in fryer Lawrence's advice when he gives Juliet the sleeping powder (2159-67), and again in his letter to Romeus (2481-84). Both these proposals involve disguise and secrecy, elements neglected or abandoned by Shakespeare when he has Friar Laurence advise Juliet (IV.i.113-117). The only trace in Shakespeare of the objections made by Romeus to Juliet's proposal that they flee together is Lady Capulet's promise to Juliet that she will have Romeo poisoned in Mantua (III.v.89-93). The effect of Lady Capulet's promise is to emphasize the continuing danger the lovers would be in if they chose open flight, but that affects very little the possibilities for successful secret flight which are stated in Brooke and Painter. Shakespeare portrays the lovers as not even thinking of the possibility of secret flight. If Shakespeare had introduced such a proposal and answered it with the sensible answers that Brooke has Romeus give (or Painter, Rhomeo), he would have lowered that passionate irresponsibility which Friar Laurence admonishes. Shakespeare makes his lovers more idealistic, more passionate, less responsible than in his source, and he handles his plot so that the luck which might have brought it off is repeatedly spoiled by someone's passion. The dramaturgic reason may be to increase suspense, but the real reason appears to lie in character

29

and to imply the psychological and philosophical meanings of the play. As Shakespeare constructed his play, it was not in character for either Romeo or Juliet to behave with circumspection, and the fact that they do not is given to Friar Laurence to point out, presumably so there'd be no mistake. These speculations upon what Romeo and Juliet might have done instead of what they do may seem less relevant to the play than they would be in real life because the additional circumstances which in real life would govern such speculations are nonexistent in the play. However, none of the members of the Elizabethan audience had heard from Northrop Frye and his predecessors that art is centripetal. They were stuck with Aristotle and had no more sophisticated way to look upon a play than as an imitation of an action; they could do no other than assume the circumstances of their own lives in the lives of these impersonations. The speculations I have offered represent the other possibilities that Elizabethans might have considered, and they also represent the presence of the free will that most good Christians and some bad acknowledge. The consequence following, that Romeo and Juliet miss avenues of escape and happy fulfillment because the strength of passion makes them blind, seems to me inescapable. I do not mean that if Shakespeare had constructed his play with circumspect and worldly lovers, it would have been a better one. It would have been a comedy. I mean that this play as an imitation of an action both implies and states alternative courses of action not taken, and the fact that they were present but not taken has philosophical implications for the play as a whole. Dowden denied the implications and plain statements that Gervinus proclaimed, but he did not account for them. His "refutation" degenerated into irrelevant sarcasm and inexcusable xenophobia:

> In accordance with his view that the friar represents the chorus . . . Gervinus discovers . . . a lesson of moderation. . . . It is somewhat hard upon Shakspere to suppose that he secreted in each of his dramas a central idea for a German critic to discover.

The alleged theme is so readily available for quotation that "secreted" seems an unreasonable way to describe it. And I don't see how it is hard upon Shakespeare, although it does seem to have been hard upon Dowden.

But if there be a central idea in *Romeo and Juliet*, can this be it? What! did Shakspere, then, mean that Romeo and Juliet loved too well? That all would have been better if they had surrendered their lives each to the other less rapturously, less absolutely? At what precise point ought a discrete regard for another human soul to check itself and say, "Thus far towards complete union will I advance, but here it is prudent to stop"?

But another critic is no more answered by indignant and sarcastic exclamations than by xenophobia or by begging the question. If indignation refutes, *Harumph!* will do it. Gervinus did not assert that they loved each other with too much self-forgetfulness; he said they indulged their passion to the exclusion of every other consideration, even such minimal prudence as might have insured the continuation of their love. Such irrational indulgence is hardly equivalent to that "loved too well." And finally, "Thus far and no further" is a mere British cliché applied without any realistic evaluation—as it so often is.

In brief, for Dowden to have refuted Gervinus logically rather than passionately, it would have been necessary for him to produce Renaissance statements putting a high valuation upon the rightness of indulgence in passion and the abandonment of all other considerations—to prove that to at least some Renaissance writers, slaves of passion were the true kings of humanity. This Dowden did not do, and he got no help from Lily Campbell. He should next have explained why the Renaissance high valuation of reason and self-control should in *Romeo and Juliet* be disregarded. This he did not do either. Finally, he should have refuted Gervinus' argument point by point; he should have explained how Friar Laurence's admonitory lines which parallel the action and foreshadow the catastrophe are to be understood in the contrary context Dowden espoused. This he attempted, but his argument is vitiated with misinterpretation and deaf indignation because his real grounds lie in the backwash from English Romanticism, not in the play.

BOAS AND DESTINY

The task of replacing Gervinus' interpretation with something more positive than Dowden's objections was performed by Prof. Frederick Boas in 1896.[12] His interpretation has been the dominant one ever since. After briefly reviewing Gervinus' opinion, he quietly rejected it as follows: ". . . it must be allowed that the hermit's moralizing phrases are introduced and repeated with what sounds like deliberate emphasis. But this doctrine of moderation in love is nowhere else found in Shakspere's writings. [We have seen that it occurs repeatedly.] Bassanio, Orlando, and Ferdinand offer whole-hearted, enthusiastic devotion to their mistresses, and no moralist rebukes them for their want of circumspection" (p. 206). This last is an unfortunate declaration: how could criticism be more uncritical than to equate these four lovers? Bassanio is a wastrel who courts the wealthy Portia in order to use her money to pay his debts and escape bankruptcy (and presumably debtor's prison) (*Merch.*, I.i.119-165). Certainly he displays no such passion as Romeo does. Orlando is an able-bodied, likeable young English philistine who wrestles well and writes comically bad verse. Rosaline twits him (*AYL,* III.ii.386-403), for being "point-device in your accouterments" and for displaying none of the signs of the fashionable love melancholy in which Romeo was so tearfully immersed in his first (and for the audience, judgment-forming) appearance. Ferdinand is more wooed than wooing: he carries wood reluctantly (*Temp.,* III.i. 28-32), apparently cheats Miranda at chess (V.i.172-175), and is vigorously instructed by Prospero in the proper morals of courtship (IV.i.14-23). Ferdinand even smiles with superiority when Prospero praises Miranda (IV.i.5-11). To lump these young men together is no more enlightening than to dismiss Falstaff as a *miles gloriosus* or a Tudor Vice. Such pronouncements are pidgeonhole criticism: they obscure significant differences that are not of degree but of kind. Romeo is unique in the Shakespeare canon. Only Antony so completely gives all for love, and he differs from Romeo in every other way. Less intemperate love than Romeo's is commonplace in Shakespeare, perhaps partly because love was thought more proper for comedy, and the nature of the genre tempered the depiction of the passion.

Boas' interpretation, that Romeo and Juliet have no conse-
quential faults and that Fate determines the tragic outcome, was
based upon a series of passages that began with the Prologue and
continued to the end of the play. All of them can be as readily
interpreted in other ways, and nothing could be more mistaken
than to apply to this play T. S. Eliot's assertion about *Hamlet,*
"There is nothing to interpret."[13]

The passages and events that Boas cited can be divided into
several groups. The first group has to do with the astrological
passages. Except for one in the Prologue—of which more presently—all these are given to Romeo:

> My mind misgives
> Some consequence yet hanging in the stars.
> (I.iv.106-107)
>
> Is it even so? Then I defy you stars!
> (V.i.24)
>
> Oh, here
> Will I set up my everlasting rest,
> And shake the yoke of inauspicious stars
> From this world-wearied flesh.
> (V.iii.109-112)

As this much constitutes the essence of the case for the destiny
or fate interpretation, it is certainly a weaker collection than
Gervinus exhibited. The remaining passages Boas cited are so
much less explicit that they are readily subject to alternative
interpretation. Indeed, one might say of the star passages also—
since all of them are Romeo's—that they constitute evidence
rather for Gervinus' interpretation, since they all represent
Romeo's abrogation of Grace to his uncontrolled, destructive
passion, felt by him as "fate." It seems like an admirable evasion
of immature man to lay the results of his passionate disposition
to the charge of a star.

The second group, passages which Boas used to bolster his
interpretation, are not explicit enough to support it except by a
certain amount of reading in. Boas called the following lines,
"passionate protests against the cruel irony of fate":

> *Rom:*   Is she a Capulet?
> O dear account, my life is my foe's debt. . . .
> *Jul:* My only love sprung from my only hate,
> Too early seen unknown, and known too late.
>   (I.v.119-141)

There's nothing here about fate at all. We have only recognition of the obstacles to their love in the hatred of their houses. The formal elements suggest an effort at passionate abandonment to love which is as readily support for Gervinus as for Boas. The latter called the following passage a "presage of woe":

>   Although I joy in thee,
> I have no joy of this contract tonight.
> It is too rash, too unadvised, too sudden,
> Too like the lightning, which doth cease to be
> Ere one can say "It lightens."
>   (II.ii.116-120)

I grant it is a premonition on Juliet's part and foreshadowing on Shakespeare's, but I have already cited it to support Gervinus because it supports him better than it does Boas. Of the fights between Mercutio, Tybalt, and Romeo, Boas declared, ". . . fate has made a mock of Romeo." Romeo does exclaim, "Oh, I am fortune's fool!" (III.ii.141), but that phrase occurs elsewhere in Shakespeare (*Lear*, IV.vi.195; *Timon*, III.vi.106), without indicating anything of destiny. One could as readily say that passion has made a mock of Romeo, for the Prince's orders had been very explicit (I.i.95-110), and Romeo remembers them (III.i.90-92). The Prince gives no subsequent sanction to brawling (III.i. 191-202; V.iii.290-295), and we must conclude that this prohibition of brawling, a prohibition from Elizabethan "real life," is part of the moral framework of the play. It is consistent with Gervinus' interpretation, but at odds with Boas'. Part of Juliet's farewell, "Methinks I see thee, now thou art so low, / As one dead in the bottom of a tomb" (III.v.55-56), Boas also called "presaging." It, too, is a piece of tragic foreshadowing; as an image in Juliet's mind, it more suggests fear as a consequence of passion than it does external fate. Boas concluded his evidence of what he called "Fortune's malignant game," with the italicized part of the following lines:

> Lady, come from that nest
> Of death, contagion, and unnatural sleep.
> *A greater power than we can contradict*
> *Hath thwarted our intents.* Come, come away.
> Thy husband in thy bosom there lies dead,
> And Paris too.
>
> (V.iii.151-156)

Boas apparently thought that "greater power" was malignant fate; it seems to me as readily understandable as Death, for death is mentioned in both the preceding and following lines, and Friar Laurence gives no evidence of believing in Fate anywhere else—and no Christian friar should, one would think.

One other piece of evidence offered by Boas remains to be considered: the Prologue. The first quatrain deals with the feud in terms of disapproval ("civil blood makes civil hands unclean"). The second quatrain deals with the lovers; it calls them "star-crossed" but says their overthrow is "misadventured." The two terms may be mutually exclusive, the former meaning "destined," the latter meaning "chanced"; or both may mean "destined," or both mean "chanced"; one has his choice of opportunities to wrest. If it be argued that "star-crossed" as "destined" has support in the text from Romeo, it can be answered that "misadventured" as "chanced" also has textual support. Prince Escalus asks,

> What misadventure is so early up
> That calls our person from our morning rest?
>
> (V.iii.188-189)

Subsequently he says, "Meantime forbear / And let mischance be slave to patience" (V.iii.220-221). "Mischance" in the context here means the events that ended in the lovers' deaths. Whatever those events may have been slave to up to this point, it certainly wasn't patience or forbearance, and the Prince's comments suggest the master of mischance might have been the patience rec-

35

ommended to Romeo by Friar Laurence, "Be patient, for the world is broad and wide" (III.iii.16), and by Balthasar, "I do beseech you, sir, have patience. / Your looks are pale and wild, and do import / Some misadventure" (V.i.27-29). Whether we think it destiny or mischance that Friar Laurence's letter "was stayed by accident" (V.iii.251), or that Juliet awoke only after Romeo had died, depends upon whether we follow Gervinus or Boas, but the incidents are not evidence for either over the other. In so elaborate a plot as Friar Laurence's, it would seem inevitable that some detail should go wrong. Two such miscarriages hardly amount to the certain operation of fate, and all the other misfortunes, the death of Tybalt, the marriage with Paris, the failure to find other solutions for the lovers, and Romeo's arrival at the Capulet tomb are all portrayed as consequences of the lovers' passion and are therefore stronger for Gervinus than for Boas.

There is also the possibility or probability that "star-crossed," although a term originating in astrological beliefs, is here used only in the sense of "unfortunate," as a modern person may exclaim, "I thanked my stars," without believing in astrology, or "I know in my heart," without believing the heart is the seat of thought. Prof. Warren D. Smith has recently discussed Elizabethan judicial astrology,[14] and has shown that the church, the state, and apparently the majority of the population rejected it. To the audience, then, "star-crossed" may merely have meant "unfortunate." Prof. Smith, although he did not discuss this play, has also shown that elsewhere in the Shakespearian canon there is no evidence that Shakespeare believed in judicial astrology and much that he did not. In *King Lear*, Gloucester, the credulous old man, believes in astrology, but as Prof. George L. Kittredge pointed out, both the good son, Edgar, and the bad son, Edmund, have no respect for astrology.[15] Certainly any interpretation that puts *Romeo and Juliet* so much out of harmony with the rest of Shakespeare's works should be received with much caution. Finally, that the Prologue is part of Shakespeare's design has been denied in recent years. E. C. Pettet doubted that Shakespeare wrote it and declared it uncharacteristic verse.[16] H. Eardley-Wilmot offered further inferential reasons for doubting Shakespeare wrote it or meant to have it included: the infrequency of prologues in Shakespeare, his apparent dislike of them, and the quality of the verse.[17] Neither of these writers could be said to have been pioneering. In the nineteenth century Ulrici noted that it had been omitted by Heminges and Condell from the first folio, said it was probably not Shakespeare's, and said of the second prologue, "It is so empty, prosaic, and barren, and so wholly pointless, that in my opinion it is impossible that it could ever have flowed from Shakespeare's pen." [18] In the eighteenth century, Dr. Johnson wrote dryly of the second prologue, "The use of this Chorus is not easily discovered. It conduces nothing to the progress of the play." [19] Although the earlier critics here are impressionistic and the later ones still only inferential, I think that any dogmatic interpretations based on the prologue must be considered doubtful.

Followers of Boas have cited other passages, particularly the allusions to fortune. "Fortune" in Elizabethan English had an assortment of meanings—chance, accident, good or bad luck, possessions, or the personification representing a superhuman force or principle. The medieval Lady Fortune was still current in the Renaissance; she is not an iron goddess of doom, but a fickle female who tumbles or exalts her subjects equally at random. In *Romeo and Juliet* it is not always clear when the use of the word represents the personification or one of the more general senses. The only unequivocal references to her are those made by Juliet, and the usual adjective, "fickle," is there applied (III.v.60-62). Only seven other references to fortune in any sense occur. Against these we might weigh the references to fortune in the other tragedies:

	All uses of "fortune"	Fortune as a Goddess
Titus	8	1
Romeo	9	2
Caesar	5	2
Hamlet	17	8
Othello	21	3
Lear	24	10
Timon	29	6
Macbeth	7	0
Antony	40	8
Coriolanus	12	2

I think this tabulation demonstrates that references to Lady Fortune and the use of the word fortune in other senses were commonplaces that can have little or nothing to do with the operation of destiny. If the recurrence of the word in *Romeo and Juliet* is so crucial that it outweighs all the parallels between Friar Laurence's injunctions and the course in the action, how much more so must destiny be operating in *Lear, Hamlet,* or *Antony and Cleopatra?* I submit that a sentimental unwillingness to see any fault in the young lovers, in spite of what Friar Laurence reiterates, has led to the necessity of finding a substitute—but specious—cause for the catastrophe.

It might be argued here that the operation of fate was in Shakespeare's source. In Luigi da Porto's *Giulietta and Romeo* the Dedication mentions "unfortunate love" and "ill-fated lovers," but also mentions the "cruel and tragic ends [to which] poor wretches in love are too often led by love itself." [20] Da Porto's tale resembles many by Boccaccio in that individualized characterization, the detailed exploration of motivation, and the statement of a universal moral code underlying and determining the consequences of action are all neglected. We have in Da Porto's tale a humanistic surface, as simple, harmonious, and bland as a Brunelleschi interior. Motivation and metaphysics remain largely to be inferred. Elements of malignant fortune, as Prof. H. B. Charlton has pointed out,[21] were added to Bandello's version of Da Porto by Pierre Boiastuau. Prof. Charlton refers to these additions as "conventionally literary," mere "tricks," and sententiousness. I suspect that they represent a transalpine necessity for an explicit ethical framework of some sort, and Boiastuau took the readiest to hand. If we look into Brooke's poem, we find forty-five references to Fortune, whether to good, to ill, to both, or to unqualified,[22] and some eight more references to the Fates, doom, stars, and destiny.[23] Brooke's poem and Shakespeare's play are of about equal length (3020 lines and 3050 respectively), yet Brooke thus has fifty-three explicit references to Fate, stars, or the goddess Fortune, while Shakespeare, as I have shown, has only five. Clearly Shakespeare has decreased extraordinarily the importance of destiny from its role in his source, just as he has decreased the lovers' maturity and self-control and increased both their passion and the Friar's admonitions of it.

Shakespeare's desired effect may have been to make more dramatic conflicts, but another consequence has been the shifts in thematic balance. In my opinion the role of fate has been reduced to an inchoate feeling and excuse in the two major characters, and responsibility for the catastrophe, if it should be thought to lie with fate in Brooke, has been shifted in Shakespeare to those characters themselves. Brooke's preface gives us no good reason to think it fate there either, and as Prof. Charlton has suggested, the role of Fate in Boiastuau and Brooke is meretricious.

To summarize: Although I don't think the conflict of grace and rude will is the complete thematic content of this play, I do think that that concept of the play is better supported by the text and the evidence of contemporaneous ideas than is the idea of destiny or malignant fate. Shakespeare's play employs fate only as a subjective feeling on the parts of the two lovers. Boas' interpretation appears to me to be the result of Dowden's and his contemporaries' intense repudiation of Gervinus' interpretation, which had been made totally inacceptable by that change of outlook, taste, and values that we call the romantic revolution.

MORE RECENT CRITICS

Professor Boas' interpretation has had many adherents. Of major editors, Neilson and Hill declared, "Shakespeare has written it clear in his text that his drama is a tragedy of fate." [24] Prof. G. L. Kittredge wrote that like *Macbeth*, it "is a fatalistic drama. . . . Only by suicide can [Romeo] defy the stars." [25] G. I. Duthie declared the play "a drama of Fate" in which the "defects of character . . . are not properly worked into the pattern." [26] Geoffrey Bullough wrote, ". . . only a blind critic could regard 'These violent delights have violent ends' as the moral text of the play." [27] He declared that Fortune is used consistently as a menace, but that Shakespeare is "working it out in terms of premonitions and the stars rather than in explicit statements." Gervinus could boast more than that: explicit statements that parallel the action.

Prof. John W. Draper in 1939 added the qualities of the humors to the influence of the stars to prove the play is a tragedy of "the hopelessness of defying the heaven's will." [28] And that's the humor of it, as Nym said; i.e., whether Shakespeare took the humors any more seriously than Elizabethans took judicial astrology remains to be proved. If it is proper procedure to suppose that popular and successful drama is to be interpreted in terms of popular trashy philosophy, then as Robert Ornstein has suggested, *A Streetcar Named Desire* should be interpreted in terms of Norman Vincent Peale. No question that Blanche and Kowalski lack the "attitude of gratitude." Prof. Draper's paper seems to me a good example of historical information misapplied. Prof. Harry Levin, in an article more concerned with formal patterns, nevertheless seems to accept the Boas interpretation also: "The overriding pattern through which she and Romeo have been trying to break—call it Fortune, the stars, or what you will —ends by closing in and breaking them." [30] Prof. Paul Siegel in a recent anthology of readings includes Dowden's comments on the play and his attack on Gervinus, along with two other selections from Dowden, but none from Gervinus himself.[31] Prof. Siegel declared Dowden "almost always right," but suggested he reduced the complexity of the play by neglecting Friar Laurence. The number of critics who had accepted Boas' interpretation by 1947 was very considerable; H. Edward Cain cited a collection of them at that time,[32] and Prof. Paul Siegel has done so again more recently,[33] so that all together they resemble the corner of a Byzantine painting with its sea of heads, some with haloes.

In the last two or three decades dissenters to one degree or another from Boas' interpretation have tended to increase. Miss Lily B. Campbell laid something of a foundation with her *Shakespeare's Tragic Heroes, Slaves of Passion*,[34] although she did not discuss *Romeo and Juliet* in that book. Prof. Arthur H. R. Fairchild has asserted that the "central issue" in all Shakespearian tragedy is reason against passion.[35] Alfred Harbage acknowledged the importance of a Gervinus-like emphasis in certain of the direct or indirect sources of *Romeo and Juliet*— Bandello, Boiastuau, and Brooke: "The moral suggested is 'the admonishing of young men, so they should learn to govern themselves with moderation and not rush madly to their own destruction'." [36] However, Harbage accepts the Prologue as indicative, although he says, "This goes beyond anything in Shakespeare in pointing out the meaning of the play as a whole." [37] In the same year Thomas P. Harrison declared that Friar Laurence represented grace; and Romeo, rude will.[38] He declared those concepts not irrelevant to a complete understanding of the play, and supported his opinion with evidence from herbals of the period. H. Edward Cain has suggested, "The theme pivots upon the simple figment that *Death* is the rival to the lovers of Juliet." [39] He cited passages at I.v.137, III.ii.132-137, III.v.200-203, IV.v.35-40, V.i.34, and V.iii.101-112. These citations do not exhaust the evidence in the play for the support of his thesis. I think he is right, that Death is an important thematic element in the play quite apart from tragic foreshadowing and the tragic catastrophe; since it needs to be and can be related to the other themes, I shall return to it presently. In an article of a year later, already cited,[40] Prof. Cain said the play was a study of the passion of anger. For evidence he cited statements upon anger and its effects from More, La Primaudaye, William Bullein, Elyot, Saviolo, and Bartholomaeus Anglicus, among others, and this thesis I also think quite correct, although also in need of being related to the other themes of the play. Prof. Brents Stirling has discussed the theme of haste in the play[41] and has shown that it appears repeatedly on both comic and tragic levels and in both language and action. But he does not relate it to the prevalence of the *festina lente* theme in Renaissance times, or elsewhere in Shakespeare, or to love, passion, reason, self-control, death, or any other themes.

Franklin M. Dickey's book on Shakespeare's love tragedies[42] seems to me an admirable example of how historical knowledge should be applied in the interpretation of literary texts. Prof. Dickey demonstrates adequately that Elizabethan attitudes toward love included the notions of restraint stated by Friar Laurence. Moreover, the grace and rude will speech (II.iii.27-30) is paralleled in *Lucrece*:

> The flesh being proud, Desire doth fight with Grace
> For these it revels, and when that decays
> The guilty rebel for remission prays.
>
> (L1.712-714)

41

As Dickey points out, the passage is authorial comment, and presumably Shakespeare's own opinion at that time. Prof. Dickey summarized his opinion of the play as follows:

> Romeo and Juliet die, critics often tell us, only as the result of a series of mistakes and misunderstandings. In this light the lovers' death is pathetic rather than really tragic. Critics are also embarrassed by Shakespeare's paradoxical treatment of the three great themes of the tragedy. On the one hand it can be demonstrated that the catastrophe develops from faults of character: Romeo's impetuous nature leads him to despair and die. On the other hand the text also gives us reason to believe that the love of Romeo and Juliet comes to a terrible end because of the hatred between the two families. And yet a third view makes fate the main cause of the final disaster: Romeo and Juliet had to die because they were "star-cross'd." . . . Against these prevailing views the following chapters propose that *Romeo and Juliet* is a true mirror of the Elizabethan concept of a moral universe although Shakespeare does not preach morality. Judged by Elizabethan standards, the play is not merely a gorgeous and entertaining melodrama but a carefully wrought tragedy which balances hatred against love and which makes fortune the agent of divine justice without absolving anyone from his responsibility for the tragic conclusion. Unlike his source Shakespeare attempts a solution to the problem of evil by fitting the power of fortune into the scheme of universal order. (pp. 63-64)

The amount of emphasis which Prof. Dickey allows to Fortune in this summary seems to me to be undermined in his subsequent discussion:

> . . . we must be careful not to make the Elizabethans, and particularly Shakespeare, seem more credulous than ourselves. The language of astrology had been part of English speech for centuries and its figurative use does not necessarily imply a literal belief in astrological prognostication. . . . In none of the early plays save *Romeo and Juliet* do the stars even *seem* to govern the plots. In the later plays Shakespeare either satirizes the attempt to explain conduct and character

by astrology or else he uses astrological predictions mainly
for ironic effects. (pp. 90-91)

> Whatever the *dramatis personae* think as individuals, the
> total meaning of each play can be found only by taking into
> account the whole structure. . . . One of the most solid fea-
> tures in the unchanging ground of Shakespeare is the belief
> in a just Providence. . . . Not fate but the corrupt will
> makes men the agents of their own destruction. (p. 91)

These comments were written before the appearance of Warren
Smith's documentation of the Elizabethan rejection of judicial
astrology, which must have been written equally independently
of Prof. Dickey's book. Prof. Dickey considers both Friar Laurence and Prince Escalus choral characters; he says Biron in
Love's Labour's Lost may be taken as Shakespeare's representa-
tive "because the action bears out his predictions" (p. 71). Surely
the same must be said of Friar Laurence.

> The ending of *Two Gentlemen,* . . . exemplifies the same
> lesson which Friar Laurence preaches to Romeo, that un-
> checked passion leads to misery. (p. 70)

Finally, Prof. Dickey has produced a quantity of evidence for
the existence of the belief that "To love extreamely, procureth
eyther death or danger" (pp. 20 and 102). Much of his evidence
is from contemporaneous writers, and the rest is from Shakespeare himself. He has shifted the probability of rightness so far
from Dowden and Boas and toward Gervinus that I doubt if the
confidence of the 1930's in the role of stars and fate in this play
can ever be restored. My only cavil is that I think his evidence
would have justified his going farther in his rejection of that
interpretation.

Prof. Irving Ribner[43] has also pointed out the moral condemnation in Brooke's preface and denied that "the 'greater
power than we can contradict' (V.iii.153) is divine providence."
He declared Romeo and Juliet were children "born into a world
already full of an ancient evil not of their own making," and
that in the face of this Romeo is developed to arrive at "a free-
willed rational acceptance of the Christian stoic view of life."
That suicide for love is either Christian or stoic I can't accept.
Prof. Ribner admits (p. 284) that it means damnation.

43

Ribner's view of the role of Christianity in the play was continued by Prof. Paul Siegel, who shifted away from Dowden and toward Gervinus:

> Since Dowden's arraignment of Gervinus, it has been customary to regard Friar Laurence as a fussy, even comical, old busybody, utterly incapable of performing a choric function. Thus Duthie speaks of him as "this well-meaning but dull, timid and unimaginative cleric" (p. xx). The man who agrees to marry Romeo and Juliet in secret and who devises the plan of the potion can scarcely, however, be called timid and unimaginative. . . . Friar Laurence supplies the moralizing with which the authors of the adaptations of *novelle* would garnish them. In Shakespeare, however, this moralizing is not extraneous to the work. . . . Friar Laurence's comments concerning the conduct of Romeo are just and foreshadow the conclusion. . . . Each utterance of Friar Laurence is balanced by one of Romeo. We should not, with Dowden, disregard those of Friar Laurence or, with Dickey, disregard those of Romeo: both sets of utterances have validity.[44]

The respective validities are of different orders, I think. Friar Laurence's is choral; Romeo's is psychological and imitative of an action. Prof. Siegel also discussed "the drive to death of the two lovers" (p. 381). In this he seems to be developing the discussion of Death as Juliet's paramour advanced by H. Edward Cain, already mentioned here. Prof. Harry Levin, who calls Mercutio's interpretation of dreams "naturalistic, not to say Freudian," [45] has also shown concern with what looks like a Freudian death-wish: "The contrarieties of [Shakespeare's] plot are reinforced on the plane of imagery by omnipresent reminders of light and darkness, youth and age, and many other antitheses subsumed by the all-embracing one of Eros and Thanatos, the *leitmotif* of the *Liebestod*, the myth of the tryst in the tomb."

LAYERS OF THEMES

In the rest of this paper I should like to consider both the equilibrium of themes in the surface of this play and the other themes that underlie them. I trust my indebtedness to certain of the foregoing critics will be as evident as my deviations and additions. If both the intellectual structure and audience appeal of the play are considered, one can reconcile the logical findings of Gervinus with the intuitive feelings of Dowden—although it may be that for some of what follows Dowden would have been as indignant at me as he was at Gervinus.

As I have explained, I think Gervinus quite right so far as he went: The play represents a conflict of grace and rude will (Christian terms, suitable for a friar); that level is the most evident and explicit, for reasons already given. But the story as Shakespeare took it over from its Italianate sources seems organized on a second level in terms of the Platonic tripartite division of the mind into the reasonable, the irascible, and the concupiscible (*Republic*, IV, 441-442). This division, which appears later in part of Richard Burton's discussion of the soul and her faculties,[46] was familiar to Italian Renaissance humanists through Ficino's translations and the general taste for Neoplatonism. Although in England Ficino's direct influence appears to have been rather limited, Prof. Sears Jayne has traced it in Spenser, Chapman, Colet, Raleigh, and Burton.[47] As he also asserts, however, other Neoplatonists—Bembo, Pico, and Castiglione—"were all extremely popular in England," and French Neoplatonists were also very influential. Certainly the contemporaneous atmosphere was favorable to the acceptance of Neoplatonic ideas, whether recognized as Neoplatonic or not. Shakespeare, in heightening events and feelings from their level in his source, has made these three elements more evident than they are in Brooke, and with thanks perhaps to Christian humanist influence, the Platonic irascible spirit has been transformed into the Christian sin of wrath. Certainly the tragic faults evident in other plays—ambition, jealousy, pride, uxoriousness, senile willfulness, treachery and deceit—are all absent here, and the action proceeds by wrath and concupiscence alone, with reason remonstrating in vain. Reason is represented in Friar Laurence, Prince Escalus, and Benvolio. Concupiscence is passionately embodied in Romeo and Juliet, fadedly in the Nurse, and obscenely in Mercutio. Ireful passion or wrath is displayed continually by Tybalt, intermittently by old Capulet, Lady Capulet, Mercutio, Montague, Romeo and the servants. The play has long been noted to be one of hot Italian passion, but this Platonic triad exhausts the major attitudes in this play, though by no means the attitudes with tragic consequences in Shakespeare.

On a third but wholly inferential level, and one that has to do only with concupiscence, the play seems to embody some of those mystical, pagan notions represented by the Neoplatonic triad of Pulchritudo, Amor, and Voluptas, a version of the three graces. To Ficino and the Italian Neoplatonists, triads were "vestiges of the Trinity";[48] all triads descended from and returned to the Beyond; in this triad, Beauty descends and gives rise to Love, who turns to the desire of Pleasure, and is then transmitted into the Beyond. This particular triad appears on the medal of Pico della Mirandola and has been explained by Edgar Wind as follows:

> The function assigned here to Amor, of mediator between Pulchritudo and Voluptas, corresponds exactly to the definition of Love first given by Plato in the Symposium, and then adopted by all the Platonists: 'Love is Desire aroused by Beauty.' . . . Only by the vivifying rapture of Amor do the contraries of Pulchritudo and Voluptas become united. . . . But to achieve the perfect union of contraries, Love must face the Beyond; for as long as Love remains attached to the finite world, Passion and Beauty will continue to clash. In the *Docta ignorantia* Cusanus explained that a circle and a straight line are incompatibles as long as they remain finite, but coincide when infinite. In the same way do Beauty and Pleasure coincide if they are projected into the Beyond, that is, if they become transcendent Graces united by the rapture of Love.[49]

These ideas, especially as outlined by Bembo in Castiglione, were conspicuously present in the environments of Da Porto, Brooke, and Shakespeare. As Prof. Olin H. Moore has shown,[50] the legend of the suicidal lovers assumes what might be called its permanent Romeo-and-Juliet form in Luigi da Porto's version. Da Porto was born into a noble Italian family in 1485 and educated at the Court of Urbino, which was at that time perhaps the most intellectual center in Italy after Florence. The seriousness of the court had been set by Duke Federigo, a great patron of the arts for forty years, and continued by his successor, Duke Guidobaldo, who was Castiglione's patron during the years that Castiglione was resident at the ducal palace, 1504-1508. *Il Cortegiano* was first drafted in 1508, and the Neoplatonic Book IV was completed by 1516, although it was not published until 1528. It thus overlaps Da Porto's *Giulietta e Romeo,* which was completed in 1524 but not published until 1530.[51] The famous discourse by Peter Bembo in Book IV was a compilation and summary of the Neoplatonic doctrine of love; Bembo and Castiglione arrived in England through Sir Thomas Hoby's translation (1561), and had wide circulation. The Neoplatonic principles cited by Wind can be illustrated for Elizabethan writers from Hoby's translation.[52]

Beauty comes from heaven and produces love: "Speakynge of the beawtie that we meane, which is onlie it, that appeereth in bodies, and especially in the face of mann, and moveth thys fervent covetinge which we call Love, we will terme it an influence of the heavenlie bountifulness, the whiche . . . stretcheth over all thynges that be created (like the light of the Sonn)" (p. 343). "Beauty is good and consequently the true love of it is most good and holy" (p. 345). "Beawtie commeth of God, and is like a circle, the goodness wherof is the Centre" (p. 348). "Good and beawtifull be after a sort one selfe thinge, especiallie in the bodies of men: of the beawtie wherof the nighest cause (I sup- pose) is the beawtie of the soule: . . . as a partner of the right and heavenlye beawtie" (p. 350). Bembo acknowledges that there may be some drawbacks: "Neyther yet ought beawtifull women to beare the blame of that hatred, mortalytie, and destruction, which the unbridled appetites of men are the cause of" (pp. 350- 351). Count Lewes (Lodovico Canossa), suggests difficulties over the role of reason: "You have saide, that they must suffre them selves to bee guided by reason, and the opinion of many is, that it is unpossible for love to stand with reason" (p. 352). Bembo presently answers, "Sins the nature of man in youthfull age is so much inclined to sense, it may be graunted the Courtier while he is yong, to love sensuallye. But in case afterward also in hys riper yeres, he chaunse to be set on fire with this coveting of love, he ought to be good and circumspect, and heedful that he beeguyle not him self, to be lead willfullye into the wretchednesse,

that in yonge men deserveth more to be pitied then blamed"
(p. 352). Pity rather than blame would certainly seem to be the
concluding attitude toward Shakespeare's lovers by the survivors
at the end of that imitation of an action. But wretchedness in
this world is not the Neoplatonic end. Bembo speaks of the stairway to a higher bliss, a union with God through love. "Emong
these commodities the lover shal finde an other yet far greater,
in case he will take this love for a stayer (as it were) to clime
up to an other farr higher then it. . . . And thus shall he
beehoulde no more the particuler beawtie of one woman, but an
universall, that decketh out all bodies. . . . This stayer of love
. . . by verye noble, and such as fewe arrive at" (p. 358). The
image of a stairway of love has great charm today because it is
so purely and innocently Freudian. "Let us clime up the stayers,
which at the lowermost stepp have the shadowe of sensuall
beawty, to the high mansion place where the heavenlye, amiable
and right beawtye dwelleth, which lyeth hid in the innermost
secretes of God" (p. 361). Bembo then concludes with a perora-
tion and prayer to love. "What tunge mortall is there then (O
most holy love) [*Amor* in the original] that can sufficientlye prayse
thy woorthynesse? . . . Accept oure soules, that be offred unto
thee for a sacrifice. Burn them in the livelye flame that wasteth
al grosse filthines, that after they be cleane sundred from the
body, thei may be copled with an everlastinge and most sweet
bonde to the heavenly beawty. And we severed from oure selves,
may be chaunged like right lovers into the beloved, and after we
be drawen from the earth, admitted to the feast of the aungelles,
where fed with immortall ambrosia and nectar, in the ende we
maye dye a most happie and livelye death, as in times past died
the fathers of olde time, whose soules with most fervent zeale
of beehouldinge thou diddest hale from the bodye and coopled-
dest them with God" (pp. 361-363).

Da Porto's version, as I have remarked, has a bland, humanistic surface in which these ideas are implicit rather than explicit.
Romeo is so beautiful that he astonishes everyone. At the Cappelletti festa he sits apart, but his beauty makes him the center
of attention. Giulietta is equally beautiful, and he tells her that
if she cannot return his love, at least he can die near her. They

have many meetings and are at length married. After Tebaldo's death they meet at Friar Lorenzo's cell and behave very temperately compared to the characters in Brooke and Shakespeare, but after Romeo's departure to Mantua, Giulietta weeps constantly and wishes for death "a thousand times a day." (The same image continues into Brooke [1981].) Romeo tries to stab himself upon hearing of her apparent death, and in the Cappelletti tomb he swallows serpents' venom (which any medicine man could have told him wouldn't work), and Giulietta seeing him die, commits suicide by holding her breath (which wouldn't work either). Notwithstanding these terminal gaucheries, the story is warm, reasonable, and humane. There is nothing about passionate abandonment. Although destiny is alluded to once at the resumption of the feud and again by Romeo in the Cappelletti tomb, Prof. Moore considers these details part of Da Porto's careful preparation;[53] they may have been the original hints for Boiastuau's exaggerations. The novelle writers often wrote exempla, and Da Porto's story appears to be an exemplum not of Bembo's discourse but of the general Neoplatonic ideas of love current at the time.

Many of the details in Da Porto which suggest a submerged foundation of Neoplatonic ideas come down into the English versions. In Painter, Rhomeo was "the comliest and best conditioned Gentleman that was amonges the *Veronian* youth" (p. 97). Nature had so adorned him with beauty that though he sat in a corner, he was "loked vpon of the whole Company, but specially of the Ladies" (p. 99). Julietta was of such "surpassinge Beautye" that to Rhomeo she was "the Chyefest place for all perfection in Beautye" (p. 100). Their readiness for death is stated repeatedly (pp. 110, 115-117, 119, 120). Julietta is very sure that she and Rhomeo will be reunited in the Beyond:

And thou my deare Lord & loyall husband Rhomeo, if there rest in thee any knowledge, receyue hir whom thou hast so faythfully loued, the onely cause of thy violent death, which frankley offreth vp hir soule that none but thou shalt ioy the loue whereof thou hast made so lawfull conquest, and that our soules passing from this light, may eternally liue together in the place of euerlasting ioy. (pp. 138-139)

49

Christians who commit suicide can not expect such an end. This is Neoplatonic reunion in a non-Christian Beyond.

In Brooke the beauty of Romeus is first among all the youth of Verona:

> One Romeus, who was of race a Montague,
> Upon whose tender chyn, as yet, no manlyke beard
> there grewe,
> Whose beauty and whose shape so farre the rest
> did stayne,
> That from the cheefe of Veron youth he greatest
> fame dyd gayne.
>
> (53-56)

At the Capelet dance the women wonder at "his sightly shape, and bewties spotles hew" (76). Juliet is so "fayre of perfect shape / Which Theseus, or Paris would have chosen to their rape" (197-198). Brooke lacks a certain delicacy. His poem is much more heavily threaded with allusions to death than is Painter's version. These many allusions[54] culminate in Juliet's final speech:

> Prolong no longer now my lyfe, I hate this long delaye,
> For straight my parting sprite, out of this carkas fled,
> At ease shall finde my Romeus sprite, among so many ded.
> And thou my loving lord, Romeus my trusty feer,
> If knowledge yet doe rest in thee, if thou these
> woordes dost heer,
> Receve thou her, whom thou didst love so lawfully, . . .
> Thinjoying of my love, which ay I have reserved,
> Free from the rest, bound unto thee, that hast
> it well deserved:
> That so our parted sprites, from light that we see here,
> In place of endlesse light and blisse, may ever live
> yfere.
>
> (2776-88)

Even in wooden Brooke the lovers seek a rapturous Beyond.

In Shakespeare's play Juliet is so beautiful that "she doth teach the torches to burn bright" (I.v.46). More significantly, she is "Beauty too rich for use, for earth too dear" (I.v.49). Juliet indirectly compares Romeo to roses (II.ii.43-45), and stars (III.ii.21-25), and she says he will "lie upon the wings of night / Whiter than new snow on a raven's back" (III.ii.18-19). On one occasion she calls him "beautiful" (III.ii.75), although it is not customary English usage to call men beautiful unless in derision. Except for Bottom when he is wearing the ass head, Romeo is the only man in Shakespeare's plays who ever gets that epithet.

I have already remarked H. Edward Cain's article upon Death as the lover of Juliet. He cited Juliet's line that her grave was like to be her wedding bed (I.v.137), her declaration that Death, not Romeo, might take her maidenhead (III.ii.132-137), her statement that her bridal bed would be in Tybalt's monument (III.v.200-203), Capulet's lament that she had been deflowered by Death (IV.v.35-40), Romeo's assertion that he would lie with her that night (V.i.34), the implication being they'd both be dead, and in its fullest form, Romeo's declaration that amorous death might be her paramour (V.iii.101-105). The additional passages that associate love with Death and the grave are many, and the references to death are more frequent in *Romeo and Juliet* than in any other Shakespearian play. I think we must conclude that the passages in question are not there merely as a form of foreshadowing or as an expression of fate, but that Death itself is one of the major themes of this play.

The major passages having to do with love and death, in addition to those already cited, are the following:

> The earth that's Nature's mother is her tomb,
> What is her burying grave, that is her womb.
> (II.iii.9-10)

The tomb-womb rhyme makes the association of death with love fairly evident. Later in the same scene Romeo says to Friar Laurence, "[Thou] bad'st me bury love," to which the Friar answers, "Not in a grave / To lay one in, another out to have" (II.iii.83-84). As the marriage becomes an evident possibility, Romeo declares:

> Do thou but close our hands with holy words,
> Then love-devouring Death do what he dare;
> It is enough I may but call her mine.
>
> (II.vi.6-8)

I have cited this before as evidence of his defying reason; the
association of love with Death is not a rational one. The third
of these lines suggests the eternal union to which the Neoplatonic lover might awake and be an emperor—in the Beyond.
When Romeo throws his tantrum after his banishment, he again
mentions the grave in connection with his love (III.iii.65-70). In
the course of the aubade after their first night together, Romeo
says to Juliet, "Let me be ta'en, let me be put to death, . . .
Come death, and welcome! Juliet wills it so" (III.v.17-24). Love
is represented visually before the eyes of the audience, but death
is sounded in their ears. Very shortly Juliet says to him,
"Methinks I see thee, now thou art below, / As one dead in the
bottom of a tomb" (III.v.56). Lady Capulet in reproaching Juliet
says first, "What, wilt thou wash him from his grave with tears?"
(III.v.71). The image is echoed with multiple ironies seventy
lines later when she says of Juliet, "I would the fool were married
to her grave!" Once Juliet is so married, none of Lady Capulet's
tears will wash her forth. When the proposed marriage with
Paris causes Juliet to visit Friar Laurence again, Shakespeare
not following Brooke, has her ring changes on the theme:

> Oh, bid me leap, rather than marry Paris,
> From off the battlements of yonder tower; . . .
> Or shut me nightly in a charnel house,
> O'ercover'd quite with dead men's rattling bones,
> With reeky shanks and yellow chapless skulls;
> Or bid me go into a new-made grave,
> And hide me with a dead man in his shroud . . .
> And I will do it without fear or doubt
> To live an unstained wife to my sweet love.
>
> (IV.i.77-87)

Her great soliloquy before she drinks the sleeping potion (IV.iii.
15-58), improved from Brooke (2349-2400), is a long compound

of images of death, love, and marriage informed with a degree of passion greater than any other thus far in the play. The scene when well done is greatly moving. The images of which it is composed are central to the thematic structure of the play.

The reunion of these suicidal lovers somewhere beyond the grave seems even more evident in Romeo's account of his dream:

> If I may trust the flattering truth of sleep,
> My dreams presage some joyful news at hand.
> My bosom's lord sits lightly in his throne,
> And all this day an unaccustomed spirit
> Lifts me above the ground with cheerful thoughts.   5
> I dreamed my lady came and found me dead—
> Strange dream, that gives a dead man leave to think!—   7
> And breathed such life with kisses in my lips
> That I revived and was an emperor.   9
> Ah me, how sweet is love itself possessed   10
> When but love's shadows are so rich in joy!
>
> (V.i.1-11)

No parallel to this passage appears in either Brooke or Painter; apparently it is Shakespeare's addition. It seems to derive its great poignancy from its calculated internal conflicts. We know Romeo is exuberant on the threshold of unexpected disaster. She *will* find him dead, but will kiss him in vain. According to Bembo, a kiss is the communion of two souls who ought to awake in the eternal Beyond; the seventh line above tells us that awakening cannot be, but the ninth line asserts in the face of reason and disaster, it *will* be. The tenth and eleventh lines are a Neoplatonic double equation: his nighttime dream of love is to his waking earthly love as his earthly love is to his love in the heavenly Beyond of his dream. The series of concepts is circular, perhaps because according to Bembo a circle is the perfect form—as well as a common symbol of eternity.

The association of love and death becomes visibly represented before the eyes of the audience in the last scene (V.iii.45-170). Romeo calles the Capulet tomb "thou womb of death." Paris asks to be laid in the tomb with Juliet. Romeo passionately harps upon death, "the lean abhorred monster" that keeps Juliet for his paramour. Death, which earlier in the play had been a mere verbal allusion gratuitously associated with love, is now visibly represented on the stage, and the passionate love which is also portrayed before our eyes is expressed in terms of death and the everlasting tomb.

A fourth level of meaning in this play is one related to the third and supported from the play by the same evidence. That theme is the equation of love with death itself. In his chapter on "Amor as a God of Death,"[55] Edgar Wind has shown that the Italian Renaissance humanists identified Eros or Amor "with Death itself, in its painful no less than in its joyous aspect." They derived this notion from their readings of Plato and Plotinus and from the many Roman sarcophagi on which they had found either the image of the deceased supported by the winged adolescent boy Amor, or figures of the mortals who had been loved by gods—Endymion, Leda, Ganymede, Rhea, Psyche, and the rest. I might add that Roman sarcophagi also sport Priapi. Wind quotes Pico's account of Alcestis, that she "did achieve the perfection of love because she wanted to go to the beloved through death; and dying through love, she was by the grace of the gods revived," and Lorenzo de' Medici, who wrote that "the beginning of the *vita amorosa* proceeds from death, because whoever lives for love, first dies to everything else. And if love has in it a certain perfection, . . . it is impossible to arrive at that perfection without first dying with regard to the more imperfect things." Wind concludes that to these Renaissance humanists, "Thanatos and the funerary Eros were one."

Not only were love and death the same, but death was the means to the greatest love to be desired. As Wind asserts, Renaissance humanists correctly understood that the figures of mortals beloved by gods which appear on sarcophagi all represented a post-mortem communion with a god through Love. This idea was employed by Michelangelo in his statue of Night on the Medici tomb, for she is really a commonplace Roman figure of Leda with an owl substituted for the swan. Wind cites Ficino, Pico, Castiglione, and Bruno, among many others, who wrote upon this mystic love union with a god through death, and he quotes Leone Ebreo, to whom "union and copulation with God Most High" was defined as a spiritual delight perfected in death.

Ebreo's is a Christianized version of the Neoplatonic idea. The gentle Reader will note that Bembo—in the quotations from Castiglione already given—twice mentions copulation with God as an ultimate objective of the lovers. Edmund Spenser in "An Hymne of Heavenly Beautie" describes Sapience as sharing God's bosome, "The soueraine dearling of the *Diety*, / Clad like a Queene in royall robes, most fit" (182-184).[56] Subsequently, Spenser speaks of "that faire loue of mightie heauens king," which he calls "sacred mysteries" (234-235). Spenser's *Sapience* is, of course, an abstraction, not a lover in a play, but Prof. Saurat has argued that the true prototype of Sapience is the Schekhina of the Cabala, and that Spenser became familiar with the idea through Agrippa or Pico della Mirandola.[57] The Schekhina of the Cabala was identified with Beauty; the relations between her and God were sexual. A much more dramatic version of the same mixture of death, piety, and eroticism occurs in Donne's Holy Sonnet XIV. The first quatrain asks for death; the last three lines are a complete fusion of religion and eroticism: "Take mee to you, imprison mee, for I / Except you'enthrall mee, never shall be free, / Nor ever chast, except you ravish mee." Similar mixtures of death and eroticism which had their remoter origins in the same late classical Neoplatonism that produced the aforementioned sarcophagi continued into Baroque times, as in Bernini's statues of the Ecstasy of St. Teresa and of the Blessed Lodovica Albertoni.

I should like at this point to summarize my interpretation so far. On the most superficial intellectual level the play represents the conflict of grace and rude will. On a second level, it represents concupiscence and irascibility arrayed against each other and reason. By the end of the play hatred has been killed with love, but also love with hatred, when reason should have overruled both. On a third level, the lovers' allusions to stars, graves, and death, together with the action, represent the Platonic translation of themselves and their earthly love from this faulty world of decay and mutability to eternal rapture in the Beyond, outside of time; in Neoplatonic terms, Pulchritudo appears on earth and through the action of Amor unites with Voluptas and returns to the Beyond. On a fourth level, death represents a desideratum, the ultimate fulfillment of ecstatic love. Shakespeare

55

omits the copulation with God. These themes are in balance: against the earthly rapture which is the shadow of the eternal love lies the shadow of death, and across all three there tolls from beginning to end the themes of *festina lente,* grace and rude will, the voices of sober reason. These complex themes, the intellectual and philosophical structure of the play, have been held in balance by Shakespeare, none dominating the others, and individual members of the Elizabethan audience were free to recognize as much as their educations and perceptions allowed and were free to stress any one theme over some other as their unconscious predilections suggested. The power with which any particular theme is carried alive into the mind so that apprehension is emotional as well as intellectual depends partly upon the quality of Shakespeare's poetry, but also partly upon the interests and ideas of the auditors—or to switch to some very post-Elizabethan diction—upon age, sex, and marital status. And so we come to another problem.

MODERN APPRECIATION

Before discussing the nature of modern appreciation, I should like to make three generalizations. The first is that although we should of course be very cautious about reading modern ideas into works of another era, we should be equally cautious about patronizing the presumed simplicity and intellectual innocence of earlier times. Because the physical sciences have produced in the last century wonders without precedent is no reason to suppose that philosophy and psychology have done the same. As some of the foregoing discussion should have made clear, it seems not only possible but likely that much art in the Renaissance or earlier is intellectually, esthetically and psychologically as complex as anything done since. In the interest of the fullest understanding, it needs all the instruments that can be brought to bear upon it.

The second generalization is that I quite repudiate the notion that art is complete in itself, "centripetal," autogenetic, autonomous, or self-contained. All art is a system of abstractions, but so is all human thought, including scientific and mathematical formulations. The latter are valuable when as in the work of

Galileo, Napier, or Newton they have some correspondence with external realities, and worthless when they don't, as in the compilations called Hermes Trismegistus. The same is true of the activities called art, and to dismiss art as wholly irrelevant to other human activity is little different in principle from treating it as exclusively self-contained—a latterday second sophistic attitude that in the absence of external ideological pressure looks plainly schizoid.

The third generalization is that the lasting appeal of the works of art we call "great" is at least partly dependent upon a validity of reference that extends outside of the work of art. The continuing appeal of classical, medieval and Renaissance art through so many centuries derives not exclusively from consummate technique, but from the appeal of that art to relatively constant ideas or to recurrent ideas—cultural patterns—in Western societies over very long periods of time. The ideas informing a specific work of art may have been articulated in some contemporaneous work of philosophy either with altered old terms, or with newly introduced ones, but the persistent reappearance of differently phrased patterns of ideas—usually in their day professing to be apprehensions of ultimate reality—argues the existence in Western culture of certain constants beneath all the obvious, conspicuous and transitory configurations that make every age unique. Whether these constants are merely beliefs of Western societies, without any objective reality, or else symbolizations of vaguely apprehended constants in human feeling, I cannot hope to say; their validation lies in other fields than criticism. But the work of art that maintains its appeal beyond its own age probably does so because it touches these constants, real or ideational; if any of those discussed below do have some objective validity, we have better reason to understand the modern appeal of this play.

Modern audiences who remain cheerfully ignorant of Christian grace and rude will, of faculty psychology and of Neoplatonic triads, nevertheless find the play either in reading or in a good performance to be tremendously moving. That a modern audience should get vicarious pleasure from the great love poetry of the play would hardly seem to need explanation, but on the other hand, the love ends in death. Logically one should think people

57

would better enjoy the play if it had had a happy ending, with Romeo and Juliet living happily ever after, but the very thought of that is ridiculous. In Western societies, at least, the love stories that have had the greatest number of versions and that were therefore presumably the most popular have all ended with the deaths of the lovers: Romeo and Juliet, Tristram and Iseult, Hero and Leander, Antony and Cleopatra, Pyramus and Thisbe. A second group ends with the death of one of the lovers and the presumed death or degradation of the other: Troilus and Criseyde, Lancelot and Guinevere, Carmen, La Traviata. All the great love stories are tragic; the happy ending is felt to be fundamentally superficial, profoundly disappointing.

I believe that the explanation of the persisting appeal of this play lies in the persistence of the ideas which provided its thematic basis and which in different terminology are still with us. The appeal may even lie in their as yet undemonstrated validity, although validity would not be necessary if belief is present to serve or if cultural patterns provide receptive ground.

The first and superficial level of meaning, the conflict of grace and rude will, has evidently withered somewhat, as Dowden and others indicate by their repudiation of it. But the second level of meaning I suggested for this play was conflicts between the parts of the Platonic and Renaissance tripartite division of the mind into concupiscence, ireful passion, and reason. I submit that Renaissance concupiscence is roughly equivalent to Plato's unruly steed (*Phaedrus,* 253-256) and to Freud's insatiable id.[58] Renaissance and Christian conscience is the conscious part of Freud's super-ego, as Freud himself acknowledged, and is also roughly equivalent to Platonic ireful virtue and to the self-righteous wrath that historically has so often beset the religious. Christian and Neoplatonic reason is equivalent to Plato's charioteer and also to Freud's ego, which is charged with mediating the conflicting demands of super-ego, id, and external reality; it declares that "to love extreamely procureth eyther death or danger." To put these three concepts into modern physiological terms, we might say that "concupiscence" is roughly equivalent to the operation of the parasympathetic part of the autonomic nervous system, and "irascibility" represents the operation of the sympathetic part. In modern physiology, as in Shakespeare's play, they are mutually exclusive modes of reaction. Reason and self-control, functions of the central nervous system, may or may not oppose, assist, or control impulses from the autonomic nervous system. This is not to say that the physiological concepts are the equivalents of the psychoanalytical; any such suggestion would be absurd; I am saying only that both sets of concepts, like the abstract and figurative concepts in Plato and Burton, appear to be describing in their different ways aspects of the same currents of human feeling and behavior. The total psychological and physical reality (if psychological and physical will really prove to be different), remains still undescribed. Shakespeare's play also involves partial apprehensions of these currents, but it blends those apprehensions with many other considerations which are emotional, philosophical, dramatic and tragic. In a general sense he is closer to truth than philosopher, psychoanalyst, or physiologist, for he portrays those apprehensions as forces operating in a social context, and he conveys them and the realization of their social consequences into the spectator's mind on the strength of emotion excited by great poetry and by sympathetic identification with seemingly concrete characters.

The third level of meaning I have suggested in this play is represented by the Neoplatonic triad of Pulchritudo, Amor, and Voluptas. The Platonic Beyond hardly has any modern scientific equivalent, although it has an approximate, Christian, coeval equivalent in the belief that the soul comes from God and returns to Him. But the third level I have discussed shades into the fourth, the equating of Eros with Thanatos in ancient and Renaissance Neoplatonic thought. I think this idea may also be explained in Freudian terms. I expect that an occasional reader may object that psychoanalysis is irrelevant to literature before 1900, and that he would do so because he really believes with G. K. Chesterton and Prof. Elmer Stoll that psychoanalysis is only a fad. I do not undertake to vouch for the "truth" of the Freudian concepts I shall here employ; indeed, I do not know what it is. But since no one has done any better at explaining the persistent irrationalities of human behavior than has Freud, it may be worthwhile tentatively to consider the Freudian explanation until more verifiable explanations come along.

In discussing infantile sexuality (imagine Dowden confronted with that term), Freud said that it included feeding and sucking, and that the deep and satisfied sleep of the infant after feeding is the prototype of the deep sleep that adults enjoy after sexual satisfaction, which he said "is the best soporific."[59] I do not know that the causation is as he suggested, but at least we have his testimony that deep sleep after love-making is very common. The symbolic equating of sleep with death is worldwide. As Prof. Chandler Beall has shown,[60] Renaissance and seventeenth-century English usage allowed the infinitive "to die" as a cant term for the sexual act. The Renaissance association of love with death was recognized as a mystery, but felt to be "right." Shakespeare has stressed death so much in this play—as we have seen, more than in any other he wrote—that we may suspect its deepest appeal is to the death instinct hypothesized by both Leonardo and Freud.

Like Freud, but much less tentatively, Leonardo suggested that all human beings secretly desire to die because the inanimate elements which have been forced into the organization of life desire to return to their simpler state:

> Behold now the hope and desire of going back to one's own country or returning to primal chaos, like that of the moth to the light, of the man who with perpetual longing always looks forward with joy to each new spring and each new summer, and to the new months and the new years, deeming that the things he longs for are too slow in coming; and who does not perceive that he is longing for his own destruction. But this longing is in its quintessence the spirit of the elements, which finding itself imprisoned within the life of the human body desires continually to return to its source. And I would have you to know that this same longing is in its quintessence inherent in nature, and that man is a type of the world.[61]

Freud's hypothesis was first put forward in *Beyond the Pleasure Principle* (1920). Recognizing that "inanimate things existed before living ones," he wrote as follows:

> The attributes of life were at some time evoked in inanimate matter by the action of a force of whose nature we can form

no conception. It may perhaps have been a process similar in type to that which later caused the development of consciousness in a particular stratum of living matter. The tension which then arose in what had hitherto been an inanimate substance endeavoured to cancel itself out. In this way the first instinct came into being: the instinct to return to the inanimate state. It was still an easy matter at that time for a living substance to die; the course of its life was probably only a brief one, whose direction was determined by the chemical structure of the young life. For a long time, perhaps, living substance was thus being constantly created afresh and easily dying, till decisive external influences altered in such a way as to oblige the still surviving substance to diverge ever more widely from its original course of life and to make ever more complicated *détours* before reaching its aim of death. These circuitous paths to death, faithfully kept to by the conservative instincts, would thus present us today with the picture of the phenomena of life.[62]

Freud pushed his speculations somewhat further than Leonardo. Against the death instincts he suggested the sexual instincts were operating like "the Eros of the poets and philosophers which holds all living things together."[63] The satisfaction of the sexual instincts removes the binding force of Eros and leaves the organism satisfied to die. It must be granted that there are some species among fish, insects and spiders that do normally die upon the completion of the sexual act. Although the parallels with Shakespeare's play are obvious, I am not vouching for the truth of Leonardo's or Freud's propositions. Leonardo was Olympian and dogmatic in tone, but Freud was properly speculative and tentative. For my part, I am only suggesting that if these propositions *are* true, they may be part of the continuing appeal of the play, and that if they are *not* true, the evident parallels nevertheless represent continuing patterns of thought.

The conclusion thus far is that the thematic structure of the play is a medley of related ideas that have occurred with different terminologies in ancient, Renaissance, and modern times. I think the profound appeal the play makes to a modern audience can be explained in modern terms which I have already shown to have had their Renaissance equivalents implicitly in the play.

The Renaissance tripartite division of mental functions into concupiscence, reason, and irascibility—upon which the plot proceeds—I have approximately equated with Freud's tripartite division of id, ego, and super-ego. If a performance of *Romeo and Juliet* is good enough for the willing suspension of disbelief to take place temporarily, we may expect all three of those mental functions in the spectator to become involved with the play. The insatiable id, which demands the passionate experience, luxuriates in the glorious love poetry and the danger which proves the validity of the love even better than the pallid preamble with Rosaline—love, love, limitless love, full speed ahead. The super-ego, especially if it is at all tyrannical, is outraged and inexorably demands punishment. The ego, which has the responsibility of mediating these demands with external reality, declares that it cannot be, that reason and self-control are being abrogated. Shakespeare's play contains characters that meet all these psychic needs. The passionate love of Romeo and Juliet is carried into the mind of the spectator by Shakespeare's great poetry; the claims of the ego for reason and self-control are met by the repeated injunctions of Friar Laurence, perhaps so that the spectator's ego does not upset that willing suspension of disbelief by declaring, "It could not be." The demands of the super-ego are met by Prince Escalus, first as threatener (I.i.89-110), then as punisher (III.i.191-202), and finally as chorus pointing the moral, "All are punishèd" (V.iii.295), and "Some shall be pardoned and some punishèd" (V.iii.308). From Romeo's dream (V.i.1-11), already cited, we may suppose that death will liberate the love of Romeo and Juliet not in the Christian hereafter, because that would be impossible for suicides, but in the Neoplatonic Beyond, free of the restraints of super-ego and ego. But though in the course of Shakespeare's drama the spectator's id may through vicarious experience feel temporarily liberated, conscience and reason do not really abrogate; there is no way they can be made to do so, short of pathology. Such passionate behavior as Romeo's they recognize must be destructive, and the symbolization of normal sleep with poetic death reassures both those functions of the mind that such abandonment has such an end. Shakespeare's play therefore meets and satisfies these three basic requirements of the human psyche. The grand passion is experienced vicariously in Romeo and Juliet, and the self-restraints that might cry alarm are satisfied with the statements of *festina lente*, grace and rude will, and the lovers' deaths. The tragic catharsis ensues from the termination of the id's satisfaction: something has been had, but the end of the play ends the satisfaction, and the sleep of death symbolizes that ending better than any "lived happily ever after," which would be a denial of the ending of the vicarious passion which the id knows is ending as the play ends. Only death is "right," for it is true to the ending of the spectator's vicarious experience of the lovers' passion, true to the spectator's own recollection of love and sleep, true to the demands of his reason, which says that such passion cannot continue, and true to the demands of Western conscience which says such passion must be punished. Finally, although the living person's physical love may not be the wildly passionate ideal desired by the id, that of Romeo and Juliet or of Tristram and Iseult *is* a representation of such heightened experience, and the death which follows, superficially a heightened symbol of sleep, is perhaps more profoundly a desire for death, illogical but mysteriously satisfying because it meets a desire so deep and inarticulate that its only conscious feeling is the grieving delusion of a will to live that knows and loves its certain doom.

The Pennsylvania State University

NOTES

[1] Gervinus, G. G., *Shakespeare Commentaries,* tr. by F. E. Bunnett, 5th ed. (London, 1892), p. 211.

[2] Textual citations are from *The Complete Works,* ed. by G. B. Harrison (New York, 1952). Globe line numbering.

[3] *Leading Motives in the Imagery of Shakespeare's Tragedies* (Oxford, 1930).

[4] *Pagan Mysteries of the Renaissance* (London, 1958), pp. 90-95.

[5] *The Tragicall Historye of Romeus and Juliet,* ed. by Geoffrey Bullough in *Narrative and Dramatic Sources of Shakespeare,* Vol. I (London and New

York, 1957), pp. 284-363. All Brooke citations and line numbers are from this edition.

6 *Rhomeo and Iulietta,* ed. P. A. Daniel, New Shakspere Society originals and Analogues, Part I (London, 1875), pp. 93-144. All citations from Painter are from this edition.

7 *Shakespeare's Young Lovers* (New York, 1937), pp. 9-10.

8 *Shakspere: A Critical Study of His Mind and Art* (New York, 1875). This and subsequent quotations are from pp. 107-109.

9 The idea of retributive justice which informs the action is explicitly stated in the following places: By Queen Margaret, I.iii.191-214, 219-227, 297-303. By Buckingham, II.i.32-40; V.i.29. By King Edward, II.i.131-133. By a chorus of characters, II.ii.59-90. By the Duchess of York, II.iv.55-65; IV.iv. 194. By Vaughan, III.iii.7. By Grey, III.iii.15-17. By Rivers, III.iii.18-22. By Hastings, III.iv.105-109. By a scrivener, III.vi.13-14. By Queen Margaret and the Duchess of York, IV.iv.39-70. By Richard himself, V.iii.204-206.

10 *Richard III,* Furness Variorum (Philadelphia, 1908), pp. 6-8. Dowden may be excused somewhat here, since this material had not been published yet when he wrote.

11 *Romeo and Juliet,* New Cambridge Edition, ed. J. D. Wilson and G. I. Duthie (Cambridge, 1955), p. xxviii.

12 *Shakspere and his Predecessors* (New York, 1896), pp. 198-214.

13 "Hamlet," *Selected Essays* 1917-1932 (New York, 1932), p. 122.

14 "The Elizabethan Rejection of Judicial Astrology and Shakespeare's Practice," *SQ,* IX (1958), 159-176.

15 *King Lear,* ed. G. L. Kittredge (Boston, 1940), note on I.ii.164-165, p. 134.

16 "The Imagery of *Romeo and Juliet,*" *English,* VIII (1950), 121-126.

17 " 'Write me a Prologue'," *English,* VIII (1951), 272-274.

18 Quoted in New Variorum *Romeo* (Philadelphia, 1878), p. 85.

19 Ibid., p. 85.

20 *Giulietta and Romeo,* tr. Jessie Benton Evans (Portland, 1934), pp. 3-4.

21 "*Romeo and Juliet* as an Experimental Tragedy," *PBA,* XXV (1939), 144.

22 The following lines in Brooke's poem contain references to the goddess Fortune: 25, 117, 154, 245, 327, 818, 828, 860, 865, 881, 908, 911, 913, 932, 935, 951, 952, 1060, 1068, 1102, 1222, 1343, 1391, 1405, 1407, 1442, 1447, 1470, 1474, 1479, 1546-54, 1588, 1591, 1606, 1667, 1668, 1754, 1897, 1921, 2040, 2352, 2484, 2745, 2758, 2840.

23 Lines 425, 500, 801, 1328-29, 1557, 1574, 1585, 1753-54.

24 *The Complete Plays and Poems of William Shakespeare* (Boston, 1942), p. 975.

25 *Romeo and Juliet* (Boston, 1940), p. xii.

26 New Cambridge Edition, p. xxxi.

27 *Narrative and Dramatic Sources,* Vol. I, p. 277.

[28] "Shakespeare's Star-Crossed Lovers," *RES*, xv (1939), 16-34.

[29] "Historical Criticism and the Interpretation of Shakespeare," *SQ*, x (1959), 3-9.

[30] "Form and Formality in *Romeo and Juliet*," *SQ*, xi (1960), 3-11.

[31] *His Infinite Variety* (Philadelphia, 1964), pp. 267-279.

[32] "*Romeo and Juliet:* A Reinterpretation," *SAB*, xxii (1947), 163-192.

[33] "Christianity and the Religion of Love in *Romeo and Juliet*," *SQ*, xii (1961), 371-392.

[34] Cambridge University Press, 1930.

[35] *Shakespeare and the Tragic Theme.* Univ. Missouri Studies, XIX, No. 2, 1944.

[36] *As They Liked It* (New York, 1947), p. 147. The quotation in Harbage is from Bandello.

[37] Ibid., p. 148.

[38] " 'Hang up Philosophy'," *SAB*, xxii (1947), 203-209.

[39] "A Technique of Motivation in *Romeo and Juliet*," *SAB*, xxi (1946), 186-190.

[40] Footnote 32.

[41] *Unity in Shakespearian Tragedy* (New York, 1956), pp. 10-25.

[42] *Not Wisely But Too Well* (San Marino, 1957).

[43] "Then I Deny You Starres: A Reading of *Romeo and Juliet*," *Studies in the English Renaissance Drama: In Memory of Karl Holzknecht*, ed. Josephine W. Bennett (New York, 1959).

[44] "Christianity and the Religion of Love," *SQ*, xii (1961), 380-382.

[45] "Form and Formality in *Romeo and Juliet*," pp. 6-7, 8.

[46] *Anatomy of Melancholy*, ed. Floyd Dell and Paul Jordan-Smith (New York, 1927), p. 141.

[47] "Ficino and the Platonism of the English Renaissance," *CL*, iv (1952), 214-238.

[48] Wind, *Pagan Mysteries*, pp. 43-51.

[49] *Pagan Mysteries*, p. 52.

[50] Olin H. Moore, *The Legend of Romeo and Juliet* (Columbus, Ohio, 1950).

[51] Moore, p. 43.

[52] *The Book of The Courtier from the Italian of Count Baldassare Castiglione.* Tr. by Sir Thomas Hoby. Ed. by W. E. Henley (London, 1900).

[53] Moore, p. 56.

[54] Lines 358, 401-402, 495-496, 513-516, 521-524, 1192, 1296-1300, 1901-1902, 1914-1915, 1981, 2021-2024, 2701-2704. Most of these are given to the two lovers.

[55] Wind, pp. 129-141.

[56] *Spenser's Minor Poems,* ed. Ernest de Sélincourt (Oxford, 1910).

[57] "La Sapience de Spenser et la Schekina de la Cabale," *RLC,* VI (1926), 5 ff.

[58] *New Introductory Lectures in Psycho-Analysis,* tr. W. J. H. Sprott (New York, 1933).

[59] "Three Essays on Sexuality. II. Infantile Sexuality," *Standard Edition,* Vol. VII, tr. James Strachey *et al.* (London, 1953), p. 180.

[60] "A Quaint Conceit from Guarini to Dryden," *MLN,* LXIV (1949), 461-468.

[61] *The Notebooks of Leonardo da Vinci,* tr. Edward MacCurdy, Vol. I (New York, n.d. [1938]), pp. 80-81.

[62] *Beyond the Pleasure Principle, Standard Edition,* Vol. XVIII, tr. James Strachey *et al.* (London, 1955), pp. 38-39.

[63] Ibid., pp. 50-52.

STRUCTURE AND THEME
IN THE FIRST TAVERN SCENE
OF *HENRY IV, PART ONE*

WALDO F. McNEIR

It has been perceived that some of Shakespeare's scenes are "so elaborately finished with a beginning, a middle, and an end as to make them little plays in their own right," [1] and it has been pointed out that in *Henry IV, Part One* "some scenes are planned like miniature dramas." [2] An excellent example of a scene having the internal structure of a miniature drama is II, iv in *Henry IV, Part One*. This does not mean that the scene has an independent existence or significance apart from the rest of the play, or that it turns inward upon itself. On the contrary, analysis will show that its light shines inward and outward at the same time, the sum of its parts constituting a smaller entity whose purpose is to illuminate both itself and the larger entity of the play. Since this is so, analysis of the organization of the scene will have to consider the interweaving in it of the serious and comic elements of the play, and its bearing on the theme of Prince Hal's education in private (ethical) and public (political) virtue.

This scene of 531 lines of prose is twice as long as the next longest scene in the play.[3] It has five "acts" or movements and an epilogue.

1. The practical joke played by Hal and Poins on Francis, the drawer (1-106).

2. The exposure of Falstaff's lies in his account of what happened at Gad's Hill (107-274).

3. The first intrusion on the revelry when Sir John Bracy arrives with news from the court (275-364).

4. The play-acting of Falstaff and Hal as they impersonate, in turn, the King and the Prince (365-464).

5. The second intrusion on the revelry when the Sheriff and the watch arrive in pursuit of the Gad's Hill robbers (465-507).

Epilogue. The inventory of Falstaff's pockets by Hal and Poins (508-531).[4]

Before we examine the remarkable internal management of the scene, we need to remind ourselves of what precedes it, for it reasserts through parallel or contrast much that comes before, just as it foreshadows much that is to follow. The opposition between Henry IV's conception of Hotspur, "the theme of honor's tongue," and his conception of his son, stained with "riot and dishonor," has been introduced in the first scene of the play. At the beginning of I, ii the Prince in seemingly idle conversation with Falstaff ridicules his old associate for asking "what time of day is it," because time is meaningless in Falstaff's world and Hal knows the time spent in that world is wasted, as shown in his famous soliloquy ending the scene, when he resolves to refute the popular—and his father's—conception of him by "Redeeming time when men think least I will." The word "time" occurs in the first and last lines of I, ii. Hal himself frames and answers the question of whether he will make a travesty of time in company with Falstaff or, in his own good time and when necessity summons, keep his appointment with history.[5] Hal makes at the beginning and the end of this scene the distinction between the false time of the little tavern world ruled by Falstaff (his surrogate father) and the true time of the great world of Britain ruled by King Henry (his real father); and his explicit loyalty to the latter despite any appearances to the contrary states an important theme of both parts of *Henry IV*. It is also in I, ii that the Gad's Hill "subplot" is initiated, and its outcome is one important movement in the first tavern scene.[6] In I, iii, one of the most powerful scenes in the history plays, Hal's rival Hotspur is tellingly revealed as he works himself up into an hysterical rage against King Henry, delaying his uncle Worcester's information about the conspiracy for seventy lines of self-defeating anger. Hotspur's real character, since his public image is as far from the

truth as Prince Hal's, comes into full view through his impetu-
osity, impatience of opposition, extravagant dreams of honor to
be won by violence, hot-headedness, touchy pride, egotism, and
rashness. Any admiration for him after this display flies in the
face of reason, but Shakespeare's intention is made even clearer
by Hotspur's repeated exhibition of the same traits.[7] The next
two scenes parody in different ways the vaunting rhetoric and
the overconfidence of the conspirators. Amid the early morning
stir in the inn yard at Rochester in II, i, bleary-eyed and scratch-
ing themselves as they prepare for the road, the two carriers talk
of Cut's saddle, moldy peas and beans, the price of oats, fleas and
chamber pots, bacon and ginger and starved turkeys; then in
preparation for the robbery Gadshill with his bluster tries to impress on his informer, the Chamberlain, that Falstaff's thieves
have powerfull allies. "It cannot choose but be a noble plot,"
Hotspur had said to his informer-uncle Worcester in assessing
the rebels' strength; and his wish that "the hours be short / Till
fields and blows and groans applaud our sport!" is closely followed by the Battle of Gad's Hill in II, ii, with the groans of
Falstaff for lack of a horse and the mock-blows from which he
and the other rogues run away to applaud the sport of Hal and
Poins. The scene in which Hotspur reads the letter (II, iii) reiterates the traits revealed in I, iii—his cocksureness, lack of caution,
romantic idea that an "honorable" plot against the King is bound
to succeed, contempt and scorn of opposition or disagreement,
ruthless self-absorption—and adds the effect of these on his relations with his loved but neglected wife, who is as ill-informed
about his plans as he is about himself. All of this will be burles-
qued by Prince Hal in the first movement of the drama now to be
examined.

The setting is the Boar's Head Tavern in Eastcheap, the capi-
tal of Falstaff's kingdom, a place of unbridled yet innocent revelry in contrast to the stiff formality of the court, although it is
not the bawdy house where drunks are "rolled" that Falstaff
tries to make it out to be in the second tavern scene (III, iii),
and that it becomes in the Doll Tearsheet scenes of *Henry IV,
Part Two*. The Prince appears as a familiar citizen if not subject
of Falstaff's kingdom. He has been "amongst three or four score
hogsheads" that he has fully sampled with "a leash of drawers"

who call him "the king of courtesy." Like Spenser's Calidore, an important part of his education is learning to behave courteously to inferiors without condescension while maintaining the distance that separates him from them.[8] And now, unlike the knight of courtesy in *The Faerie Queene,* he is half-drunk. But he has won the admiration and loyalty of "all the good lads in East-cheap" by his gesture, which will stand him in good stead at Agincourt. The jest which he and Poins now play on the boy Francis is neither unimportant nor pointless,[9] even though it does launch the scene with an elementary vaudeville turn on a crude level of comedy, for it parallels several themes of the play. When Hal asks, "But, Francis, darest thou be so valiant as to play the coward with thy indenture and show it a fair pair of heels and run from it?" we think of Falstaff's flight at Gad's Hill, a coward-ice that the fat ruffian is soon to call courage. Unconsciously, the Prince's suggestion is analogous to his own running away from or shirking his apprenticeship to his father in kingcraft. When Hal returns to his suggestion with "Wilt thou rob this leathern-jerkin, crystal-button, etc.," the Gad's Hill robbery is echoed again, and the questions of master-servant relationships and of personal loyalty to a master, themes to be developed later by Heywood and Dekker, briefly resound. But the suggestion is not seriously made, for Hal is not corrupting the boy as Falstaff's page is corrupted in *Henry IV, Part Two,* and moreover Francis is too distracted by Poins's repeated yelling for service and his own "Anon's" in reply to follow the intentionally jumbled threads of the Prince's verbiage. As both of them call him and, as the stage direction says, "The Drawer stands amazed, not knowing which way to go," his dilemma resembles on a lower level Hal's own situation in which he is called by the claims of the court and drawn by the attractions of the tavern at the same time, providing a moment of suspension in comic indecision that is resolved when the Vintner, the boy's master and the representa-tive of authority, orders him off to where he belongs. He must at-tend to "the guests within," not stand irresolutely beguiled by the Prince's specious fun-making. Here Hal in jest plays Falstaff to Francis's childish version of himself, anticipating the more overt impersonations in the fourth movement of the scene. Poins asks what the point is of "this jest of the drawer." As a practical joke invented by Hal and lacking any further comic possibilities, it is different from the practical joke of Gad's Hill invented by Poins, the comic outcome of which lies just ahead in the exposure of Falstaff. We have seen, however, that the jest is of some thematic importance in Shakespeare's design. Hal's reply, "I am now of all humors," confirms his readiness for anything, either mirthful or serious, that may occur. He proves equally capable in both modes in what follows. Still keeping Falstaff "with half-a-dozen more" waiting at the door, Hal has one more private joke in mind, this one at the expense of Hotspur. The transition from comically serious to seriously comic is made through a natural psychological process in Hal's association of the inarticulateness of Francis, who has "fewer words than a parrot . . . his eloquence the parcel of a reckoning," with the single humor of "Percy's mind," ever-dwelling on war and so indrawn that he is incapable of communicating even with his wife. Hotspur is consistently mistaken in his judgment of others, including Prince Hal,[10] as well as of himself. In contrast, the Prince's burlesque here of the immediately preceding scene between Hotspur and Kate (II, iii) is shrewdly penetrating. Its humorous effect depends on the ironic mimicry of the passionate Hotspur, whose ranting fulminations we have listened to at length, as a man sparing of speech, as wordless and abstracted as the childish drawer. It is not thus, of course, that Hal will speak of his enemy at Shrewsbury (V, i and V, iv), but now he is "of all humors," ready to "play Percy, and that damned brawn," who is still champing outside, "shall play Dame Mortimer his wife." In view of the heights of play-acting achieved by Hal and Falstaff in the fourth movement of the scene, of which this is another anticipation, we wish this hilarious idea of Hal's had been carried out. But it is time to admit Sir John.

The great second movement is pivotal in the structure of the scene and of the play. Just as Hotspur's distended sense of honor as a thirst for military glory founded on rash courage has been deflated by Hal's irony, so now Falstaff's shriveled sense of honor as a rejection of military glory founded on cowardice is exposed by Hal's account of what actually happened at Gad's Hill. Hal throughout represents the Aristotelian virtue or mean of rational courage between the two vices or extremes of Hotspur's fool-hardiness and Falstaff's cowardice.[11] Avoidance of both the excess and the deficiency of courage is one of the lessons he must learn before he can govern either himself or the kingdom. Falstaff's unconsciously self-damning refrain, "A plague of all cowards," occurs five times before he begins his version of the fight at Gad's Hill. With each iteration he puts his head further into the noose with which he will hang himself. His lament that "There lives not three good men unhanged in England; and one of them is fat and grows old" echoes the ambiguous exchange between him and Hal in I, iii concerning Falstaff's position in the new regime when Hal becomes king.

> *Falstaff.* Do not thou, when thou art king, hang a thief.
> *Prince.* No; thou shalt.
> *Falstaff.* Shall I? O rare! By the Lord, I'll be a brave judge.
> *Prince.* Thou judgest false already. I mean, thou shalt have the hanging of the thieves and so become a rare hangman.

Aside from the fact, unnoticed by critics, that this is the first clear forecast of the rejection of Falstaff, the prediction that he will one day be his own hangman is prepared for with every repetition of "A plague of all cowards." Falstaff's narrative consists of three overlapping parts: the number of men who attacked him and his companions, the number with whom he fought alone, and the number he dispatched. His arithmetic constitutes a tissue of prevarications which diminish in magnitude, those at the beginning being more outrageous than the ones which follow. There were "a hundred upon poor four of us," Falstaff begins, and he fought "with a dozen of them two hours together." By his own testimony, at the odds of twenty-five to one he did rather less than half his share. A few lines later he says he fought with "fifty of them . . . two or three and fifty upon poor old Jack." Only later does he come to the two, four, seven, nine, and at last eleven "rogues in buckram suits," of whom he killed at first two and finally "seven of the eleven." Only last of all does he invent the "three misbegotten knaves in Kendal green" who came at him from behind in the dark, the comparatively minor lie that traps him. The progress of his recital when analyzed in this way makes it unlikely that Falstaff, who whatever else he may be is not clairvoyant, senses from the start that the "incomprehensible lies" foretold by Poins when concocting the Gad's Hill scheme (I, ii) are expected of him, and therefore obliges by knowingly entering the trap to provide entertainment for the Prince.[12] More significant is the fact that nothing Falstaff says can be believed; his whole life is a lie; he is, as the Prince puts in, the father of lies, Satan himself, "gross as a mountain, open, palpable." When cornered, his evasions or attempts to avoid the detection of his lies and the exposure of his cowardice fall into three parts, balancing the three parts of his recital. His first evasion is a reasonable refusal to "give you a reason upon compulsion." This is thoroughly modern, no more than the rule that a man can not be compelled to testify against himself. His second evasion as he tries to ward off the inevitable is completely irrational, the animal-like reaction of a man who sees the circle relentlessly closing: he snarls name-calling insults at Hal. The most revealing of the epithets he hurls is the last one—"you vile standing tuck," i.e., an unbending, unpliant rapier, one that will not yield to pressure, for the metaphor perfectly describes the Prince's determination to confront, if not to shame, Falstaff with the truth. When the truth is out, the third and most gymnastic evasion follows: "By the Lord, I knew ye as well as he that made ye . . . The lion will not touch the true prince." This is no modern principle known to jurisprudence, but a thoroughly medieval notion of folklore origin.[13] Thus the first and third of Falstaff's evasions epitomize the two conflicting aspects of kingship, the modern and the medieval, that Shakespeare expresses in his history plays.[14] But are Falstaff's evasions effective? Does he gain anything from them? His lies about his heroic conduct at Gad's Hill and his lies about his cowardly conduct, when the truth is revealed by Hal, are usually spoken of as if Falstaff wins a victory by his skill in verbal fencing which more than compensates for any incapacity or faintheartedness in actual fencing. On the contrary, his self-exposure is his self-condemnation in Hal's eyes, whose attitude of amusement mingled with disgust marks the beginning of Falstaff's fall.[15] And it is obvious that old Jack's

cowardice is a matter of record before Shrewsbury. To the Elizabethans, steeped in a chivalric past that Shakespeare was re-creat-
ing for them in his English history plays, personal cowardice was
a comic vice, both funny and sinful. This was the impression of
it presented in Udall's Roister Doister, Lyly's Sir Tophas, Sidney's Dametas and Clinias, Spenser's Braggadochio, Trompart,
Malbecco, and Coridon, and Jonson's Captain Tucca. Shakespeare had already presented it in that light in Thomas Horner
and Peter Thump in *Henry VI, Part Two,* and he was to do so
again in Sir Andrew Aguecheek and Parolles. Of course, Falstaff
acknowledges no defeat as he worms his way out by pronouncing
himself "a coward on instinct." Incapable of shame, and as self-
deluded as Hotspur, he gladly believes he has regained Hal's
affection and gleefully learns the loot from the robbery is intact.
Elated by the sorry role he has—in his own view—so successfully
played, he wishes to undertake another. "Shall we have a play
extempore?"—yet another anticipation of the fourth movement.
Now Hal could show his contempt by casting him as Hotspur's
wife, as he had thought of doing, but that would dishonor the
lady as well as let Falstaff off the hook too easily. "Content," he
replies, "and the argument shall be thy running away." Falstaff
is not eager to play himself; in fact, he always prefers any other
role to that. Hal's suggested argument for the "play extempore"
is another unconsciously ironical commentary on his own situation, for he is still running away from the court where his duty
awaits him. So ends the second movement, the longest in the
miniature drama of the scene.

In a sense, then, both Hal and Falstaff are saved by the diver-
sion caused when Sir John Bracy arrives with word for the Prince
from his father. This, the first of two intrusions on Falstaff's un-
real domain of idle revelry by the real world of serious affairs
where history is in the making, constitutes the third movement
in the scene. Its timing and the change from the headlong pace
and uproarious tone of what precedes it make it dramatically
important. Again, Shakespeare uses it to intertwine more com-
pactly the themes and issues of the scene itself in relation to the
larger design of the play. Yet again, the interruption gives a
breathing spell between the swift turns and dodges, the witty
thrusts and counterthrusts, the exhilarating verbal and mental

exercise in the exposure of Falstaff and the more leisurely, more sophisticated high comedy in the brilliant play-acting of the episode to follow. Falstaff does not welcome the invasion of his sovereignty.

> *Falstaff.* What doth gravity out of his bed at midnight?
> Shall I give him his answer?
> *Prince.* Prithee do, Jack.

This symbolic gesture of sending Falstaff to turn away the intruder signifies that Hal is not yet ready to assume the responsibility he is evading in the company of his tavern companions. The time is fast approaching when he must assume that responsibility, but he wishes to prolong the present moment. He is still "of all humors." Having triumphed over Falstaff he is willing to continue the fun, although, as in all of Shakespeare's greatest comic scenes, a serious vein almost of sadness underlies the action from this point on. In fact, it is just because of this added dimension of depth that the whole scene looks beyond the sunlit comedies to the darker tragi-comedies that lie a decade ahead. While Falstaff is disposing of Sir John Bracy, with what impudence we may imagine, the Prince takes advantage of his absence to learn more of his perfidy in the Gad's Hill affair. This is the epilogue of the subplot that began in I, ii. Falstaff's hacking of his sword, now confirmed by Peto, is repeated by the cowardly Parolles in *All's Well That Ends Well*. Hal's ridicule of Bardolph's hypocritical remorse and his calling him an inveterate thief—"thou stolest a cup of sack eighteen years ago"—is more noteworthy than the joke about his fiery red nose. The first looks ahead to Bardolph's ignominious fate in *Henry V;* the second merely anticipates Falstaff's corruscating wit on the subject of Bardolph's nose in III, iii.[16] At the end of his brief bout with Bardolph, Hal's pun on choler (i.e., collar)-halter points once more to his rejection of Falstaff and his crew, of whom Bardolph is to be the last survivor in *Henry V*. When Falstaff returns to report to the Prince that "There's villainous news abroad . . . you must to the court in the morning," the serious plot casts its shadow across the comic plot, and the moment draws nearer when tavern time will be replaced by historical time with the Prince's acceptance of his destiny. Word of the Percy rising has reached the King perhaps sooner than it would have except for Hotspur's indiscretion revealed in II, iii. The anticlimatic arrangement of Falstaff's list of the rebel leaders, which begins with "that same mad fellow of the north, Percy" and proceeds through "that sprightly Scot of Scots, Douglas" to "one Mordake," makes it a parody of the epic catalogue of heroes. Dramatically, it shows that Falstaff is still smarting from Hal's exposure of his cowardice, as with sly malice he endows the rebel chiefs with the supernatural powers of fallen angels—"that fiend Douglas, that spirit Percy, and that devil Glendower"—implying that Hal should fear such enemies "upon instinct"—"art thou not horrible afraid?" The Prince sees through this little maneuver, and we do not question his calm reply, "Not a whit, i' faith. I lack some of thy instinct." It is one of the most revealing moments in the relationship between the two, indicative of a widening rift and the weakening of Falstaff's influence. The two antagonists of the Prince, the two obstacles to his attainment of social maturity and political wisdom are fused in Falstaff's perverse praise of Hotspur. Hal defeats Falstaff against odds at Gad's Hill, just as he conquers Hotspur against odds when he confronts his other opponent in the last act.[17]

The link with the fourth movement, the impersonations scene, is in the line, "You must to the court in the morning." During the discussion which follows between Falstaff and the Prince, this summons from the King is in the back of both their minds. Thus the argument of the "play extempore" suggested by Falstaff at the end of the second movement is jointly and simultaneously conceived. Falstaff will play the King—not Lady Percy and not himself, as Hal had suggested earlier—and Hal will play himself as they rehearse the confrontation of father and son; the exchange of these roles, which produces the apogee of Shakespearean comedy in the history plays, is not foreseen. The humor of the three major movements, leaving aside the two interruptions, advances from the farcical business of the practical joke played on Francis to the wit of the verbal fencing in the exposure of Falstaff—really the culmination of another practical joke—and finally reaches the level of intellectual comedy with the superb inventiveness of the two actors in this play within the play within the play.[18] In casting his substitute father as his real father, the Prince seems once more to commit an unconsciously symbolic act. It is as close as he ever comes to disrespect toward the King, an echo of the traditional Prince of *The Famous Victories* whom Shakespeare meant to replace with his own portrayal of the character. Yet, as compensation, the signs of Falstaff's assumed royalty in throne, sceptre, and crown are reduced by Hal's literal directness to what they are—a joined-stool, a leaden dagger, and a bald crown. If "the cushion of luxury is worn in emblematic parody of crowned royalty," [19] the cynicism is Falstaff's, not the Prince's, whose respect for the crown he will one day wear is clear from the beginning. Any ambiguity on the Prince's part is secondary, however, for Falstaff is the center of fascinated interest to his "nobility," the denizens of the Boar's Head, as he puts on his kingliest air. The simple minded Mrs. Quickly, laughing while she admires his acting, becomes his "tristful queen." Only this prologue to Falstaff's audience with the Prince and his address from the throne is done "in King Cambyses vein." Preston's antiquated tragedy of *ca.* 1565 is one of the memories of Falstaff's youth more than thirty years before, and his reference to it unerringly dates him. So does the outdated Euphuistic style of some twenty years earlier adopted for his speech to Hal, a style already parodied by Shakespeare in *Love's Labor's Lost*. Falstaff's notions of how a modern monarch would act and speak are ludicrously old-fashioned, so that in an important sense his parody of royalty turns back on himself. What "King" Falstaff begins in jest he finishes in earnest, for it is not the dramatic or rhetorical style of his performance with which he is chiefly concerned, although that is what his audience of subjects chiefly enjoy, but the opportunity his role gives for self-praise and self-justification to Hal. Amid the complicated cross currents of ironies, motives, and self-revelations crowding together here, more pathos than fun belongs to the father's plea to the son he is supposed to be reproving when he begs, "there is virtue in that Falstaff. Him keep with, the rest banish." The old man has enjoyed his sense of intimacy with the Prince, who represents to him the son he never had. He wants to keep him for himself, as shown by his special jealousy of Poins, and he is becoming aware that his hold on Hal's interest is waning. The Prince on his side has been amused and diverted by

Falstaff, nothing more. It is inevitable that political reality, which the Prince grasps and which Falstaff never understands, should in the end come between them. But a heavier blow is to follow. Hal speaks only two lines during Falstaff's serio-comic masquerade, and he says nothing in his own defense; he is not accountable to Falstaff for anything. "Dost thou speak like a king?" he asks mockingly as he prepares to exchange roles. "Do thou stand for me, and I'll play my father." He does so in deadly earnest. Good Counsel's denunciation of "that reverend vice, that gray iniquity, that father ruffian, that vanity in years" is wholly in the Morality tradition. Its object understands its import better than Hotspur understands his uncle Worcester's lecture in III, i, which this parallels and anticipates, for Falstaff reacts in self-defense and fear. His plea ending with "Banish plump Jack, and banish all the world!" contains the irony of an unintended implication—banish "the world, the flesh, and the devil," which makes it as self-condemnatory of "that old white-bearded Satan" as Hal's denunciation. The words, "I do, I will," are not only the emotional climax of the relationship between the two in both parts of *Henry IV*, since the Prince moves henceforth along a direct line that leads to the rejection at the end of *Part Two*, but also the structural climax of the internal drama of the first tavern scene.[20] The complete fusion in this movement of the scene of the two levels of spirited comic action and serious significance is one of Shakespeare's greatest achievements, a paradigm of the perfect balance between comedy and history found in *Henry IV, Part One* but not in any other play of the two tetralogies.

To Falstaff's dismay, the make-believe of the "play extempore" is broken off at its most intense moment. There is no more dramatic interruption than the Sheriff's knock at the door,[21] not even the arrival of Mercade in *Love's Labor's Lost*. "Enter Bardolph, running." The Sheriff and his posse have traced the Gad's Hill robbers to the Boar's Head.[22] This, a far more threatening invasion of Falstaff's realm than the first, constitutes the fifth movement of the scene and its last structural division. It serves, like the first interruption, as counterpoint to the tavern revels. Falstaff again resents the intrusion, but more bitterly than before. "Play out the play. I have much to say in the behalf of that

Falstaff." So he has, but he will never have a chance to say it, for the "play" has ended for him. Will Hal turn him over to the law's authority? The whole world of Falstaff hangs in the balance, as his terrified adherents know, while the Prince makes up his mind. During the suspenseful interval Falstaff pleads not for favor but for sufferance. "Never call a true piece of gold a counterfeit. Thou art essentially mad without seeming so." I would interpret this to mean: "Never mistake a true friend like me for a false one. Just as you are fundamentally mad without seeming so, I am fundamentally good without seeming so." [23] Hal's answer, "And thou a natural coward without instinct," gives him no encouragement, and Falstaff is prepared to be delivered to the Sheriff. But Hal has decided otherwise. In yet another swift change of roles, he drops the attitude of condemnation and becomes the merciful Prince as he postpones Falstaff's judgment day. "Go hide thee behind the arras." In contrast to the symbolic gesture with which he had sent Falstaff to deal with the first intrusion on the comic world by the real world of history, the Prince in another symbolic gesture deals with the Sheriff himself, signifying that the moment of his prophesied return from the comic world to the real world of history is imminent. His equivocation with the Sheriff, "The man, I do assure you, is not here" (i.e., in this room), is overheard by Falstaff behind the arras, and at that instant he probably falls asleep, safe in the knowledge that for the time being he has been spared. Thus the Prince with complete composure engineers and stage manages the most important of all Falstaff's evasions, whereas he had exposed all the lesser ones, based on more monstrous lies, in the second movement of this scene. The present movement, in which Hal stalls off the Sheriff and saves Falstaff for later retribution, anticipates the way in which he will carelessly allow Falstaff to claim credit for killing Hotspur at Shrewsbury in V, iv. The first and fifth movements in the drama of this great scene are symmetrical: in the first Poins was hidden while Hal played with Francis, and here Falstaff is hidden while Hal plays with the Sheriff; in the first we see Hal with a juvenile denizen of the tavern world, while here we see him with an adult harbinger of the court world, a representative of the good government that is antithetic to all Falstaff stands for.

79

The symbolism in the hiding of Falstaff is continued in the epilogue to the internal drama of the secene, when he is revealed asleep and snoring behind the arras.[24] The devil who haunted Hal in the likeness of an old fat man has been exorcized. Falstaff's sleep foreshadows his playing dead in V, iv, and the comic inventory of his pockets—"Item, Sack two gallons"—foreshadows Hal's discovery of a bottle of sack in his holster in V, iii. A serious undercurrent accompanies the laughter of Hal and Poins[25] over the contents of the pockets, and the Prince in closing the scene is quietly serious as he looks forward to his meeting with his father that morning (III, ii). "We must all to the wars" is the theme of the rest of *Henry IV, Part One,* of its sequel, and of *Henry V.* When the Prince returns to the upper world of his father from which he had fled, he carries with him into the light of day all the inhabitants of the subterranean tavern world of Falstaff. The announcement of Falstaff's charge of foot looks ahead to the recruiting scenes in both parts of *Henry IV,* and the Prince's enjoyment of the prospect of Falstaff's having to march looks back to the plight of the horseless knight at Gad's Hill. The epilogue provides a quiet ending to the drama of the first tavern scene.

So it is that this scene in *Henry IV, Part One* is constructed like a miniature drama with a beginning, middle, and end. Its structural parts—the five "acts" or movements and the epilogue, as I have designated them—are perfectly articulated with each other. At the same time, the sum of the parts is greater than the whole, for each movement in the internal drama of the scene looks beyond itself, either echoing something that has preceded it or foreshadowing something that is to follow it. And, as we have seen, the second part of *Henry IV* is significantly anticipated. The design of the scene, exhibiting as it does both structural and thematic unity, therefore reveals something of Shakespeare's total conceptualizing grasp of his material when he is writing at the top of his bent as he is throughout *Henry IV, Part One.* The same conceptualizing grasp resulting in an almost miraculous integration of structure and theme no doubt exists in other scenes scattered throughout his thirty-seven plays; and just as surely, in other scenes no such integration occurs. My aim here has been to show that in II, iv, of *Henry IV, Part One,* con-

structed like a miniature drama, the relationship between structure and theme and the implications of this relationship are vital,
complex, and demonstrable. Here Shakespeare's sense of dramatic design has both the balance, symmetry, and proportion of
Renaissance art and the involute multiplicity of Baroque art.

University of Oregon

NOTES

1 Hereward T. Price, *Construction in Shakespeare,* University of Michigan
   Contributions in Modern Philology, No. 17 (Ann Arbor, 1951), p. 19.
   Price's plea that "We badly need a study of Shakespeare's methods in the
   single scene" has gone largely unheeded, perhaps because the critic goes
   too far when he immediately adds, "His typical scene is a miniature play
   with its internal logical structure, its beginning, middle, and end" (p. 21).
   It is impossible to imagine a play, by Shakespeare or any other playwright, consisting of a succession of "typical" scenes of this kind. Price's
   idea of construction is, by implication at least, simple and unitary; Shakespeare's is complex and multiple, as I want to show.

2 M. A. Shaaber, ed., *The First Part of King Henry the Fourth,* Pelican
   Shakespeare (Baltimore, 1957), p. 19. He mentions as examples the scene
   at Glendower's house (III, i), the scene between the king and the prince
   (III, ii), and the second tavern scene (III, iii); he does not mention the
   first tavern scene. As a matter of fact, all the history plays contain such
   scenes. In *Richard II* they are especially conspicuous: the lists at Coventry
   (I, iii), the death of Gaunt (II, i), Richard's return from Ireland (III, ii),
   the confrontation of Richard and Bolingbroke at Flint Castle (III, iii), the
   deposition (IV, i), and the Oxford conspiracy (V, iii).

3 My line numbering is that of the Cambridge edition of W. G. Clark and
   W. A. Wright (9 vols.; Cambridge, 1863-1866). The next longest scene,
   I, iii, has 302 lines; but it is entirely in verse, so the statement holds. The
   second tavern scene (III, iii) has 193 lines of prose and twelve lines of verse
   at the end.

4 William R. Bowden, "Teaching Structure in Shakespeare: 1 *Henry IV,
   Twelfth Night,* and *Hamlet," College English,* XXIII (1962), 525-531, gives
   a brief outline of II, iv in *Henry IV, Part One:* "Hal & Francis; Falstaff's
   story; play-acting; Falstaff's pocket picked" (p. 526). He thus omits the two
   structurally vital interruptions, the third and fifth movements in my outline. Derek Traversi in his discussion of this scene in *Shakespeare from
   "Richard II" to "Henry V"* (Stanford, 1957), pp. 66-77, recognizes the
   same structural phases that I do, but he does not interpret them as having the structure of a miniature drama.

⁵ The soliloquy tells the audience, "I know you all expect me to be the prodigal of legend and of *The Famous Victories,* who had no thought of the future while reveling with low companions, but then, without reason or warning, turned into a great king; so I will for a while present the character you expect, and my father and everyone else will think ill of me, but you will know better." Shakespeare is saying, "For the earlier stage Prince was a reprobate, and this is not the man."

⁶ Shaaber says, pp. 18-19, "The story of the robbery on Gad's Hill, a series of scenes [I, ii; II, i, ii, and iv] which might be called a subplot if it did not come to an end before the play is half over, obviously gathers momentum as it develops and reaches its own peculiar climax."

⁷ I fail completely to understand F. M. Salter's discovery in *Henry IV, Part One,* of what he calls "the Tragedy of Hotspur," and his attempt to find in its protagonist "the hero of great and noble quality but damned by a fatal flaw" such as we see in Shakespeare's tragedies, just as I disagree completely with his statements that "the Falstaffian scenes . . . constitute a complete play which is meaningful in and by itself," and "not a single thing in this formless comedy, or droll, depends upon the historical matter of *1 Henry IV* for meaning." See his "The Play Within the Play of First Henry IV," *Transactions of the Royal Society of Canada,* 3rd Series, Section 2, XL (1946), 209-223.

⁸ Traversi in his unhistorical criticism of this history play stresses the Prince's detachment from his low companions as a deficiency of his coldly calculating character. To Shakespeare—as to Spenser—such detachment would have been made inevitable by a prince's birth and aristocratic social status.

⁹ Traversi, p. 68; Gareth Lloyd Evans, "The Comical-Tragical-Historical Method: *Henry IV,*" in *Early Shakespeare,* Stratford-upon-Avon Studies, 3 (London, 1961), p. 150. J. Dover Wilson, *The Fortunes of Falstaff* (Cambridge, 1943), p. 49, thinks the main purpose of the scene with Francis "is to keep the audience waiting, agog for [Falstaff]." Falstaff, this early in the play, is not that engrossing—nor in my view, does he ever become so.

¹⁰ He shows contempt for him in his first mention of the Prince in *Richard II,* V, iii, an attitude maintained in his reference to "that same sword-and-buckler Prince of Wales" in I, iii of this play, and similarly throughout.

¹¹ E. M. W. Tillyard, *Shakespeare's History Plays* (London, 1944), p. 265. The Aristotelian element in these oppositions is brought out by William B. Hunter, Jr., "Falstaff," *South Atlantic Quarterly,* L (1951), 88-89. Spenser makes the same point in Book II of *The Faerie Queene* in the contrast between Guyon's courage, Pyrochles' rashness, and Braggadochio's cowardice.

¹² This theory has been endorsed by those critics who attribute all the complexities of Falstaff's derivation—from the Lord of Misrule, the Fool, the Buffoon, the Boy Bishop, the morality Vice, the Cozener, the Braggart Soldier, the Euphuistic Courtier, the Religious Hypocrite, and indeed what not besides?—to Falstaff himself. See, for example, S. B. Hemingway, ed., *King Henry the Fourth, Part One,* A new Variorum Edition of Shakespeare (Philadelphia, 1936), p. 144; George L. Kittredge, ed., *King Henry IV, Part One* (Boston, 1940), p. xi; Wilson, pp. 50-56; Traversi, pp. 71-72.

[13] It is widespread in the medieval romances, e.g., in Josian's lion in *Bevis of Hampton,* and it reappears in Una's lion in *The Faerie Queene.*

[14] Tillyard, pp. 245-263. Although he treats the subject in another connection, S. L. Bethell has made some interesting observations on the anachronistic past-present comparisons or juxtapositions in the history plays, seeing them as a characteristic of Baroque art and poetry, in "The Comic Element in Shakespeare's Histories," *Anglia,* LXXI (1952), especially pp. 100-101.

[15] Evans, p. 152, sees the mock-trial, the fourth movement in the scene, as the beginning of Falstaff's fall.

[16] A. Haire Foster in *Wit, Humor and the Comic in Shakespeare and Elsewhere* (New York, 1956), p. 3, says "Wit is the arrow, the comic is the target. . . . Bardolph's large and lurid nose is a comic object, Falstaff's remarks on it are wit."

[17] Hunter, p. 89.

[18] Wilson, pp. 56-57, dismisses this part of the scene, saying it "raises no problems that need disentangling." Traversi, p. 73, believes that not until the parody of the interview between the King and his son, "is the connection between the 'serious' action and its 'comic' underplot made finally clear," which is surely wrong. The relation between the historical and the comic action is never explicitly formulated; but the complex interweaving of the two, beginning with Hal's soliloquy at the end of I, ii, has been finely treated by C. L. Barber, *Shakespeare's Festive Comedy* (Princeton, 1959), pp. 192-213.

[19] Bernard Harris, "Dissent and Satire," *Shakespeare Survey,* XVII (1964), 137.

[20] This double significance of Hal's words was strongly apparent in the production of *Henry IV, Part One* at the Royal Shakespeare Theatre in Stratford in 1964. Prince Hal (Ian Holm) stands on the table where Falstaff (Hugh Griffith) had lately sat. Falstaff stands close below him with suppliant upstretched arms as he makes his plea. At the crucial words, "I do," spoken quietly, Hal takes both of Falstaff's hands in his own, one might almost say in parody of the marriage ritual, and fixes him with an intense gaze. There is a full stop, not the comma of the text, before the next words are spoken. With "I will," Hal's voice becomes harsh, and he flings Falstaff's hands away with a gesture of resolute rejection.

[21] Evans, pp. 152-153.

[22] Traversi, p. 77, curiously believes that news of the Sheriff's arrival "adds little to what has gone before."

[23] See Samuel B. Hemingway, ed., *The First Part of King Henry the Fourth,* Yale Shakespeare (New Haven, 1917), p. 124, for the interpretations of Malone, Wright, and the editor.

[24] Wilson, pp. 58-59, says of this only that because of Falstaff's audible snores, "The sleep also adds the crowning fun to the greatest of comic scenes."

[25] The Peto of the text is almost certainly an error.

HAMLET AND THE
NAME OF ACTION

MATTHEW N. PROSER

I

It is correct to think of *Hamlet* as a tragedy whose "center" is only hinted at by the complicated metaphor of language and action which is the play itself.[1] This hint is like a centripetal force, compelling our attention away from the questionable logic of events toward a fascinating and dangerous unknown. Yet in another sense, the play is its own mystery and to experience the play is, emotionally at least, to divine the mystery: those "thoughts beyond the reaches of our souls" awakened in Hamlet by the appearance of his father's ghost. For the play is pre-eminently a play about knowledge—indeed self-knowledge—or the lack of these. That is why we always think of the terms "illusion" and "reality" when we think of *Hamlet*. Whatever his failings, our sympathies remain with Hamlet because he cannot fully penetrate our mystery, but only live it, and feel it, as we do, in his few brief hours upon his "stage of life." No simple metaphor, he seems the essence of our searching selves. His scrupulosity is his only armor. If Hamlet is Man, we must admire him because against destiny he is all but defenseless. A bare bodkin can only confirm his end.

At the outset of *Hamlet,* there is only one unquestionable reality: the physical fact of the old king's death. Though the young prince may come to doubt the ghost is a "true" ghost or feel it necessary to prove Claudius a killer, it is impossible to question this single reality, except to inquire into its nature. The ghost, unshriven, gives a partial answer to this inquiry:

> But that I am forbid
> To tell the secrets of my prison-house,
> I could a tale unfold whose lightest word
> Would harrow up thy soul, freeze thy young blood,
> Make thy two eyes, like stars, start from their spheres,
> Thy knotty and combined locks to part
> And each particular hair to stand on end,
> Like quills upon the fretful porpentine.[2]
>
> (I.v.13-20)

Doomed to purgation of "foul crimes" done in his "days of nature," the ghost, who for Hamlet was the paragon of men and kings, witnesses the end of the *best* of lives, and simultaneously demands revenge. But despite Hamlet's impulse to sweep to his revenge, the description of the ghost's unhappy punishment perhaps remains with him. Or at least, if the ghost's words do not remain with him, Hamlet is surely capable of doubting in his own right the peace in death:[3]

> To die; to sleep;—
> To sleep? Perchance to dream! Ay, there's the rub;
> For in that sleep of death what dreams may come,
> When we have shuffl'd off this mortal coil,
> Must give us pause. . . .
>
> (III.i.64-68)

"The dread of something after death" comes to Hamlet because his contemplation of suicide is not simply academic. It is a mode of action which occurs to him with some seriousness. But Hamlet knows the edicts against self-slaughter, and even if he did not give them full credence, they surely impress him enough to make him hesitate:

> Thus conscience does make cowards of us all;
> And thus the native hue of resolution
> Is sicklied o'er with the pale cast of thought,
> And enterprises of great pith and moment
> With this regard their currents turn [awry],
> And lose the name of action. . . .
>
> (III.i.83-88)

The "enterprises of great pith and moment" are both the suicide and the revenge upon Claudius, or so it would seem, unless we feel Hamlet is generalizing completely beyond the context of the present situation. This may be possible, but it is hardly likely. Professor Harrison's suggestions that Hamlet is simply meditating upon the book he holds and that the introductory words of the soliloquy, "To be or not to be," are a traditional medieval formula appropriate to such "a common topic for philosophic discussion" [4] take, perhaps, too much emphasis off our notion of Hamlet as a creature vitally concerned with his own fate. Even if Hamlet's remarks are philosophic generalizations, they would be bolstered, if not for him, at least for us, by the immediacy of his situation. And the immediacy of the situation offers Hamlet the alternatives of satisfying the ghost, escaping from the responsibility for revenge, or questioning the very situation. At moments Hamlet is capable of considering each of the three. The initial and reiterated dedication to revenge and the contemplation of suicide suggest the first two alternatives. But the questioning is persistent throughout and takes two main forms, at least in the first acts. Hamlet "rebels" against the imposition of his fate:

> The time is out of joint;—O cursed spite,
> That ever I was born to set it right!
> (I.v.189-190)

He seeks to prove the ghost is a "true" ghost and Claudius a real killer:

> The play's the thing
> Wherein I'll catch the conscience of the King.
> (II.ii.633-634)

Hamlet must murder to satisfy the ghost, but to pacify his conscience, he must capture Claudius' conscience to make sure the ghost's end will not be his own. Destiny at his very birth threw the burden upon him;[5] for he is his father's son and the presumable heir to the Danish throne.

86

As son and heir Hamlet has certain responsibilities which an Elizabethan audience would have acknowledged. (One, as a matter of fact, could probably say as much about any audience.) Whether an Elizabethan audience would have morally demanded that Hamlet avenge his father's death with violence is arguable. But they certainly would have expected Hamlet to take an immediately active part in exposing and condemning the killer. They also would have expected him to correct the political situation in the land by taking the usurper off the throne. Regarding the political situation, it is of little use to say that Claudius conducts himself as an energetic and diplomatic king once he has attained power.[6] Claudius' power in the first place derives from an illegitimate act that must necessarily lead to dangerous consequences once the truth is out. Shakespeare makes sure the truth comes out very early in the play, and puts that truth into the ghost's mouth. The truth is a cruel truth, a kind of infectious virus, but its infectiousness is accountable to the infectious quality of the poison Claudius poured into the old king's ears. Poisoned deeds lead to poisoned words. These enter the ear too and infect the mind with images of death, corruption and revenge. Murder leads to revenge: the revenge is "justified," but revenge itself is a kind of murder. Hamlet's "conscience" is divided. He is caught, as Professor Heilman puts it, between two "imperatives," and each has "its own validity." "Hamlet and Orestes . . . cannot avenge their fathers, the victims of evil deeds, without themselves committing evil deeds." The two imperatives cannot, apparently, be reconciled.[7] The idea of murder leads to the question of the moral responsibility of the potential murderer: that potential murderer is Hamlet. Therefore we might take certain words of Hamlet to Ophelia as more than an exhibition of feigned madman's palaver:

> . . . I am myself indifferent honest, but yet I could accuse me of such things that it were better my mother had not borne me. I am very proud, revengeful, ambitious, with more offences at my beck than I have thoughts to put them in, imagination to give them shape, or time to act them in. What

should such fellows as I do crawling between heaven
and earth? We are arrant knaves all; believe none
of us. Go thy ways to a nunnery. Where's your father?

(III.i.123-132)

We need not construe every word literally, but we can say at
least that Hamlet is aware of the infection within him and that
he protests against it, just as momentarily earlier on the parapet
he protested against the very nature of his responsibility:[8]

O all you host of heaven! O earth! What else?
And shall I couple hell?

(I.v.92-93)

This "rebelliousness" against the violent nature of his responsibility is a reaction quite characteristic of Hamlet. And clearly the
rebelliousness is connected with the sense of corruption he feels
within himself, a sense of corruption engendered by the role he
is forced to play, not through his own doing, but the doings of
others. For the role of avenger violates his aspirations as courtier,
soldier and scholar. It mocks his desire to be a man of grace,
sensitive deliberation and dignity. The role of avenger makes impossible that image he would wish to fulfill—Horatio's, whose
conduct, standing as it does outside the immediate situation, is
ideal, incorruptible and rational. It is as if Hamlet had suddenly
been cast in some sordid melodrama, which is, in one light, precisely the case.

Yet this sense of corruption and "rebelliousness" is reflected
even before Hamlet knows the truth about his father's death,
only when he suspects it:

O, that this too too solid flesh would melt,
Thaw, and resolve itself into a dew!
Or that the Everlasting had not fix'd
His canon 'gainst self-slaughter! O God! God!
How weary, stale, flat, and unprofitable,
Seems to me all the uses of this world!
Fie on't! Oh fie, fie! 'Tis an unweeded garden,

That grows to seed; things rank and gross in nature
Possess it merely. That it should come to this!
But two months dead! Nay, not so much, not two.
So excellent a king; that was, to this,
Hyperion to a satyr. . . .

(I.ii.129-140)

If ever there were a Shakespearean soliloquy that was more than conventional, this surely must be it. Hamlet's isolation on the stage, the intimacy of his language, and his heartfelt ejaculations make it clear that these are words which Hamlet takes to heart even as we do. His mind, turning forward and backward upon itself, releases a sequence of images from his instinctive "conscience"—that very conscience which will jointly impel and impede revenge.

An examination of this soliloquy suggests not only how Hamlet views his mother's conduct and the contrasted moral qualities of his two fathers, but how Hamlet views himself. When Hamlet says this world is ". . . an unweeded garden,/That grows to seed; things rank and gross in nature/ Possess it merely," we have more than a combination of images which project Shakespeare's thematic material: the internal corruption in the state of Denmark and its king and queen. Specifically, we have the prince morally positioning himself in regard to this state of affairs. His earlier cry, "Fie on't! Oh, fie, fie!" defines his reaction; but his initial statement, "O, that this too too solid flesh would melt," in conjunction with the vision of the rank garden, defines Hamlet himself, and from this conjunction we can infer the extent to which he already feels that rank garden is his own, the garden which is Eve's as well as his mother's. He sees himself, whether consciously or not, as man cursed, fallen in his original, and in being so fallen, heir to the destroyed garden that should have been his Paradise. And this fall is laid upon him by factors outside himself, even as his burden of revenge will be. It too is "inherited."

Out of his agonized reaction and the information the ghost delivers (corroborating the intuitions of his "prophetic soul") grows the heroic role he must seek to adopt:[9] the attempt to restore the garden, a metaphor of moral, psychological and political order, but by means of revenge. He must, as it were,

89

become his murdered and cuckolded father, the old King Hamlet, and assume in corporeal reality the martial form and vigorous bearing the ghost presents. He must assume this role because fate has made him his father's son and the presumable heir to the throne, because the inherited burden of responsibility requires him now to be the Dane, even in the face of conflicting moral reservations which seem to indicate that to become the Dane is in one sense only to confirm his fall—the fall imposed upon him by being man. At the same time, to become the Dane is, this being true for the punished ghost quite literally, to purge his nature, even as he confirms it, to release the condemned spirit of his father from its purgatorial bondage, even as through thought and finally action, he at last releases his own. For the great "enterprise" whose name is action is Claudius' death, but the title "the Dane" is the name of action which comprehends in its telescopic terseness and ambiguous dignity the name of man in the highest moral, political and social action, at the same time it comprehends that "mole of nature" about which Hamlet expatiates so eloquently in Act I, scene iv, when he speaks of Danes and men.

II

Given the common denominator of corruption the epithet "the Dane" appears in part to suggest, to become the Dane in its laudatory sense alone poses complex problems. For the implications of kingship are not simply personal, but social and political as well.[10] What is curious about Hamlet is that he fails for the most part to identify clearly his social and political role. His failure to do so is curious not only because we would expect a well-educated prince to think about the social and political consequences of assassination—and surely Hamlet strikes us more as a Renaissance Prince than a Medieval one, despite his historical date; it is curious because for Hamlet to have thought socially and politically would have perhaps taken a great burden from him by simplifying his choices. A less morally sensitive prince might have written off the required revenge as a duty to state and left the matter at that. Or he might have brought his own political ambitions more strongly into play. But Hamlet, "the expectancy and rose of the fair state" scarcely thinks politically at all. Furthermore, there is an extreme irony in the fact that Rosencrantz and Guildenstern, indeed Hamlet himself in Act III, scene i, should make the accusation of "ambition," when we in certain respects might accuse Hamlet of not being ambitious enough.[11] In reality Hamlet's reactions to the murder of the old king are for the most part personal and moral. We might expect them to be, considering that the king was his father and the usurper has married his mother. On the other hand, to have focused upon the political ramifications of his projected revenge might have freed him to act. Though it occurs to Claudius that the "rabble" love the young prince, the idea simply does not seem to make its way into Hamlet's mind. He does not consider appealing to the populace; he does not make plans to organize a court faction; he does not ask Horatio to help get military aid from abroad. Instead he feigns madness and has a play put on by professional actors.

It is the ghost himself who might have served as a model for the active and politically conscious man Hamlet must emulate at this point in order to act decisively. The emphasis on action, bold, deliberate and offensive in nature is announced upon the ghost's first appearance on stage:

> What art thou that usurp'st this time of night
> Together with that fair and warlike form
> In which the majesty of buried Denmark
> Did sometimes march?
>
> (I.i.46-49)

The "warlike form" of the ghost which is questioned by Horatio, as well as the very fact of the ghost's appearance, implies to Horatio, Marcellus and Bernardo that "something is rotten in the State of Denmark" that demands action. This emphasis upon offensive action is supported by references to the ghost's arms and armor during the earlier scenes of the play. When the ghost first materializes before us, Marcellus asks of Horatio: "Is it not like the king?" Horatio responds: "As thou art to thyself. Such was the very armour he had / When [he] th' ambitious Norway combated" (I.i.58-61). Later Bernardo, having heard Horatio's explanation for the military preparations in Denmark, remarks about the ghost: "Well may it sort that this portentous figure / Comes armed through our watch, so like the king / That was and is the question of these wars" (I.i.109-111). Horatio describes the ghost to Hamlet as "A figure like your father,/Arm'd at all points exactly, cap-a-pie. . . ." (I.ii.199-200). Hamlet questions Marcellus and Bernardo a few lines later in the same scene:

> *Ham.* Arm'd, say you?
>
> {*Mar.*
> {*Ber.* Arm'd my lord.
>
> *Ham.* From top to toe?
>
> {*Mar.*
> {*Ber.*   My lord, from head to foot.
>
> (I.ii.226-227)

Armor in these excerpts suggests not only the art of war which gained the forfeiture of certain lands from Old Fortinbras, the art of war whose preparations Denmark has begun in order to protect those same lands from young Fortinbras; armor and arms also suggest the directly offensive tactics the old king would take against his brother. They suggest too the political importance of the situation.[12] For just as the state is threatened from the outside by young Fortinbras, it is threatened from the inside when "the royal bed of Denmark" becomes "a couch for luxury and damned incest," and when the head of state has suffered a terrible and unpunished assassination.

Yet if arms and armor connote offensive action, they also suggest self-protection: defense. Armor can ward off the blows of sword or mace, and in doing so ward off the slings and arrows of outrageous fortune. Significantly too, the man of action like Fortinbras or Laertes (and even, one presumes, the old king himself in his days of power) carries his assurance that his cause is just like a coat of armor. His sense of righteousness may well eliminate recognition of the doubtfulness or foolishness in even the best of acts, and thus protect him from the onslaughts of "conscience." "Purpose needs ignorance," as Professor Heilman says. A man needs to eschew self-knowledge in order to act violently. Or purpose needs "a rush of emotion, a rush so powerful and self-justifying that it seems truth itself. . . ."[13] Fortinbras never doubts the justice in his cause. "Of unimproved mettle hot and full," his obligation to his father, or so he must feel it, his obligation to his own young honor, is to conquer the conqueror Denmark and regain the lost lands. Indeed, only his old uncle Norway can restrain him, and restrained, Fortinbras must fulfill his ambitions by attacking the Poles for a worthless piece of land. Similarly, Laertes, bereft of his father, has no doubts about his duty where the punishment of Hamlet is concerned. When Claudius asks what he would undertake to show himself his "father's son in deed/More than in words," his response is as automatic as it is audacious: "To cut his [Hamlet's] throat in the church." The lack of self-knowledge of these men and their emotional sense of self-righteousness protect them from intellectual doubt, from the kind of "conscience" Hamlet so amply illustrates. Fortinbras does not recognize his foolishness in attacking the Poles; nor does Laertes recognize that in the end he will prove capable of killing Hamlet in Claudius' sordid plot. Fortinbras and Laertes are "armed against a sea of troubles" not by virtue of their perspicaciousness, but by virtue of an emotional commitment they simply do not question. They are willing to do their "duty" and be damned. Moreover they have backing for their exploits, and thus make an impression upon the courts of the world. Fortinbras is sustained by the army he controls, Laertes by the "rabble" who call him lord and demand him for their king.

But Hamlet to all intents and purposes is alone, whether this be due to his own nature, his actions, or the decree of fate. All witnesses to the ghost's appearance have been sworn to secrecy, and Horatio remains uninvolved directly in the play's action. Although Hamlet can cry vehemently for revenge and curse himself with passion for not having yet executed the deed, his language most characteristically eschews the spontaneous, unthinking dedication of Laertes, but rather evokes his sense of isolation and of emotional decrepitude:

93

> Now I am alone.
> O, what a rogue and peasant slave am I!
> (II.ii.575-576)

Nevertheless Hamlet's sense of isolation and impotency must not be understood necessarily as Shakespeare's commentary upon him. Quite to the contrary, in Hamlet's very lack of self-assurance, in his apparent defenselessness we can see the weakness that is his special virtue. Because Hamlet is unarmed by a sufficiently strong sense of unassailable "rightness," the pretended madness, in fact language itself, keenly edged and pointed, become the only weapons he has against the ambiguous decree of fate which requires an act at the end of whose fulfillment may lie some unknown spiritual punishment like his father's. At moments he must flagellate his spirit by "gross examples" which indicate his dereliction of duty to stimulate sufficient emotion to lay the basis for action:

> What's Hecuba to him, or he to Hecuba,
> That he should weep for her? what would he do,
> Had he the motive and cue for passion
> That I have? . . .
>   Am I a coward?
> Who calls me villain, breaks my pate across,
> Plucks off my beard and blows it in my face,
> Tweaks me by th' nose, gives me the lie i' th' throat
> As deep as to the lungs? Who does me this?
> (II.ii.585-602)

Who, indeed, but Hamlet? In his very questioning he reveals that awareness of self which alternately "puzzles the will" or forces him to "unpack" his heart "with words,/And fall a-cursing, like a very drab,/A scullion." Yet it is this very same self-awareness in Hamlet that implies his moral and intellectual superiority; not his self-knowledge (for with such language Hamlet reveals how much he does not know himself, but how he is seeking *to* know himself). It is the vague awareness that the very justice in his cause may be his undoing, because no cause is ever so unambiguously just. This awareness is suggested by the

94

manner in which he must reconfirm his cause to himself, even as he uses that cause to prove his dereliction of duty:

> Rightly to be great
> Is not to stir without great argument,
> But greatly to find quarrel in a straw
> When honour's at the stake. How stand I then,
> That have a father kill'd, a mother stained,
> Excitements of my reason and my blood,
> And let all sleep, while to my shame I see
> The imminent death of twenty thousand men,
> That for a fantasy and trick of fame
> Go to their graves like beds, fight for a plot
> Whereon the numbers cannot try the cause,
> Which is not tomb enough and continent
> To hide the slain? O, from this time forth
> My thoughts be bloody, or be nothing worth!
>
> (IV.iv.53-66)

Yet despite such momentary efforts to emotionally define and confirm the justice of his cause, Hamlet's typical mode of action, barring the impassioned and accidental slaying of Polonius, scarcely fulfills his cry for blood. Moreover, it is Hamlet himself who makes us aware of his failure to take decisive action, not supersubtle critics of the play. It is Hamlet who says, "I do not know/Why yet I live to say, 'This thing's to do,'/Sith I have cause and will and strength and means/To do't." It is Hamlet who accuses himself of being "a dull and muddy-mettled rascal," a "John-a-dreams, unpregnant" of his "cause." However, we may add that Hamlet's difficulty is not that he chooses inaction, but that he chooses particular kinds of action: the kind which seeks to prove or the kind which allows the latitude for "escape"; because the feigned madness is only a "pretense" and the "mouse-trap" is only a play, and the essence of both is the mirrorlike quality which reveals truth at the expense of "decisive" action: the thrust of the sword which concludes a final commitment to a frightening and perhaps soul-defiling end.

The open opportunity to murder Claudius while at prayer is an excellent example of the kind of attitude which prevents direct action on Hamlet's part:

> Now might I do it pat, now he is praying;
> And now I'll do't—and so he goes to heaven;
> And so am I reveng'd. That would be scann'd.
> A villain kills my father, and for that
> I, his [sole] son, do this same villain send to heaven.
> Oh, this is hire and salary, not revenge.
>
> (III.iii.73-79)

This is an instance of Hamlet's "scrupulosity" which works in two directions. Surely his motivations have nothing to do with conventionally humane impulses. His wish to kill Claudius when the king is "about some act/That has no relish of salvation in't" so that "his soul may be as damn'd and black/As hell, whereto it goes" characterizes a murder far more horrible than the one he would have achieved by killing Claudius on the spot, had Claudius actually been successfully praying. Is it not then a "scrupulosity" concerning his own soul which is perhaps revealed?[14] If we compare his attitude with that of Laertes when he is seeking the identity of his father's killer, we are bound to notice that reflections on the moral state of the intended victim after death do not participate in Laertes' judgments:

> Conscience and grace, to the profoundest pit!
> I dare damnation. To this point I stand,
> That both the worlds I give to negligence,
> Let come what comes; only I'll be reveng'd
> Most throughly for my father.
>
> (IV.vi.132-136)

Laertes' blind dedication to his revenge has a double significance in relationship to Hamlet's attitude. First of all he does not scruple to condemn his own soul to eternal damnation as long as he achieves his vengeance. Secondly he gives no thought to the condition of his victim's soul in a future world. This is emphasized later when he suggests he would be willing to cut his victim's throat "i' th' church." He does not consider that Hamlet's presence in a church might "sanctuarize" his death and fail to accomplish Hamlet's damnation as Hamlet considers when he sees his uncle at prayer (as if in a church). Nor, apparently, does the fact that to kill in a church is sacrilege seem to concern Laertes. As Claudius instructs Laertes: "Revenge should have no bounds." Revenge, John Lawlor suggests, is and must be in its nature rash, disproportionate, and we might add unthinking and uncaring about the ultimate ramifications of the vengeful action.[15] Here, then, is the second sense in which perhaps Hamlet "scruples." He demands that his revenge be strictly proportionate in relation to the death his father suffered. If the old king died with his sins upon his head, then the new king must die in precisely the same condition. But if Hamlet is correct in saying that to murder Claudius at prayer is "hire and salary," perhaps it is also correct to say that what Hamlet wishes to dispense is not revenge but that "even-handed justice," an eye for an eye, in a world where action in its very nature is always either too little or too much.[16]

One comes to feel, at long last, that it is precisely "some craven scruple/Of thinking too precisely on th'event" which characterizes Hamlet's failure to take advantage of the one clear opportunity he has had to "drink hot blood" and fulfill his father's command. Indeed one comes to feel that it is precisely this scrupulosity in the moral and intellectual sense which required him to prove that the ghost was a true ghost and the killer a true killer, although whether this scrupulosity is "craven" is quite another matter. For is it not, after all, quite reasonable to mistrust the possible "equivocations" of a possible "fiend" that could be lying "like truth"? And is it not laudable to question an act which may have the taint of damnation in it? It is in reality Laertes who would act in "bestial oblivion," not Hamlet, although it is to himself that Hamlet attributes this possible character when reprimanding himself for his failure to fulfill the ghost's demand for revenge.

The murder of Polonius, if not that of Rosencrantz and Guildenstern, appears to bear out the suspicion that "conscience" and "consciousness' are the elements which prevent Hamlet from dispatching his uncle at prayer. In the murder of Polonius, it is exactly these elements which are missing. Polonius, behind the arras in the queen's closet, believing that Hamlet is about to attack his mother, has scarcely time to cry, "What, ho! help, help, help!" before the prince has run him through: "How now!

97

A rat? Dead,/For a ducat, dead!" Here is spontaneity of action, speed, passion and thoughtlessness:

> *Queen.* O me, what has thou done?
> *Ham.*   Nay, I know not.
>   Is it the King?
> *Queen.* O, what a rash and bloody deed is this!
>
>   (III.iv.25-27)

What complicates interpretation of Hamlet's spontaneous killing of Polonius, whom, it appears Hamlet believed to be the king, is the fact that the killing takes place under the very kind of circumstances Hamlet had just promised himself he would utilize should the proper opportunity to kill the king arise; that is, when Claudius is "about some act/That has no relish of salvation in't." The pressure of the dialogue, however, seems to be on the spontaneity and rashness of the act, which might suggest that the sequence should be read ironically. Hamlet does exactly what he had calculated upon doing, but significantly, without calculating, and with such a degree of rashness that he unthinkingly kills the wrong man.

It seems possible to assume, then, from the manner in which the tragedy develops, that in order for Hamlet to kill Claudius he must disengage himself from his divided "conscience" and extreme "self-consciousness," but that he must also prevent the kind of spontaneous but blind "rashness" which led to Polonius' death. For although "rashness" clearly leads to action, when it literally cannot see its enemy and identify him, it can scarcely be called efficient. Rather it can lead to the kind of misadventure Polonius' death seems to represent. Passion evidently must be a question not of blind rage, but a secure sense of the righteousness of one's cause and an experienced knowledge of oneself and one's adversary. This is one possible way out. Or action must become "disinterested" to the degree that the avenger can envision himself as an instrument in the hands of powers outside himself, be such powers political or in some way providential. To put the matter another way, Hamlet must once and for all come to accept his destiny and the role accorded him by Fate, even if such an acceptance commits him to his own self-sacrifice or the sacrifice of an innocence he knows has already been partially lost. In short, he must make the hard recognition of his own human limitations and accept his own humanity in order to act as best he can.

III

In a recent article, Charles W. Eckert discusses the relationship of several north and south European "myths" to certain ancient rites and rituals once prevalent in the northern and Mediterranean areas of the continent.[17] A number of remarks made by the author are pertinent to the subject at hand because the northern "myth" Eckert refers to is the Hamlet story as it appears in Saxo Grammaticus and Belleforest. Moreover, Eckert's discussion proves inadvertently an illuminating one in regard to the question of Shakespeare's Hamlet's delay. Mr. Eckert first notices that there are a number of rituals and rites which have in them elements analogous to plot features in his illustrative tales. These rituals concern purgation and regeneration in connection with New Year's festivals. The social and symbolic meanings of these rituals are perhaps relevant where the social and political aspects of Shakespeare's *Hamlet* are concerned. Eckert says:

> The festival takes place at a critical moment when a society stands in need of a ritual death and rebirth. This macrocosmic crisis is seen to be analogous to the microcosmic crisis that occurs when young boys are about to become men and puberty initiations are therefore performed during the New Year's Festival. . . . Only when the young men have been initiated can the larger rites of regeneration be completed. In our myths the hero appears at a time when society stands in need of regeneration, when the house of Atreus, or Rome, or Denmark is rotten. But before he can act effectively he must himself be regenerated through rites of initiation in which madness, animalistic behavior, misogeny [to break the silver cord], sacrifice, instruction, travel

[as in Hamlet's leaving for England], symbolic death [as in the case of Hamlet who is believed to be dead by the usurper], and rebirth, investment, and the attainments of the status of manhood are the constants. When these personal rites are completed, the social rites may also be completed and the hero becomes the wielder of fire and sword, the purger of his society.[18] [My brackets]

It is not Eckert's purpose to discuss the relationship of these mythic and ritualistic elements to Shakespeare's *Hamlet*. Furthermore, we need not be surprised that many of these elements make an appearance in Shakespeare's *Hamlet* since the play derives in part from what Eckert terms the "myths" of Saxo and Belleforest. The rites of initiation through which the mythic hero must pass may well be seen in "translation" in the figure of Shakespeare's Hamlet: his feigned madness, his misogeny, his voyage to England, Claudius' belief in his death, his unexpected return to Denmark, his "investment" with the "sword" which allows him to become purger of his society—all bear undeniable relationships to the madness, misogeny, travel, symbolic death, rebirth and investment which confer manhood and maturity upon the mythic hero. Yet these are all "rationalized" more or less representationally in the plot of Shakespeare's play and their ramifications extend beyond the "primitive" into the concerns of a more sophisticated society. What these parallels and relationships do seem to point to in each case is a similar concern with the role of leadership in the society: with the role of the hero or king and the kind of sacrifice he must make, the sort of maturity he must attain, in order to discharge his obligations to a society which is corrupt either simply because the year has come to its conclusion, or because, as in the case of Shakespeare's *Hamlet* (and even in Saxo and Belleforest), there is an element of corruption in the court and, therefore, the country, which must be purged.

In the case of the *Hamlet* "myths" and their related rituals, the mode of maturity the hero (a potential king) must attain is relatively simple. His personal purgation, achieved by passing through his "initiation" leads, as it were, automatically to the purgation of the land. The maturity he displays and gains by passing the "tests" forced upon him by his predatory uncle confers upon him the role of purger of his society. In the stories by Saxo and Belleforest there is no ambiguous element of delay. To begin with Amleth and Hamblet are too young at the time of the former king's death to take revenge. Furthermore Amleth-Hamblet's feigned madness and the accompanying pattern of strange conduct can be explained either by the fact that the hero is defending himself against his uncle, or the pattern can be explained as the result of the ritualistic elements by which the hero is initiated into his role. That is, to effect the personal purgation of the hero, obviously a "ritual" is required. This will necessarily slow up direct action on the part of the hero. Whatever the explanation, there is no mystery about Amleth-Hamblet's motivations as there is about Hamlet's.

In the case of Shakespeare's *Hamlet,* however, although we are free to acknowledge the mythic basis of such factors as the feigned madness, or Hamlet's "misogeny," the trip to England or his "investment" with the purging "sword," this mythic basis is not sufficient to explain them entirely because the whole question of "maturity" is complicated by the introspective nature of the hero, the ambiguity of his "conscience" and the high degree of political sophistication in the court and its characters. It is easy for the mythic hero to fulfill his role because the traits he proves by his personal initiation are automatically transformed into public virtues. Private self merges into public with great gains, but little or no significant loss. This is especially true of the Hamlet of Saxo and Belleforest. But for Shakespeare's Hamlet to assume his public role means the loss of the private identity which suggests his morally and intellectually sensitive nature. For Hamlet to kill the king is in a sense for him to accept, not simply purge, his *own* corruption in order to purge the rotten state of Denmark. Privately speaking, to kill the king means to witness the shadow of those purgatorial fires his father so vividly evokes on the parapet at the beginning of the play. For the mythic hero life is relatively uncomplex. To kill the usurper might necessitate the private sacrifice of the hero's life (as a matter of fact it does not in the *Hamlet* "myths"), but there is no question about what happens to his spirit. It is either passed on to the next king or venerated. For Shakespeare's Hamlet the sacrifice of life may be easy. But what might lie beyond life in the way of punishment suggests the sacrifice of those nobler human features: reason, self-command, grace, dignity, with the accompanying reduction of Hamlet to the level of his uncle by the enactment of a deed like his uncle's. And one grows more and more to feel that this is what is disturbing Hamlet. Nevertheless, there is this relentless truth: in order for Hamlet to lay the ghost which haunts the kingdom to rest, to bury the body which one might say still lies unburied —or which keeps reappearing in the shape of a stabbed Polonius or a drowned Ophelia (*Hamlet* being a play with a body perpetually behind an arras)—it is precisely his personal "conscience" he must sacrifice and his own corruption he must confirm in order to act.

To confirm that corruption, however, is to affirm his humanity, and to witness that humanity is to locate and accept his role in the face of death and the unknown quantity which lies beyond the grave. It is Act V which metaphorically delineates this transformation.

In the graveyard scene, the images of physical corruption and the theme of moral corruption which permeate *Hamlet* coalesce in an extended dramatization of human insufficiency. Although the interview between the two clowns has a surrealistic quality —the contrast between the seriousness of their task and the lightheartedness of their humor opening vistas upon the transience of life and its values as against the permanence of the graveyard—Shakespeare is careful to keep our eyes on the specific subject, death's latest victim, Ophelia. It is the same Ophelia who went mad because her father died at her lover's hands, and who met her own end dragging her garlands into the brook's "muddy death." Behind Ophelia, whose madness unlocked the treasure house of her innocence to reveal those bawdy songs which strike the audience so pathetically, lies the body of Polonius whose "guts" were lugged by Hamlet "into the neighbor room," and whose body, according to Hamlet is "compounded . . . with dust, whereto 'tis kin" and then "bestowed" at a "supper," "not where he eats, but where he is eaten." Behind Polonius lies the old king himself, killed by a "leperous distilment" whose effects are to "curd, like eager droppings into milk,/The thin and wholesome blood" and scab the "smooth body with a vile and loathsome crust."

All three are victims; yet all three have been touched by a moral corruption, however slight, which is mirrored forth to us by the imagery of filth and physical decay associated with their deaths. Old Hamlet dies with his sins still on his head; Polonius dies spying upon the privacy of others; Ophelia dies, having spied for her father and the king, and having given us a glimpse at the sexuality of even the most innocent. In each case the "privacy" of the individual, his soul, is at issue. Old Hamlet is given no time at his death to save his soul. The innocence of Ophelia's soul, though embalmed with flowers, reveals the minute worm at its root. Polonius, who adjured his son to be true to himself, is disastrously true to his own advice. In his purely practical attitude toward life, his role as functionary, he sacrifices his own private soul in sacrificing the privacy of others.

When the first clown asks his riddle and receives his first answer from the second clown, one wonders if in the answer there is not some pertinence, however vague, to those victimized dead as well as to the guilty living:

> *1. Clo.* What is he that builds stronger than either
> the mason, the shipwright, or the carpenter?
> *2. Clo.* The gallows-maker; for that frame outlives a
> thousand tenants.
>
> (V.i.46-50)

If the emphasis is moral in this first response, however, the second response stresses not the moral quality in life, but the perfect equality of all men and sinners in death and the permanence of death in contrast to the transience of life. The second clown cannot tell the answer, so the first explains it to him:

> *1. Clo.* Cudgel thy brains no more about it, for your
> dull ass will not mend his pace with beating;
> and, when you are ask'd this question next, say
> "a grave-maker"; the houses that he makes lasts
> till doomsday. Go, get thee to Yaughan; fetch
> me a stoup of liquor.
>
> (V.i.63-68)

103

The responses to the riddles are jokes, of course, but they are serious enough in light of Hamlet's reactions in the churchyard. Hamlet jokes too, but there is a crucial perception of reality at the heart of his irony that makes us realize how his growing acquaintance with the dead, those in the churchyard and those with whom he has more intimate connections, is in a certain sense a meeting of equals on very common ground. That acquaintance is shadowed forth now in the graveyard, whose tenants, the once living, were formerly prospective dead like himself.

With his father, with Polonius, Rosencrantz and Guildenstern, and now even Ophelia behind him, from one perspective it could be said that Hamlet's acquaintance with death has been his initiation into life. Claudius, it appears, was right when he said "reason's" common theme "is death of fathers," although he might have extended the statement to include lovers, sons, men. Yet Hamlet's acquaintance with death, highly concrete as it has been, is to some degree, if not to him, then to us, a kind of metaphor for the permanent corruption in human nature, a corruption which has displayed itself in the killings, the subterfuges, and the spying which have characterized the past action of the play. This corruption, linked to the physical corruption of the grave, may be observed in such physical manifestations as that congregation of worms who are our final masters. And these are but a token symptom of death, a state whose permanence masters the master worm. In the end, it is the predicament of our annihilation that relates us. The whole process by which Hamlet recognizes his own humanity, and even accepts his own necessary end is caught in the graveyard scene, not without a sense of his bitterness, not without a certain wonder, but with, at last, a feeling of Hamlet's acquiescence to his destined role. It is an acquiescence too, which in its temporary world-weariness, will simplify his moral awareness by reducing the significance of human life while magnifying the eternal kingdom of worms and dust.

The catalyst, of course, is Yorick's skull; and it is interesting that Shakespeare should have used this skull, not simply because the death's head has the obvious function of a *memento-mori*, but also because the skulls of men suggest man in the ideal fulfillment of his potentialities: his reason, his imagination, his morality. As Hamlet himself said earlier, ironically enough, to two of his future victims:

104

. . . What a piece of work is man! How noble in reason! How infinite in faculty, in form and moving! How express and admirable in action! How like an angel in apprehension! How like a god! The beauty of the world! The paragon of animals; . . .

(II.ii.315-319)

How significant too that Hamlet should have added as early as Act II, scene ii: "And yet, to me, what is this quintessence of dust?" The theme is born out in Act V as Hamlet expostulates upon the skull of the jester who was once his friend:

Let me see. [*Takes the skull.*] Alas, poor Yorick! I knew him, Horatio; a fellow of infinite jest, of most excellent fancy. He hath borne me on his back a thousand times. And [now] how abhorred [in] my imagination [it] is! My gorge rises at it. Here hung those lips that I have kiss'd I know not how oft. Where be your gibes now, your gambols, your songs, your flashes of merriment, that were wont to set the table on a roar? No one now, to mock your own jeering. Quite chop-fall'n? Now get you to my lady's chamber, and tell her, let her paint an inch thick, to this favour she must come. Make her laugh at that.

(V.i.202-215)

The pattern here, though a variation, fundamentally repeats that in the earlier speech. Yorick may not have been "noble in reason" or "infinite in faculty," but his "excellent fancy" and "infinite jest" parallel the earlier references, suggesting if not the nobility in life, at least its joy, its freshness, its amazingly vivid reality. But here the mocking turn of attitude is not limited by a sentence. It is expressed in detail, and explores further the apparent valuelessness of a life which in the face of death is only mocked, a death's head becoming the apt reflection of the lady who paints an inch thick or the clown who jibed (as Hamlet jibes now in his own fashion), now jibed at forever.

But this skull has been preceded by another, and Hamlet's

first speculations as to each skull's former possessor encompass a microcosm of the court:[19] "The pate of a politician," offers Hamlet as the clown throws the skull to the ground as if it were, significantly, Cain's, the first murderer's jawbone; or the skull of a courtier, or of a lawyer, or of a land buyer. Such considerations as have developed around these skulls lead inevitably to the greatest contrast: that between a world conquerer and his end:

> . . . Alexander died, Alexander was buried, Alexander returneth into dust, the dust is earth, of earth we make loam, and why of that loam whereto he was converted might they not stop a beer-barrel? Imperial Caesar, dead and turn'd to clay, Might stop a hole to keep the wind away. O, that that earth which kept the world in awe Should patch a wall t' expel the winter's flaw!
>
> (V.i.231-239)

After the murder of Polonius, Hamlet had remarked that "Your fat king and your lean beggar is but variable service, two dishes, but to one table; that's the end" (IV.iii.24-26). The politic worm was "your only emperor for diet." In his remarks on Alexander and Caesar, the levelling process of death is insisted upon even more rigorously. If kings and beggars provide food for worms, the greatest of kings and emperors are in the end nothing more than clods of earth fulfilling undignified functional services. Curiously, however, there is a certain unconscious aptness in Hamlet's reference to Caesar that goes beyond the purely literal. If Caesar's dust stops the hole in a wall "to keep the wind away," the emperor's service during life is at least metaphorically akin. He serves, theoretically at least, to ward off anarchic nature through the sacrifice of his personal life in the execution of a public role. In mythic times this sacrifice might very well have meant the sacrifice of the king himself to propitiate the gods and confirm the fertility of nature. But even in more modern times, the king had to "die" to personal consequences, indeed give up his personal life, for the sake of that public order which nature seeks to reduce through the threatening processes of destruction and decay. The king's function, in this sense, was to maintain the permanence of his kingdom against these hostile aspects of nature.

The entrance of Claudius following Ophelia's coffin at the end of Hamlet's speech (Ophelia who was as much Claudius' victim as Hamlet's) sets in contrast the usurper who has joined nature's anarchic forces by killing his brother and his king, against the young prince, who, matured by his acquaintance with death, and having learned the insignificance of individual lives, will accept his role as "king" and "minister" of justice in the name of a providential order of which he makes himself the tool.[20] Paradoxically he will have to harden his conscience in order to do so: or at least that portion of his conscience which fears his own punishment, and that portion which might have felt more strongly the guilt for what he had done to others.[21]

The first sign that Hamlet has come to see himself in a new way occurs during his strong reaction to Laertes' protestations of grief at Ophelia's grave. To begin with, Hamlet reacts with spontaneous passion to Laertes' theatrical demonstration of love. The violence of Laertes' grief seems indeed more like that of a lover than a brother:

> Hold off the earth a while,
> Till I have caught her once more in my arms.
> [*Leaps in the grave*]
> Now pile your dust upon the quick and dead,
> Till of this flat a mountain you have made
> To o'ertop old Pelion, or the skyish head
> Of blue Olympus.
>
> (V.i.272-277)

Hamlet responds in kind. It is as if he were protesting against Laertes' assumption of *his* private role as chief mourner in Ophelia's funeral. By the grave stands the usurper who has taken his kingdom, and now young Laertes' preempts a position in the funeral which Hamlet evidently feels belongs to him. It is important to notice also that the sudden exposure of Hamlet as he advances toward the grave is as much a challenge to Claudius as it is to Laertes. Hamlet, moreover, takes the trouble, even in his passion, to publicize his appearance and his role. And it is a role that we can see now is more than private in nature. There is a distinctly public side to it. One might say that "privately" Hamlet challenges the figure of Laertes as chief mourner, but that simultaneously he "publicly" challenges the figure of Claudius as king. His language, addressed to to the king and his entourage as well as to Laertes, mocks the exaggerated quality of Laertes' words and conduct, while he, in his very mockery, makes use of a similar kind of rhetoric, sonorous and formal, which confers dignity upon himself. This language, in content and style, is in a very essential sense a publication of identity:

> *Ham.* [*Advancing*] What is he whose grief
> Bears such an emphasis, whose phrase of sorrow
> Conjures the wand'ring stars and makes them stand
> Like wonder-wounded hearers? This is I,
> Hamlet, the Dane!
>
> (V.i.277-281)

This is the only time Hamlet refers to himself by the title of the Danish kings. With it, he, the son, confers his father's title upon his head and sets himself in direct competition with the usurper, who by this time has not simply taken Hamlet's father's life, but has in fact directly sought after his own. The name brings with it his father's grandeur, and his humanity. It brings with it as well all the public responsibility of kingship.

Thus if it can be said that Hamlet rejects the lover's role in the "nunnery" scene, he reassumes that role now as he leaps into his beloved's grave, crying:

> I lov'd Ophelia. Forty thousand brothers
> Could not, with all their quantity of love,
> Make up my sum. What wilt thou do for her?
> (V.i.292-294)

The "bravery" of Laertes' grief puts Hamlet into the "towering passion" with which he confronts Laertes' rant.[22] Emotion, not godlike, but not blind either, is the catalyst that allows Hamlet an open confrontation with the brother who has "usurped" his role in the funeral. And in this case, unlike that of Laertes' father Polonius behind the arras, he sees and knows his adversary. His violent grappling with Laertes in the grave is filled with a sense of the "justice" in his cause. Without calculation or scrupulosity, Hamlet, for better or worse, has found a means of acting in order to define himself in his relationship to Ophelia.

Likewise, Hamlet finds a way, but a different one, to deal with his father's cause—a way to assume his father's role and regain his usurped name. Having observed the insignificance of individual life in comparison with the necessity of his cause and having perhaps accepted the corruption his own humanity implies, he can assume the perspective of his father's ghost and translate it into his own. In scene ii of Act V he says to Horatio:

> Does it not, thinks't thee, stand me now upon—
> He that hath kill'd my king and whor'd my mother,
> Popp'd in between th' election and my hopes,
> Thrown out his angle for my proper life,
> And with such cozenage—is't not perfect conscience
> To quit him with this arm? And is't not to be damned
> To let this canker of our nature come
> In further evil?
>
> (V.ii.63-70)

The recognition of death's enduring kingdom has obliterated the division of conscience which characterized Hamlet's frame of mind. Moreover the new public sense of his identity has freed him to feel not despair, melancholy or helpless outrage over his personal affronts, but rather a kind of poised indignation, which rapierlike, cuts through moral subtleties and reduces the case to a series of hostile acts aimed directly at himself. To kill now is not only a matter of revenge; it is a matter of self-protection, of self-defense. Hamlet's sense of the justice in his cause gives him the arms and armor for any action which may come.

Furthermore, as a man forced to defend his honor and himself in a world which has attempted to annihilate him, he can afford to dismiss his responsibility for the deaths of Rosencrantz and Guildenstern with a certain *hauteur*:

> Why, man, they did make love to this employment;
> They are not near my conscience. Their [defeat]
> Doth by their own insinuation grow.
> 'Tis dangerous when the baser nature comes
> Between the pass and fell incensed points
> Of mighty opposites.
>
> (V.ii.57-62)

Having sealed their death warrants with his "father's signet," "the model of that Danish seal," Hamlet acted through hard necessity with the perspicacious dispatch of a mighty king. In his reaction to their passing there is no anguished recognition that he has destroyed two former friends, even though they have been misguided and acquiescent tools of Claudius. Rather he sees them from the height of royal power, and what impresses us in his argument is the distinction he makes between their intrusive "baser nature" and the greatness and power of himself and his rival. This sense of "great enterprise" frees the actor to make a public claim that satisfies his private goals. As "the Dane" confronting a usurper, he is a private man seeking to adjust his wrongs; but he is also the kingdom of Denmark, heroically marked and royally caparisoned, defending itself from a dangerous social infection.[23] And he is Man, aware of his "dram of evil," having accepted the awful necessity of his own sacrifice, his own duty, and his own end.

For the moral issues have now been resolved and simplified. Damnation is no longer a question of acting, but a question of what it would mean not to act. It is "perfect conscience" to kill Claudius because he is the canker in the state and nothing more. To be damned is to allow the canker to live. Hamlet's conscience has knitted itself into a kind of wholeness. It is vitally necessary for Hamlet not to see anything more. He will now eschew plots because he sees or feels that providence has made him its tool. The "interim" is his because the moment of his destiny will come to him whether he seeks it or not: "A man's life's no more than to say 'One'." His own life and death, even what may lie after death, are insignificant in the face of his greater destiny. If the impending duel with Laertes is a trap, then that destiny will come. And if that destiny is to include the death of Claudius, it too will come. The significant element is that Hamlet submits to his fate whatever it may be. Hamlet need only patiently wait. When the moment comes, he will know how to act. For he has been schooled now in both killing and dying.

> . . . we defy augury. There's a special providence in the fall of a sparrow. If it be now, 'tis not to come; if it be not to come, it will be now; if it be not now, yet it will come; the readiness is all. Since no man has aught of what he leaves, what is't to leave betimes. [Let be.]
>
> (V.ii.230-235)

This speech is one of kingly resignation and maturity.[24] For the first and only time in the play Hamlet uses the sovereign form "we" in reference to himself. He claims both royal dignity and public prerogative for himself. His readiness for the final sacrifice, in which he will prove both killer and victim, is less a sign of personal despair than an acknowledgment of his social obligation as a prince, a very special public and private fulfillment. In submitting to "providence" he submits to a moral necessity he himself cannot fully understand except in the terms he has at long last found for himself.

When, at the duel, Hamlet sees his mother fall, and hears Laertes cry, "—The king, the king's to blame," he knows how to act. He stabs the king and forces him to drink the dregs of the infamous potion. His passion is direct and spontaneous, his conduct as just as human conduct can be, even as Claudius' plot was devious and calculated, his conduct cruel. Hamlet's death by the poisoned tip of Laertes' sword, Claudius' death by the tip of the same sword, two acts which strangely unite and separate the prince and usurper, answer that call for blood which was the ghost's first cry. Purged, the state draws life from the spilling of the poisoned blood. Rivals in their "days of nature," Hamlet and Claudius, true to the temper of the graveyard, unite in death. What lies beyond for the king, killed at long last "about some act/That hath no relish of salvation in't" is self-evident. What lies beyond for Hamlet is implied by the human tribute accorded him by Fortinbras of Norway, that most active of princes—but not without our sensing a terrific irony on the quality of human action even at its best:

> Let four captains
> Bear Hamlet, like a soldier, to the stage,
> For he was likely, had he been put on,
> To have prov'd most royally; and, for his passage,
> The soldiers' music and the rites of war
> Speak loudly for him. . . .
>
> (V.ii.406-411)

University of Connecticut

NOTES

[1] A number of contemporary critics have stressed the idea that *Hamlet* is a play which poses questions rather than a play which gives answers. Harry Levin gives the most extensive exposition of this point of view in *The Question of Hamlet* (New York, 1959). His book actually contains the most complete refutation to T. S. Eliot's suggestion that the play fails because Hamlet lacks a sufficient "objective equivalent" to justify his emotions: *Selected Essays* (New York, 1950), p. 125.

[2] All quotations are taken from *The Complete Plays and Poems of William Shakespeare,* eds. William A. Neilson and Charles Jarvis Hill (Cambridge, Mass., 1942).

[3] C. S. Lewis, like G. Wilson Knight in *The Wheel of Fire* (London, 1959), p. 31, notes that "the subject of Hamlet is death." However Lewis qualifies his statement by adding that Hamlet's hesitation is accounted for not by "a physical fear of dying," but by "a fear of being dead; that is, a fear of what follows death." See *Hamlet: The Prince or the Poem.* Proceedings of the British Academy (London, 1942), pp. 13-14.

[4] G. B. Harrison, *Shakespeare's Tragedies* (London, 1951), p. 100.

[5] John Lawlor in *The Tragic Sense of Shakespeare* (London, 1960), p. 58, stresses how Hamlet is "condemned" to revenge "by the inescapable authority of a father from beyond the grave." Irving Ribner, *Patterns in Shakespearian Tragedy* (London, 1960), p. 65, notes how Hamlet "comes into a world full of ancient evil not of his own creation."

[6] Knight, p. 33.

[7] Robert B. Heilman, *Shakespearean Tragedy and the Drama of Disaster* (Vancouver, B.C., 1960), pp. 8-9.

[8] See Lawlor, p. 57.

[9] John Holloway discusses the question of role in *Hamlet*, but from a slightly different perspective in *The Story of the Night* (London, 1961), pp. 26-27. For a good discussion of Hamlet in relation to the "actor" image and the theater metaphor characteristic of the play, see Anne Righter, *Shakespeare and the Idea of the Play* (London, 1962), pp. 161-164 especially. For another such analysis, see C. R. Forker, "Shakespeare's Theatrical Symbolism and Its Function in Hamlet," *SQ*, XIV (1963), 215-229.

[10] See Francis Fergusson's discussion of the "imposthume" in Claudius' state, with its political, cultural and religious implications: *The Idea of a Theater* (Garden City, N.Y., 1949), pp. 113-124.

[11] Dover Wilson in his introduction to *Hamlet*, Cambridge edition (Cambridge, 1934), p. liii ff., sees Hamlet as ambitious and understands the political issue as being significant to an interpretation of the play. Although one can agree about the significance of the political issue, Wilson's evidence for Hamlet's "ambition" is based only on two references to the loss of the crown: one at III.iv.99 and the other Hamlet's words describing how Claudius has "popped in between th' election and my hopes." These two short references do not seem to give sufficient warrant for our making claims about "Hamlet's ambitious designs." Fergusson's idea, however, and one he attributes to Wilson, that "Hamlet has lost a throne, and has lost thereby a social, publicly acceptable *persona*," which he seeks throughout the play like a "disposed" ghost is a significant insight. See p. 112.

[12] Theodore Spencer, "Hamlet and the Nature of Reality," *ELH*, V (December, 1938), 269.

[13] Robert B. Heilman, " 'Twere Best Not Know Myself," *SQ*, XV (Spring, 1964), 91. G. Wilson Knight in *Wheel of Fire* uses a phrase similar to Heilman's "purpose needs ignorance." Knight says "passion implies purpose," but in the context of a statement which notes that Hamlet cannot "feel anything passionately for long." In a sense this is true; however, Knight adds that "One element in Hamlet . . . is the negation of any passion whatsoever," pp. 41-42. To say as much rather stretches the point.

[14] Coleridge calls Hamlet's failure to kill Claudius at prayer "motive–mongering" [*Coleridge's Shakespearean Criticism*, ed. Thomas M. Raysor (London, 1930), I, 33.] Bradley says that the interpretation that the failure "is an unconscious excuse for delay is now pretty generally agreed . . . ," *Shakespearian Tragedy* (London, 1960), p. 134ff.

[15] Lawlor, pp. 47-50.

[16] *Ibid.*, p. 47. See also Ribner, p. 77.

[17] Charles W. Eckert, "The Festival Structure of the Orestes-Hamlet Tradition," *CL*, XV (Fall, 1963), 321-337.

[18] *Ibid.*, p. 335.

[19] Leo Kirschbaum, *Character and Characterization in Shakespeare* (Detroit, 1962), p. 96.

[20] Fredson Bowers discusses the distinction between Hamlet's conduct as "scourge" and his conduct as "minister" in "Hamlet as Scourge and Minister," *PMLA*, LXX (September, 1955), 740-749.

[21] Ribner accentuates Hamlet's acceptance of providence in a manner somewhat parallel to my own. His emphasis on Christian providence, however, is more strenuous than mine. Ribner says, citing V.ii.230-235 ("There's a special providence in the fall of a sparrow. . . ."): "This is the answer to which Shakespeare finally leads us, the resolution of the paradox in the ghost's command. Such a faith is the only plan that Hamlet needs to combat the evil of the world. The ineffective schemer of the first three acts is no more; Hamlet has become a passive instrument in the hands of divine providence," p. 81. Ribner also feels that the pattern of maturation revealed in *Hamlet* is one which moves away from passion toward the "reason" reflected in his acquiescence to divine providence. Hamlet's purpose, Ribner thinks, formerly had been "blunted by . . . passion," p. 70.

[22] I cannot accept Ribner's notion that "Hamlet does not abandon himself to the 'towering passion' which Laertes' words provoke," and that his speech to Laertes (V.i.297-307) is merely "one of scornful derision," p. 86. It is, after all, Hamlet who says he was in a "towering passion." Moreover, "towering passion" and "scornful derision" are by no means mutually exclusive.

[23] Bowers, p. 748, says that Hamlet at the end of the play is no longer "a private revenger, but one seeking public vengeance and justice."

[24] For an alternative, yet related, interpretation of the graveyard scene and the recognitions which follow it, see Ribner on Hamlet's role "as a symbolic portrait of the human life-journey" and the accompanying pattern of maturation, pp. 79-90.

THE CHRONOLOGY
OF SHAKESPEARE'S JACOBEAN
PLAYS AND THE DATING
OF *ANTONY AND CLEOPATRA*

J. LEEDS BARROLL

I

The assignment of certain chronological positions to Shake-speare's tragedies is often a circular process. In the absence of definite dates for plays, assumptions as to an order of artistic development are frequently productive of reasoning which es-tablishes dates for additional plays, estimates based on the dates already "known." Such a process can be misleading especially if a consequently "traditional" ordering of Shakespeare's tragedies then influences an approach either to the general shape of Shake-speare's career or to the evaluation of an individual play. For obviously if we consider *Anthony and Cleopatra* and *Coriolanus* as late, and thus as "further development" or "reiteration" of certain tragic principles, we are likely to approach these dramas in a manner that we might not necessarily accord to, say, *Romeo and Juliet* or *Julius Caesar*. Therefore, a consideration of the date of *Anthony and Cleopatra* seems worth attempting once more, for this play especially has suffered from its position, tend-ing to be interpreted, *a priori,* as a kind of "final statement." But our aim need not be a polemic one. A number of scholars have carefully investigated the problem of Shakespeare's tragic chro-nology, and nothing very different can arise here, if only because most of Shakespeare's plays, in the relatively brief period of his Jacobean career, are usually dated in estimates of two-year spans. Rather, let our purpose be to attempt to define the kinds of ques-

115

tions that might be asked about the dating of Shakespeare's Jacobean tragedies and to consider ways in which such questions can, in theory, be answered.

If we are indeed attempting to locate a Shakespearean tragedy in time, we might first inquire as to the kind of date which is the object of search. Short of authorial declaration, for instance, it is obviously difficult to determine by "internal evidence" when a play was completed, for certainly a writer can retain his own manuscript indefinitely before he releases it to a scribe. And no matter how enticing it might be to fall into ethical or philosophical orderings that serve to reconstruct Shakespeare's career into a symmetry, there is, as yet, no method which can trace chronologically the turning of a mind from one task or one mood to another. The problem of "stylistic evolution" might be a case in point, even though the notion of such evidence, not often precisely defined, has been a strong factor in moulding traditional assumptions regarding the chronology of Shakespeare's tragedies. Present awareness of compositorial error, of the difficulty of evolving any system of scansion according to which metrics can be adequately described, and of the problem of comparing lines of verse on a page to whatever might be their equivalent "units" either in the structure of Elizabethan phonology or in the utterances of the actors on the stage, all these matters are too difficult to allow us to speak of "metrical tests" with any confidence.

Yet Chambers is typical of much thinking on this point, as when he observes, in his dating of the tragedy, that "the metrical character of *Antony and Cleopatra* forbids us to put it before *Macbeth* or *Lear*." For such pronouncements underlie many of the great theatrical historian's conjectures as to date, and the conjectures themselves have often served as points of departure for essays on, or casual references to, the matter of Shakespearean chronology. Chambers himself devoted part of a chapter to some analysis of the problems inherent in the use of metrical criteria, and though these *caveats* are still valid, it is significant that after he reproduced and corrected a number of the standard "metrical tables" such as Fleay's, Chambers produced one himself, an extract from which follows.[1]

	(1) Full Lines (5+6 foot)	(2) Split	(3) Unsplit	(4) Unsplit with Pauses	(5) (4) as % of (3)
J. C.	2161	129	2132	437	20
Ham.	2290	194	2096	552	26
M. M.	1460	148	1312	398	30
Oth.	2362	268	2094	694	33
Lear	2043	243	1800	691	38
Mac.	1595	246	1349	494	37
A. C.	2589	470	2119	935	44
Cor.	2413	394	2019	749	37
Cy.	2537	393	2144	1027	48
W. T.	2049	330	1719	699	41
Tp.	1378	227	1151	481	42
Per.		84	564	209	37

Explaining Column 4 as full lines in which there is "the use of a period, colon, semicolon, interrogation mark or exclamation mark in the *Eversley* text," Chambers assumed, as he remarked elsewhere, that the percentage figure is obviously the significant statistic. Thus the burden of his observations is in the last column.[2] But if these figures are indeed Chambers' rationale for the statement that "the metrical character" of *Anthony and Cleopatra* "forbids" us to put it before *Macbeth* or *Lear,* the implications of only this last column are interesting. For solely according to ascending percentages, Chambers' obvious chronological criterion, "metrical tests," would reveal the following chronological order of some of the plays in this table. *Measure* (30%); *Othello* (33%); *Macbeth* (37%); *Pericles* (37%); *Coriolanus* (37%); *Lear* (38%); *Winter's* (41%); *Tempest* (42%); *Anthony* (44%); *Cymbeline* (48%).

The metrical character of *Anthony and Cleopatra* would not only forbid is to place it before *Lear* and *Macbeth* but also before *Coriolanus, Tempest, Winter's,* and *Pericles* (with which *Anthony* was entered in the Stationers' Register). But *Coriolanus* is dated by Chambers as follows: "The evidence of style and metre puts *Coriolanus* between *Antony and Cleopatra* and *Pericles*." Or again, for *Cymbeline*: "A date of production in 1609-10 would fit the evidence of metre and style, which links the play with *Winter's Tale* and *Tempest*." But "the style and metre group *Winter's Tale* with *Cymbeline* and *Tempest*, and it may reasonably be placed between them." [3] According to Chambers' table, however, if we can operate as he himself does, we may reasonably put *Anthony* before any other play from which it deviates by seven percentage points. Chambers' chronology of *Cymbeline, Winter's,* and *Tempest,* for instance reflects the percentage-sequence 48-41-42, and the series *Anthony, Coriolanus, Pericles* reflects the percentages 44-37-37. But in this context, would not a sequence of 44-38-37 be quite as consistent and would it not enable us to construct from Chambers' figures a chronological series *Anthony* (44%), *Lear* (38%), *Macbeth* (37%)?

It would seem that such results might be sufficient to weaken the rather strong language Chambers has used in his conjecture regarding the chronological relationship of *Anthony* to *Macbeth* and *Lear*. We can perhaps make the point again, by evolving our own percentages from the table Chambers has offered by comparing Column 2 to Column 1. The criterion is at least as objective as that of Chambers and there are ascending percentages too if we ask what proportion of all the lines in each play are fragmented so as to be divided among two or more speakers. We find: *Measure* (10%); *Lear* (11%); *Othello* (11%); *Cymbeline* (15%); *Macbeth* (15%); *Tempest* (16%); *Winter's* (16%); *Coriolanus* (16%); *Anthony* (18%). But we know for a fact, do we not, that *Anthony* was entered in the Stationers' Register in 1608? In truth, any table such as this can hardly claim to make distinctions in dating according to three or four percentage points, if only because the principle of random variation is an important factor in statistics. If such variation includes a penchant in one play for splitting lines, the figure of 18% for *Anthony* does not necessarily convey chronology; it simply states that there is a greater percentage of split lines in this play than in others, and that *Anthony* was one play in what seems to have been a general trend towards splitting lines on Shakespeare's part.

Several other standards may finally be presented in this matter of "stylistic tests." Table I of Chambers' Appendix H presents a count of the total number of lines in each play (including prose) and the total number of lines of prose in each play. This count is Chambers' correction of Fleay. Using these figures, we can readily enough compute the percentage of prose lines (discounting for the moment compositorial problems) to the total number of lines in each play, surely as reasonable a criterion as any of the foregoing. We find: *Caesar* (7%); *Macbeth* (7%); *Anthony* (9%); *Othello* (20%); *Coriolanus* (24%); *Lear* (27%); *Hamlet* (30%). According to this table *Julius Caesar* and *Macbeth* are roughly contemporaneous. If, lastly, we allude to the matter of feminine endings, still a popular criterion, let us produce the figures from Chambers' Table III for percentages of such endings in certain plays, the figures compiled by König represented by the first number and those of Hertzberg by the second number. We find: *Caesar* (20%, 18%); *Hamlet* (23%, 25%); *Macbeth* (26%, 23%); *Anthony* (27%, 26%); *Coriolanus* (28%, 28%); *Othello* (28%, 26%); *Lear* (29%, 27%). The span is from 5% in *1 Henry IV* to 35% in *Tempest,* and if the figures are accurate, there does seem to be a general increase of feminine endings over the period of Shakespeare's career, but the foregoing calculations are hardly definitive enough to date each of the plays relative to the other. The fact is that any characteristic of a play, including, say, the number of speaking parts, which can be counted and thus transformed into quantitative terms, will form figures that can be grouped into any combination of purely *numerical* categories. To assume that such categories will have any precise chronological relevance, however, is to play with numbers, to instigate a *spiel* which should not be confused with what certain disciplines imply by the word "test." The science of calculating percentages does not necessarily allow those percentages to be used as chronological indices. The proposition that "metrical tests forbid" any chronological placements of certain dramas may itself be mathematically phrased, but the precise correlation between ascending percentages and the passage of time in the life of an individual has yet to be demonstrated.

If, in our inquiry regarding the question of finding the composition date of a play, we balk at metrical tests, we should, though to a lesser extent, also be cautious about the matter of topical allusions, if only because of other kinds of assumptions we are required to make. Certainly it is possible to establish *termini a quo,* as when, for instance, we view the procession of the descendants of Banquo in *Macbeth,* for this masque shows an eventual ruler of England descending from a Scottish noble, and it can be assumed, practically if not theoretically, that the play contains material written after the accession of James I. But other cases are far less certain. For there is the problem of the defining concept underlying the theory of "topical allusion"— that a playwright is likely to have his characters allude to current events no matter what the immediate dramatic context of his speech. Sequences in comedy do utilize topics of current common interest as the basis for some humorous sallies, as in the reference to the Brownists in *Twelfth Night,* but to derive chronological orientation from more generalized speech or activity on stage seems less sound methodology. Given the large number of publications and manuscripts surviving from the sixteenth and seventeenth centuries, and given the *modus operandi* of selecting passages in a play with no discrimination as to context, there are bound to be "correlations." If Gloucester mentions "these late eclipses" and thus theoretically keys the writing of *King Lear* to a date just following a real eclipse, might we not with equal relevance allude to the violent tidal storms of March 29th and 30th, 1606, for there certainly seems to be a storm in *Lear.* There is a storm too in *Othello, Macbeth,* and in *Tempest,* as well as *Twelfth Night.* The methodology in all cases would be the same: first, the selection of some event or topic of conversation in the play, then the discovery of a similar topic or event current at one point in English life outside the play. Knowing the date of the latter, we use that date as chronological orientation for the play itself. There was a dearth of corn in 1608; there is a dearth of corn in *Coriolanus,* hence, etc. Might we not, by the same logic, date *Coriolanus, Julius Caesar, 1* and *2 Henry IV,* and *Richard III* according to the Essex conspiracy? There are conspiracies against the government in these plays. If this is not acceptable, what then precisely is the rationale underlying the "topical allusion"?

Circularities in these respects reach their peak in observations on *Macbeth.* K. Muir has already noted that allusions to equivocation are to be found as early as in *Hamlet,* but there remains much emphasis on the matter of Malcolm's lines when he feign-ingly observes to Macduff that he would "poure the sweet Milke of Concord into Hell,/Uprore the universall peace, confound/ All unity on earth." H. N. Paul, the most detailed exponent of a date for *Macbeth* as during the visit of Christian of Denmark, has alluded to the street pageant of July 31st which greeted the progress of the two monarchs into London.[4] The allegorical figure of Concord speaks of peace and unity in this pageant, and Paul suggests first that this presentation alludes to James's slogan of Love, Peace, and Unity, as it probably would, and, secondly, that *Macbeth* itself alludes to the pageant, in the lines of Malcolm above. But the weakness of this kind of argumentation lies in its circularity. If Christian and James saw *Macbeth* in the summer of 1606, during Denmark's visit, and if Shakespeare's play was presented after July 31st before the two kings, then the Malcolm lines, by a stretching of the sense, just might be chronologically pertinent. But if *Macbeth* was not presented at this time, then the lines would not be specifically topical. The "allusion" does not demonstrate that *Macbeth* was presented before James and Christian: in order to be considered as an allusion at all, it de-pends on the play having been presented before Christian and James in the first place. Chronology certainly cannot be estab-lished on the basis of a prior chronological speculation.[5]

Theories of topical allusion, especially when there exists no Stationers' Entry for a play in question, cannot reveal the time at which a play was written, for if the allusion is not minutely specific, the concept of topical allusion actually assumes the date which it is theoretically attempting to determine. Were there no dearths of corn before or after 1608? To select an event in the first place is already to assume that the play in question was written after the event, and, in effect, a chronological conclusion already exists. And what is to be done if the original assessment, before the topical process, is based on an unproved assumption that the dramatist is in the habit of having his characters or plots allude to current events?

There would thus seem to be every reason to define that date for which one searches in connection with a specific play as a date not of composition, but of performance, if only because such a quest at least poses a query that is theoretically answerable.

Of course even this kind of date produces no biographical certainty in terms of artistic development, for clearly the first record of a performance is not necessarily the record of a first performance. But as an heuristic maneuver, the very search for a first performance may impose a discipline enabling us more successfully to evade the slips into aesthetic orderings to which any interested and intelligent student of Shakespeare is, at one time or other, bound to be prone.

II

If performance is to be the criterion for chronological inquiry, the problem is complicated by the fact that the acting of the King's Men was by no means a continuous affair, but of course dotted with several kinds of interruptions. There is not only the problem of endemic plague but the question, too, of Lenten prohibition. G. E. Bentley, in a recent article, has observed the possibility that, after 1615, playing in Lent may have been a matter of purchasing a "Lenten dispensation" as Sir Henry Herbert termed it,[6] but evidence for the period of our own interest here, before 1615, is somewhat scantier. In 1605, Lent begins on February 13th, but the Prince's Men were paid for acting on the 19th of this month before the Prince at Whitehall.[7] Similarly, in 1607, the King's Men acted before James on February 27th, Ash Wednesday having been February 18th. In 1608 there is lion-baiting at Whitehall before the Prince and Lady Elizabeth on February 22nd, Lent having begun on the 10th, but perhaps this show, courtesy of Henslowe and Alleyn, might be regarded as the kind of special performance that Bentley sees as characteristic of Lenten stage practices after 1615. Possibly royal performances were an exception to the rule, yet even in the week before Queen Elizabeth's death, stage plays may have been restrained in town until further notice on the 19th of March,[8] and Lent was already in progress, Ash Wednesday having fallen on the 9th of March.

At any rate, Chambers observes that there seems to have been strict enforcement of a Lenten break established by Council orders of 1600 and 1601, and, indeed, in one year, the permission by James to resume playing, plague conditions having presumably abated, is dated Easter Monday, April 9th, 1604, when the companies are permitted to act again, "the time of Lent being now passt." [9] In a similar vein, too, there is perhaps vague evidence from the spring of 1607 when the plague was continuing at a light rate. Easter was April 5th, 1607. One week after this, on Sunday, the Mayor wrote to the Lord Chamberlain asking for a restraint of "such comon Stage Plaies as are Daylie shewed and exercised" on the grounds of an increase in plague "for theis two or three weekes of late." [10] But for the seven weeks of February 26th through April 12th, the day of the letter, death figures from plague were as follows: 20, 30, 33, 22, 13, 13, 23, the last figure representing the last Thursday report from which the Mayor could have derived his comments of Sunday, the 12th.[11] If the companies had been acting throughout Lent, it would seem as if the Mayor might have had better grounds for his complaint earlier in this series, especially since the 1604 permission to act again had also established thirty deaths a week as a plague-level prohibitive for acting. What could be suggested is that a Lenten prohibition, implied in the April 1604 letter, still applied to Lent, 1607, and that the actors began playing immediately in the week after Easter as if the ending of Lent were a reasonable excuse, despite the continued presence of mild plague.

Finally, there are several remarks emanating from the 1608 Lenten season in the account of the College Revels of St. John's, Oxford, which extended from October 31, 1607, to February 13th, 1608. At one point in this account, allusion is made to unsuccessful arguments against the presentation of a tragedy at the college "because itt was neere Lent and Consequently a season vnfitt for plaies." But the tragedy *Periander* is given, yet the Epilogue does interrupt himself to remark: "But wee forgett times limitts; Nowe tis lente." A remark, too, adduced by Chambers from Middleton's *Mad World My Masters* (S. R. Oct 4th, 1608), would seem confirmatory here: " 'Tis Lent in your cheeks; the flag's down."[12]

There would seem to be some justification, then, for concluding that Lent was a time when plays were prohibited on the public stage, whatever the practice might have been at court. And with an awareness of possible Lenten interruptions, together with our approximate knowledge of plague conditions, it seems possible to organize a search for dates of possible first perform- ances not only of *Anthony and Cleopatra* but also for a number of Shakespeare's other plays, particularly the tragedies, by isolat- ing Shakespeare's Jacobean chronology according to interims in which public acting was not theoretically prohibited. This can be accomplished rather conveniently at the beginning, since the last Shakespearean play to be accounted for prior to the accession of James is *Troilus,* entered February 7th, 1603. The plays that remain to be recorded at this point are *Measure, All's Well, Macbeth, Anthony and Cleopatra, Lear, Coriolanus, Timon,* the "final" comedies, *Henry VIIII,* and *Two Noble Kinsmen.*[13] It would therefore seem convenient to begin Shakespeare's Jacobean chronology in terms of the *Troilus* entry, since in less than two months, James would be king. A summary of conclusions below will be found in tabular form on p. 134

I. *Troilus* is entered, February 7th, 1603. Lent extends from March 9th to April 24th. Acting was restrained on March 19th. Elizabeth's death occurred on March 24th, and it is uncertain whether acting resumed after Easter Sunday, April 24th, for Elizabeth was not buried until April 28th.[14] Seven days later, Henslowe mentions that "we leaft of playe now at the kynges coming," while four days after that, on the 9th of May, Henslowe speaks of "begininge to playe agayne by the Kinges licence." On the 19th of May, however, the Royal Patent for the King's Men gives them allowance to play only "when the infection of the plague shall decrease."[15] Cognizance has therefore presumably been taken of a rise in the plague death rate, from 18 in the week of May 5th-12th, to 22 for the week following. Thus, our first interim, from its arbitrary starting point with the entry of *Troilus,* is rather irregular, possibly totalling something like four and a half weeks before Lent and perhaps fourteen days at the most between Easter and the issue of the Patent for the King's Men: an interrupted period of about six weeks.

II. The plague dominated at least from May 19th, 1603, to Christmas, 1603. Puzzlingly enough, Joan Alleyn observes on

October 21st, 1603, that the companies are back in London.[16] "About vs the sycknes dothe Cease," she says, but deaths for the week of October 13th-20th are 642. Possibly the players had been misled by the September 16th proclamation postponing Michaelmas Term "from the Utas of the same, until the fourth returne," that is, from its traditional beginning on the 6th of October until about October 27th (the beginning of the fourth return). Three days before Joan's letter, a second proclamation (October 18th) further adjourned the term from the fourth return to *cras Martini* (November 13th) when the term would begin again, but in Winchester.[17] Possibly the first proclamation influenced a reasonable assumption by the actors that the plague would wane with autumn and that they would have their Inns of Court audiences by October 27th. At any rate, they must have left town again, for they were summoned to Wilton to play before the king on December 2nd, and they had to come from Mortlake where possibly they were sojourning through the courtesy of Augustine Phillips who had a house there.[18]

During this holiday season, beginning with December 2nd, Shakespeare's company gives nine performances, the last on February 19th, the only known Shakespearean work possibly being *MND* on January 1st.[19] Times are obviously bad for the company, for when Burbage, instead of the usual Hemming, is given £30 on the 8th of February, the Chamber Account notes that the money is "for the mayntenaunce and releife of himselfe and the rest of his Company being prohibited to presente any playes publiquelie in or neere London" by reason of the plague.[20] It seems clear that the King's Men are not performing much unless they tour. Thomas Pope had made his will, too, the previous summer, July 22nd, 1603, leaving his interests in the Globe to Mary Clark, and the will was being proved on February 13th, 1604. Chambers notes also that the names of Lowin and Cooke appear for the first time in the cast-list of *Sejanus*, possibly performed before the end of 1603. There were thus internal disturbances, not only in the business affairs, but in the constitution of the acting group. In Lowin's case, there must have been the problem of learning parts. He had been with Worcester's Men in 1602-03 at the Rose, and appears to have been with the King's Men only after March 12th, 1603.[21]

Ash Wednesday is February 22nd, 1604, but Paul's Boys,

Queen's Revels, Prince's and Henslowe's omnipresent bears monopolize Shrovetide, the last play given by King's being on Shrove Sunday, the 19th. The King's Men march in the coronation procession on March 15th, and on Easter Monday, April 9th, 1604, the players will be authorized to act again, as we have seen. Thus concludes a span of time beginning December 2nd, 1603, and ending on April 9th, 1604, in which the King's Men possibly gave nine performances. In fact, ever since the plague had closed in, on May 19th, 1603, these nine performances may represent the totality of plays produced in eleven months up to April 9th, 1604. One can only speculate on the affairs of Shakespeare during this interim. If, as a principal member of the company, he had time to turn from the various corporate problems to a rapid production of tragedies, they were apparently not being acted, except perhaps at court during the Christmas holidays, depending on what authors the company divided its eight performances among.

III. Following Easter, April 9th, 1604, acting would seem to have continued unhindered for several months, but, as Wilson observes (p. 116), a bill was read in May "for the charitable Relief and ordering of persons infected with the Plague." Such a bill, and the delay in the convocation of James's first Parliament until March 19th are not conclusive signs of an alarmist attitude since, on the one hand, relief might be intended for sufferers from the ravages of the fall previous, and, on the other hand, James's aversion to and delay in the convocation of Parliaments as a general principle are well known.[22] Molin, whom Wilson uses for his plague figures here, is perhaps a more satisfactory indication. On May 2nd, the Venetian ambassador begins to feel alarm, and on May 9th, growing concern until, on May 28th, as Wilson observes, Molin notes that everyone is beginning to look for a house in the country. The abnormally cold weather that Wilson alludes to will begin to be described by Molin on June 20th, and death figures plummet. During the summer, Molin closely follows the progress of the epidemic which is raging in the country outside of London while he observes that the city itself is the healthiest place in the kingdom. But he only stops reporting weekly plague figures, never above thirty in the city between May 28th and September, on October 23rd, 1604.[23]

126

It is difficult to gauge the attitude of the city authorities in all this. Molin reports plans first to cancel and then to go ahead with Bartholomew Fair (August 24th) which was cancelled the previous year, but the Fair probably had no real relevance to acting prohibition.[24] In the spring, deaths had been at 20 when acting was allowed after Lent. When Molin first expressed alarm on May 2nd, figures were at 19 for the week previous. They then rose, with Molin's concern, to 20, 20, 24, 34. If one must venture a guess, it seems reasonable to assume that by May 29th, the occasion of the last figure, acting had been suspended for the summer despite the coming onset of bitter cold which would not, after all, grip London for several more weeks. If the ending of term time in the spring has any relevance to acting, Easter Term probably would have been over on Friday, May 18th (the day after Ascension). Relevant here too is the fact that the King's Men were at Oxford between May 7th and June 16th.[25] Later, in the summer, from August 9th-27th, the King's Men are at Somerset House in attendance on the Spanish ambassador. Perhaps we can assume a total span of public acting in this interim as extending from April 9th, 1604, to some point in May.[26]

IV. In the fall, term time was kept (or, at any rate, not cancelled), presumably the theatres were open, and the holiday season at court began with an All Hallow's Day performance at Whitehall by the King's Men. They presented eleven plays at court, performing finally on Shrove Tuesday, February 12th, 1605. We may, then, assume normal acting conditions for Shakespeare's company for about five months, September, 1604, to February, 1605.

V. Easter is March 31st, 1605, and there seems to have been little plague of theatrical significance through the spring although there does exist a Bill of Mortality for the week of March 22nd-29th in which plague deaths are differentiated from other kinds. Nineteen deaths are listed in this bill, well below the limit of thirty. In May, too, the Lord Mayor wrote that the physician which James recommended as an expert on the plague is welcome but cannot be used at this time (May 15th) because "of late" only two or three a week have been dying of the plague.[27] By May 13th, however, when his will is proved, Augustine Phillips is dead. There is no provincial performance this summer, but

Shakespeare may have been at Stratford, for he purchased the tithes on July 24th, we recall. Presumably acting came to an end in the late spring, and, if so, we have a season of three months at the most for this interim, the spring of 1605.

VI. Fall ushers in plague again, and, on October 5th, 1605, the Privy Council prohibits stage plays. If the King's Men had already come back to town in early October, they were out again on the 9th, performing at Oxford.[28] Although acting is not permitted again until the letter of the Privy Council on December 15th, court performances may have begun earlier. The payment to the King's Men in the warrant of March 24th, 1606, simply specifies ten several plays "in the tyme of Christmas laste," but the Prince's Men were paid in a document alluding to specific dates: they played before the Prince at Whitehall on December 1st. At any rate, after December 15th, there is presumably both court and public acting until Ash Wednesday, March 5th, 1606, and these three months might thus present us with another chronological entity.[29]

VII. This period is a difficult one to assess. In March, 1606, the plague again became noticeable, and Wilson observes that "the authorities quickly and vigorously enforced the plague-orders."[30] Easter is April 20th, 1606. The problem is whether there were any performances in the spring. In the summer and autumn, plague figures were quite high, but between March and the middle of June, deaths were never, except in one case, even as high as twenty per week. On the other hand, they never went below nine. The figures for March, when the authorities took steps, were 7, 9, 14, 17. For April, they were 13, 27, 12, 11, and for May, 17, 13, 13, 14. On April 30th, when the royal patent for the Prince's Men was issued, there was no proviso, as there was in the patent for the King's Men, that the warrant would be effective after infection should cease. On the other hand, the license for Queen Anne's Men, issued April 15th, 1609 (Easter Saturday), contains no plague qualification either, even though figures will be high that spring. On May 27th, 1606, the Acte to Restraine Abuses is promulgated, and it is difficult to see how, at this particular time, authorities could be aggravated by the use of holy names "in any Stage play, Interlude, Shewe, Maygame, or Pageant" if there had been no playing since March. On the other hand, the wording of this particular prohibition specifies "any tyme or tymes, after the end of this present Session of Parliament" so that provision for the future may be the intent here. The term "Maygame" too is equally suggestive considering the date of the Act itself, and Maygames or pageants might as easily have provoked the order.[31] It is, furthermore, possible that the infection of the previous fall had the authorities sufficiently nervous to act quickly when actually warm weather was in the offing.

Plague figures are high throughout the summer, but this summer is also the occasion of the visit of the King of Denmark before whom Shakespeare's company performed two plays at Greenwich and one at Hampton Court between July 17th and August 10th.[32] When fall comes, however, there is presumably no acting in the city. The Mayor acknowledges a letter from the Privy Council in October, and informs them of the steps taken to preserve the city from infection. Plague deaths are over forty until the last two weeks of November. On the 6th of this month, Zorzi Giustinian, Venetian ambassador to England, writes that Parliament will reconvene, now that the plague has ceased, but Third Session does not begin until the 18th.[33] It is difficult to tell whether acting was yet permissible. As November is ending, deaths go down to 22. On the 9th of December, as Wilson has observed (p. 119); the Keeper of Newgate is allowed funds for relief of the prisoners as long as the infection should continue, and for the five weeks of December, death figures from plague are 45, 38, 28, 38, 38. Performances at court begin on St. Stephen's Day and a normally full holiday drama season at court extends through Shrovetide, Ash Wednesday being February 18th, 1607. As far as public acting after Christmas was concerned, the matter is problematic for the period before Lent. Weekly figures for January are 26, 16, 14, 28, and in February, 33, 20, for the weekly reports before Lent. Chances are that acting was not permitted, and if we are to sum up this interim extending from Easter, 1606, to Lent, 1607, it very much looks as if possible performances in the provinces and performances before Denmark and then at Court during Christmas were the only opportunities for acting. That is to say, there were three performances before Denmark, ten performances given at Christmas, and any possible number of performances in the provinces, for this period, acting probably being prohibited in London.

VIII. Easter is April 5th, 1607, and a week later, as we have observed, the Lord Mayor must assume that plays are in progress when he asks that they be repressed because of the rising of the plague. At the same time, we must again deal with the problem confronting us for the previous year. For the plague figure of the week preceding the Mayor's request is only 23, and whatever the Privy Council saw fit to do about the Lord Mayor's complaint, deaths (with one exception) averaged in the twenties for subsequent weeks, never, however, going below ten. It was in July that they began to rise into the seventies and upwards. But it would seem dangerous to posit sporadic public acting for this spring of 1607. For instance, the last three weeks of April report deaths as 27, 26, 43. Can one assume that the players would act for one week after the weekly report, and be forced to abstain in the week following? The city authorities would have every right to fear the worst with summer coming on, for the previous year might have served as a model.[34]

Assuming, in any event, the usual summer exodus, Easter term ending on May 15th, we find the King's Men in Oxford during September of 1607, and although Michaelmas Term seems to have been held, plague persists throughout the fall, deaths never going below 40 until the report of November 22nd is in. Between November 26th and December 9th, the figures are 21, 19, 28, but on December 8th, a hard frost sets in, and still another on the 22nd, with the result that the plague decreases drastically.[35]

The Prince's Men are performing at Whitehall on November 19th, but the King's Men begin the season at court on St. Stephen's and they give thirteen performances during the holidays, their largest number yet at court.[36] There is presumably public acting too, especially in January; however, Ash Wednesday is early, falling on February 10th, 1608. In sum, we appear to be faced with the same kind of acting situation for Easter 1607, to Lent, 1608, as we were for the previous year. Plague seems to have made all but private performances impossible during the year, always excepting the provinces and with the qualification here of the month of January, 1608.

130

IX. Easter is March 27th, 1608. Plague figures do not even go as high as eleven per week until the end of May, so, with one possible exception, we may assume a normal acting season. The exception has to do with the matter of a possible prohibition of acting because of Chapman's *Byron*. The two documents serving as the grounds for such a possibility are, however, ambiguous. One, dated March 11th, 1608, is the letter from Sir Thomas Lake to Robert Lord Salisbury, which, as is well known, refers to a Blackfriars production not only offensive to the French ambassador but also offensive to James in its references to his project regarding the Scottish silver mine. We gather from Lake that the king has vowed these actors "should neuer play more but should first begg their bred." The second document is more specific, however, about general prohibition, as La Boderie writes about "comédiens à qui j'avois fait deffendre de jouer l'histoire du feu mareschal de Biron." Mentioning that the players have mocked James's "mine d'Escosse", the French ambassador notes that James "a fait deffense que l'on n'eust plus à jouer de Comédies dedans Londres" and that "pour lever laquelle deffense quatre autres compagnies qui y sont encore, offrent desja cent mille francs, lesquels pourront bien leur en redonner la permission; mais pour le moins sera-ce à condition qu'ilz ne représenteront plus aucune histoire moderne."[37] As familiar as these documents may be, the problem remains as to whether there was, indeed, any acting prohibition. Giustinian, the Venetian ambassador in England, first refers to the king's interest in the silver mine on December 17th, 1607, when he reports that James ordered the Council to make provision "for working the mine discovered some years back in Scotland." Still guiding ourselves by Giustinian's information, we note that samples from the mine were then brought back and that "The people are filled with vain hopes of great riches" on February 18th, 1608, and on March 24th, Giustinian notes that "the analysis of the Scotch mine gives a net annual yield of two hundred thousand crowns." [38]

The order of events, then, is as follows. As we have noted, after plague, acting probably resumes in the middle of December and continues until Lent, Wednesday, February 10th, 1608. On March 11th comes the letter from Sir Thomas Lake, while La Boderie's letter, if his date of April 8th is in continental style, is written March 29th, Old Style. Easter is March 27th. There are thus several possibilities. The Blackfriars play could have been given in December when James's interest was first aroused in the mine, and, if the play mocked this venture, before the optimistic reports came back from Scotland. If so, all of James's threats could have been made during Lent—they were possibly made before Easter—and the London companies would have been scrambling to avert postponement of their after-Easter season. The tenses used by La Boderie, however, are ambiguous. At any rate, there is never any reference to a closing of the theatres, only to a banning of a particular Blackfriars play and to James's threats about the future. We may speculate here that there is no evidence of general prohibition in effect, but only in potentiality, La Boderie's letter suggesting that the matter has been resolved. Lake seems to suggest offences in sequence by two companies. All these could have taken place before Lent, and it could be that no immediate steps were taken because Lenten prohibition had suspended acting anyhow so that there was no question of immediate steps to close theatres. On the other hand, if the Blackfriars group played in Lent, then we should reconsider the matter of Lenten prohibition as regards Blackfriars in general.

Easter term presumably ends on May 6th, and in July plague figures begin to mount. There is no autumn season because of plague, but twelve plays are presented at court. We may thus assume, for this period, a spring acting season, and a Christmas court season. Lent, 1609, is irrelevant, since there are, for instance, 90 deaths in the second week of February, 1609, Lent being March 1st, 1609. For this period then, we may suggest an acting season in the spring of 1608, but after that court performances only through to the following Lent.

X. Easter is April 16th, 1609, but the death rate from plague is prohibitive of acting throughout the remaining spring, through summer and autumn, until December, in which month the figures never went below 23. In January and February, deaths are 32, 19, 31, 27, 21, 11, 18, Ash Wednesday falling on February 21st, 1610. For this interval of Easter, 1609, through Lent, 1610, there could then have been the usual holiday court presentations and public acting from December, 1609, through February, 1610, but the March 10th, 1610, payment by the king to Shakespeare's company for private practice "for his Majesty's service" would seem to suggest no public acting before Lent (see *n.* 73).

XI. Easter is on April 8th, 1610, and the allusion to a performance of *Othello* at the Globe seen by Prince Lewis of Württemberg on Monday, April 30th, 1610 (N.S.) suggests a spring season this year, Easter term ending on May 18th. However, by the first week of September, deaths were 96 in one week, the figures having started to rise in July. Towards the end of December, the figure is down to zero and we may assume, perhaps, December, January, and early February performances until Ash Wednesday which is February 6th, 1611.[39] In this period of Easter, 1610, to Lent, 1611, then, we may assume normal spring performances in public, but nothing during the summer or fall until about December after which the King's Men might have acted for two months, and of course gave their (fifteen) performances at court. The warrant of February 12th again gives a plague reward, this time of £50.

XII. Easter is March 24th, 1611. Plague, ironically, has ceased to be a problem—ironically because in the following fall, November 1st, *The Tempest* will be given at court, and Shakespeare will have written his last (undisputed) play. In the spring, Forman's somewhat dubious document describes performances of *Macbeth, Cymbeline, The Winter's Tale,* and *Richard II.*[40]

With the end of Interim XII, we have covered the period of time which produces specific allusion to most of Shakespeare's canon remaining after *Troilus,* with several exceptions. *Henry VIII* will be recorded in 1613, and *Two Noble Kinsmen* much later. *All's Well, Coriolanus* and *Timon* will not be recorded until the appearance of the First Folio, unless we take a payment to the King's Men for the holiday season of 1612-1613 as a reference to *All's Well.*[41] To summarize these interims, the following table will perhaps be convenient, each Roman numeral referring to what might be styled an "Interim" in the chronology of possible Jacobean first performances of Shakespeare's plays since *Troilus.*

I.   a. Feb. 7th, 1603, to March 19th, 1603.
      b. April 29th to May 5th; May 9th to May 19th, 1603:   *six weeks.*

II.   Dec. 2nd, 1603, to Feb. 19th, 1604: *nine performances.*

*III. April 9th, 1604, to May, 1604:   *two months.*

IV.   Sept., 1604, to Feb. 13th, 1605: *five months.*
     Nov. 1st: *Othello*
     Dec. 26th: *Measure for Measure*

V.   March 31st, 1605, to May/June, 1605:   *two months.*

VI.   December 15th, 1605, to March 5th, 1606:   *three months.*

VII. a. Denmark's visit.
      b. Christmas at court to Feb. 27th, 1607   *thirteen performances.*
     Dec. 26th: *King Lear*

*VIII. a. A few weeks in April, 1607?
      b. Dec. 26th, 1607, to Feb. 10th, 1608   *two months?*

IX.   a. March 27th to May/June, 1608:   *three months*
      b. Christmas at court to March 1st, 1609.   *twelve performances.*

X.   Christmas at court to Feb. 21st, 1610   *thirteen performances.*

XI.   a. April 8th, 1610, to May/June 1610:   *two months*
      b. Dec. 1610, to Feb. 6th, 1611: *two months.*

XII. a. March 24th, 1611, to May/June, 1611   *three months*
      b. Oct., 1611, to Nov. 1st, 1611 *one month.*
     Nov. 1st: *Tempest*
     Nov. 5th: *Winter's Tale*

* Doubtful seasons

134

If our speculations have any accuracy at all, it would seem that between February 7th, 1603, and November 1st, 1611, a little less than nine years in which Shakespeare completed his canon, there were available to him not more than twenty-eight months of public performance, and, in addition, forty-seven court performances when public playing was not possible. Assuming the tentative accuracy of this table, as far as possibilities are concerned, we should then be able to refine our guesses as to the dating of Shakespeare's Jacobean tragedies, assuming we are dating according to first performance either at the Globe or at court—but not in the provinces. We can only speculate as to whether or not the Privy Council order of June 22nd, 1600 (reaffirmed Dec. 31st, 1601), continued further restriction into the time of James. We recall that, after limiting the number of playhouses to two, the order went on to specify that the two houses "maie play each of them in there seuerall howse twice a weeke and noe oftener and especially that they shall refraine to play on the Sabboth daie vppon paine of imprisonment and further penaltie and that they shall forbeare altogether in the time of Lent and likewise at such time and times as anie extraordinarie sicknes or infeccon of disease shall appeare to be in and about the Cittie." It would be interesting to determine whether, in truth, acting continued to be confined in this manner, for the possibility of two performances a week would further narrow chronological possibilities.[42]

III

The only fact known regarding the date of *Anthony and Cleopatra* is the Stationers' entry for 1608:[43]

> 20 Majj. Edward Blount. Entred for his copie under thandes of Sir George Buck knight and Master Warden Seton A booke called. The booke of Pericles prynce of Tyre. vj[d].
>
> Edward Blount. Entred also for his copie by the like Aucthoritie. A booke Called Anthony. and Cleopatra. vj[d].

The nature of this joint entry has, of course, given rise to much conjecture, but little has changed since E. K. Chambers' estimate of the situation which is worth quoting here as the center of reference for subsequent discussion:[44]

> There is no reason to doubt that the S. R. entry of 20 May 1608 relates to the play, although Blount appears to have forgotten it when the entry for F I was made. This gives a limit of date. But there is reason for putting *Antony and Cleopatra* earlier than 1608. In 1607 Samuel Daniel issued a new edition of his *Certain Small Workes,* and herein made considerable changes in his *Cleopatra* of 1594. [Chambers here refers to *The Eliz. Stage,* III, 275.] These, as carefully analyzed by Case, seem to me clearly to show the influence of Shakespeare's play. There are some parallels of idea and phrase. Dialogue often replaces narrative or soliloquy. Dircetus and Diomedes are introduced for the first time. Charmian, Iras, and Gallus are elaborated. A new scene relates, through the mouth of Dircetus, events leading up to the death of Antony, as given by Shakespeare. One may recall a probable similar use by Daniel of *Richard II.* . . . The metrical character of *Antony and Cleopatra* forbids us to put it before *Macbeth* or *Lear.* But it may have been produced early in 1607, and of this there is confirmation in Barnes's *Devil's Charter* (1607), 2546-69, where Alexander Borgia uses asps, which he calls 'Cleopatraes birds,' to poison two boys. *Devil's Charter* was given at court as early as 2 February 1607, but thereafter 'renewed, corrected and augmented' for the reader, and registered on October 16. Parallels to iv.14.2 in Chapman's *Bussy d'Ambois,* iii.1.23 and to i.4.20 in the anonymous *Nobody and Somebody,* 36, may be left out of account. Probably both plays are earlier than *Antony and Cleopatra* and the ideas are in both cases of still older standing [Refs. to ES III. 214, 253; IV. 37].

Clearly we retain only a *terminus ad quem* for Shakespeare's play: Friday, May 20th, 1608, the day on which the play was entered by Edward Blount, and to establish a *terminus a quo* is then our primary task. This may exist in Walter Cope's well known letter to Cecil, referring to the holiday season of 1604-

1605 (Interim IV). "Burbage ys come," observes Cope, "and sayes ther ys no new playe that the Quene hath not seene, but they have revyved an olde one cawled *Loves Labore Lost,*" and the play itself is recorded as having been performed in January.[45] If the letter does allude to an actual situation in which the King's Men are suffering a scarcity of new plays (including ones by Shakespeare), a glance at the performance records, rather abundant for this season, enables us to speculate as to what Shakespeare's Jacobean production might have been as of January, 1605.

Bearing in mind the entry for *Troilus,* in February, 1603, and recalling that, by then, only *Julius Caesar, Hamlet, Romeo,* and *Titus* had been accounted for, among Shakespeare's tragedies, we note that *Othello* has been performed on November 1st, 1604, and *Measure for Measure* on December 26th, 1604. Both of these plays are "new" in the sense that they are the first new plays of which there is any record since the entry of *Troilus.* But aside from these two dramas, the King's Men, in the holiday season of 1604-05, present *Merry Wives* on November 4th, *Errors* on December 28th, *Henry V* on January 7th, *LLL* "betwin Newers Day and Twelfe day," and finally *Merchant* twice: on February 10th, and again, by the king's command, on February 12th, 1605. Since the latest of these plays cannot be dated, in terms of S. R. entries, after 1600, it seems quite clear that the King's Men are presenting Shakespearean material which is at least four years old, and the performance of such plays might confirm our notion of a shortage of Shakespearean material.[46] Possibly *Othello* was new, catering as it did to the same court interests to which Jonson's *Masque of Blackness* may have been responding when, on Twelfth Night, this "Maske of Moures" was presented, but both *Othello* and *Measure* might easily have been performed in Interim III or even II, since James, in the case of *Merchant of Venice* at least, did not seem to mind repetitions.[47]

Thus, Cope's letter, taken in conjunction with the detailed list of plays actually presented, might conveniently serve us as a *terminus a quo* for all the remaining tragedies and the "final comedies." Such a *terminus* is reasonable too if we recall the "time of troubles" which Shakespeare's company underwent coincidentally with the accession of James. Always acknowledging

137

that *Lear, Anthony, Macbeth, Timon,* and *Coriolanus* could have been conceived and written at any time prior to the holiday season of 1604-05, a first performance of these tragedies does not seem likely to have occurred yet, unless we wish to place one or all of them in Interims I, II, or III. Utilizing this admittedly assumptive reasoning, we might then "bracket" Shakespeare's *Anthony and Cleopatra* within the following period: *terminus a quo:* the end of Lent following the 1604-05 holiday season, Easter Sunday, March 31st, 1605; *terminus ad quem:* S. R. May 20th, 1608. What remains to be done is to narrow the brackets.

It is appropriate at this point to consider the two plays which Chambers and others have brought forward as indicators of the date of *Anthony and Cleopatra.* These are Samuel Daniel's revision of his own closet drama, *Cleopatra,* and Barnabe Barnes's *The Devil's Charter.* Arguments concerning the Daniel play have centered around the possible influence of Shakespeare on Daniel's revisions. Norman's study, the most recent, summarizes the relevant scholarship, alluding, among other things, to Schanzer's important point that the new addition by Daniel of a quasi-Shakespearean scene in which Dircetas brings Anthony's bloody sword to Caesar was already in the Countess of Pembroke's translation of Garnier's *Marc-Antoine.*[48] Norman's own argument about verbal correspondences is highly suggestive of a relationship between Daniel's and Shakespeare's versions, but such correspondences do not demonstrate priority, such a point being essentially undemonstrable by parallels of sense. For granted that Daniel had one version of Cleopatra in 1605, and granted that his changes in the 1607 edition suggest a similarity to motifs and words in Shakespeare's play, there is no purely logical reason why Shakespeare could not then have been following a revised Daniel, for we cannot assume that expanded phrases or motifs are necessarily later ones, or that unadorned motifs and phrases are necessarily earlier ones.[49] The more obviously apprehensible possibility is that, though Shakespeare may have entered into the matter somehow, Daniel revised the larger structure of his *Cleopatra* to make it conform to Lady Pembroke's *Antonie.* Daniel acknowledges her as a model in his dedicaton, and, for the 1607 revision, he greatly enlarged this dedication too, and it could seem as if his writing of a Dircetas scene was inspired by Lady Pembroke's example. Given such an argument, perhaps allusion here to a specific and minor move on Daniel's part will nevertheless support the possibility that Daniel's revision followed a viewing or a reading of Shakespeare's play.

When Anthony asks Eros to kill him, Shakespeare is basically paralleling information in Plutarch:

> Now he had a man of his called Eros, whom he loved and trusted much, and whom he had long before caused to sweare unto him, that he should kill him when he did commaunde him: and then he willed him to keepe his promise[50]

Plutarch's Eros then kills himself, and North's marginal gloss reads "Eros Antonius servant, slue him selfe." The Countess of Pembroke's translation follows this closely, as Dircetas recounts Antonie's death to Caesar and Agrippa in Act IV:

> So said, forthwith he *Eros* to him call'd,
> *Eros* his man; summond him on his faith
> To kill him at his nede. He tooke the sword, etc.[51]

The suicide follows.

Shakespeare works differently, but characteristically, for he has combined two figures from the source into one, as he did with another character in the play.[52] For although Plutarch tells the reader at this point that Eros had promised to kill Antonius, Shakespeare nevertheless reached back for an event which occurred during the long Parthian expedition, an earlier portion of the *Life of Antonius*. Here, as Plutarch describes it, Antonius was so desperate at the rebelliousness of his soldiers that he

> called for one Rhamnus, one of his slaves infranchised that was of his gard, and made him give him his faith that he would thrust his sword through him when he would bid him, and cut of his head: bicause he might not be taken alive of his enemies, nor knowen when he were dead. (p. 51)

If we then recall the account of Eros' suicide and finally glance at the suicide passage in *Anthony and Cleopatra,* its antecedents in both of these Plutarchan passages are clear.

> Thou art sworn, Eros
> That when the exigent should come, which now
> Is come indeed: when I should see behind me
> The inevitable prosecution of
> Disgrace and horror, that on my command,
> Thou then wouldst kill me.

"The Gods withold me," answers Eros; "Shall I do that which all the Parthian darts,/ Though enemy, lost aim, and could not?" Anthony, in the process of further persuasion, then says

> Draw that thy honest sword, which thou hast worn
> Most useful for thy country.
> *Eros*   Oh, sir, pardon me.
> *Ant.* When I did make thee free, swor'st thou not then
> To do this when I bade thee? Do it at once,
> Or thy precedent services are all
> But accidents unpurpos'd.

Two points may be observed here. Shakespeare, in the process of elaborating on the account of Eros from the source, deviates in a planned way by drawing on the Parthian episode for additional background. The Shakespearean Eros is created into a freedman who alludes to Parthia, who has served his country with a sword which he now wears at his side, who is at least a soldier, and perhaps a guard. We will recall a possibly intimate and military relationship betwen the two, for not only does he put on Anthony's armor, he also writes for him to the deserting Enobarbus, and fights with him in the second battle. Then, the second point, the talk about Eros having been manumitted becomes part of the structure of Anthony's persuasion, because this manumission operates as an argument final enough to make Eros take some action.

Daniel's approach to this extremely minor point is thus rather interesting. He follows Lady Pembroke by having Dircetas give the account of Antonius' death, and Dircetas describes Antonius as saying:

Come *Eros,* doe this seruice for thy Lord,
The best and greatest pleasure thou canst doe:
Imploy this weapon here; come, make this sword
That wone me honor, now to saue it to.[53]

The narrator continues: *"Eros,* his late infranchis'd seruant, takes/ The sword, as if he would haue done the deed" etc. And it is this word "infranchis'd" which may claim our attention if we recall the options for Daniel at this point. Revising his Cleopatra by putting in a description of Antonius' death, he might, for instance, have reread Lady Pembroke's version, reread Plutarch, or simply used his own imagination, drawing on his recollection of and general familiarity with the Cleopatra story in Plutarch. But if he reread Lady Pembroke's work, Daniel would never have gathered the idea of Eros as freedman, or "infranchis'd" servant: our glance at Lady Pembroke's passage has shown as much. Nor would a reading of the incident in Plutarch have given Daniel such an idea; in fact, as we have seen, the marginal gloss specifically describes Eros as "Antonius servant." We are thus left with the possibility that, by coincidence, Daniel and Shakespeare both thought of this minor invention independently, or that one followed the other. If we reject coincidence, which writer then would have been first?

Shakespeare's is the structured alteration, a re-creation of Eros into someone who has been in Parthia and worn a sword most useful to his country. And because he was writing for the stage, Shakespeare, in the suicide scene, had to be specific, too. For at that point, he will need not one, but two swords on stage. Thus Eros can stab himself with his personal sword, and Anthony, instead of taking a sword out of the body of Eros, can use his own. By comparison, Daniel's account would seem to be somewhat ambiguous, or at least not alert here. His Antonius tells Eros, as we have seen, to use a sword, but it reads as if the hero himself is holding it out: "Make this sword/ That wone me honor, now to saue it to./ . . . *Eros,* his late infranchis'd servant, takes/ The sword." Then (sig. G8ᵛ), Daniel's Antonius makes a speech over the dead Eros and "With that he takes his sword, and down he falls/ Vpon the dismall point." Which sword? Are there two? The questions are unnecessary because Daniel is not faced with a problem in stage production here.

141

Finally, if Daniel's Eros is "infranchis'd," why does his Antonius say in the speech over his body, "must both a woman, and a slaue/ The start before me of this glory haue?" Although here, "slaue" may be (rather inappropriately) an aristocratically derogatory figure of speech, it would seem as if Daniel has an ambiguous, or at least a careless, concept of his "infranchis'd" Eros. Lady Pembroke's version is actually more consistent for it reports the Plutarchan information that Eros had merely made a promise. Daniel's Eros has made no promise, is not allowed to speak, is given no identity beyond that of an "infranchis'd" servant, and is referred to as a "slaue." Of course, there is no reason at all for Daniel's Eros to be infranchised, in fact, and Eros is nowhere else ever in such a state except in Shakespeare's play where the information is a major point in the scene.

We might, in effect, ask, if Shakespeare had not written his own play, would Daniel, considering the way he has written, ever have assumed that Eros was infranchised? The very minor nature of the point seems significant. For it would seem natural that Daniel might be influenced by Shakespeare's emphasis into assuming such details to be factual, at least as regards sources. Daniel is obviously making little effort to follow the spirit of Shakespeare's uplifting of Eros here, and his erroneous assumption of a meaningless "fact," goes against anything in his usual sources. This would urge Daniel's work as the later one, merely because Eros' precise (and erroneous) status is so irrelevant to Daniel's own purpose.[54] Logically, of course, Daniel might have somehow gotten the idea into his head, and Shakespeare, seeing the possibilities, might have elaborated on a notion he actually received from Daniel. But this line of direction is actually more difficult to demonstrate. It requires positing that, given the fact that Daniel is the least interested in Eros of the three, Lady Pembroke, Shakespeare, and himself—Daniel does not even mention Eros' promise to slay Antonius—he will nevertheless associate this one odd detail, which no one other than Shakespeare has mentioned, with the insignificant character, even despite the fact that Plutarch's obvious gloss says the opposite. If we may speculate more freely for the moment, it would seem as if Daniel not only mistakes Shakespeare's version as factual, but vaguely recalls the Shakespearean speech with which Anthony tells Eros to draw his sword: "Make this sword/ That wone me honor, now to saue it to."

Finally, it might be mentioned that Shakespeare's own approach to this suicide has already been hinted at in *Julius Caesar*. For a comparison of Plutarch with Shakespeare's own change here will emphasize the poet's possibly prior claim to a version he will use again in *Anthony*. In the description of Cassius' death, Plutarch observes that "he gotte into a tent where no bodie was, and tooke Pyndarus with him, one of his freed bondsmen, whom he reserved ever for suche a pinche, since the cursed battell of the Parthians, where Crassus was slaine, though he notwithstanding scaped from that overthrow: but then casting his cloke over his head, and holding out his bare neck unto Pyndarus, he gave him his head to be striken of. So the head was found," etc. (p. 226) Shakespeare's slightly altered version is similar to what he does in *Anthony*, showing, too, that the association of freeing and resultant gratitude was one he consistently made.

> Come hither, sirrah.
> In Parthia did I take thee prisoner;
> And then I swore thee, saving of thy life,
> That whatsoever I did bid thee do,
> Thou shouldst attempt it. Come now, keep thine oath
> Now be a freeman; and with this good sword,
> That ran through Caesar's bowels, search this bosom.
> Stand not to answer

Hence, as Norman and others have suggested, the *terminus ad quem* for Daniel's revision could enable us to infer a similar *terminus* for Shakespeare's play, but not, we would suggest, a *terminus a quo*. For even if the earlier version of Daniel's *Cleopatra* did last appear in 1605, there is nothing to gainsay Daniel's having revised his *Cleopatra* in 1604 and then waited to publish it until he had all the other material for his 1607 edition ready. For this edition is extensively altered, and we err if we assume even tacitly that Shakespeare himself would have been a primary cause for Daniel's revised version. Nevertheless, it seems possible to consider Daniel's play as an influence on our concept of the *terminus ad quem* of Shakespeare's drama, if the foregoing analysis of the relationship of the two versions has been acceptable.

But there is no Stationer's entry for Daniel's 1607 edition, so if we would move back the *terminus ad quem* for Shakepeare's play from May 20th, 1608, it is a question of whether we move it back to March 24th, 1607/08, or to December 31st, 1607/08— of whether John Windet, Daniel's printer, dated Old Style or New Style. Greg's statement on printers' practices in general, as well as specific evidence, suggests that, in fact, Windet began his year on January 1st.[55] One of his printings (STC 20905) was entered on January 15th, 1605/06. This title, *The Returne of the knight of the poste from hell,* is cancelled, however, on February 17th, 1605/06. Records of the Court of the Stationers' Company suggest the reason. "Vpon the hearinge of the matter in controu'sie betwene them: ffor thendinge thereof yt (is) ordered, that M[r] windet in recompenc' of the hindrance he hathe done M[r] East & for coste of sute" was to pay East forty shillings in two installments, terminating March 25th.[56] Whatever the actual basis of the dispute, it is clear that it terminated in a decision against Windet and in a cancelling of this title entered to N. Butter. It seems clear too that East had sufficient justification to be awarded damages payable before Lady Day. May we not then assume that the title in question was already in print and that Windet was paying damages for this reason? If so, it is sufficient to note that while the whole process of litigation, beginning with the entry and culminating in the deadline for payments extended between January 15th and March 25th, 1605/06, Windet's title page itself is dated "1606."

The possibility that Windet dated New Style is supported further by a case in which Windet printed the volume of Latin poems in memory of Sir Philip Sidney (STC 4473). Alexander Neville, who edited the volume, dated the preface February 16th, 1586, and it is obvious that he had to be dating Old Style because Sidney died in the fall of 1586. Windet's title page and colophon both give the date "1587," and the title page imprint specifies the day of the month, just as Neville does: "Febr. xvj." Clearly the identity of February 16th in the dating of both Neville and Windet rules out the possibility of coincidence, of the chance that Windet printed the work exactly a calendar year later than Neville's signing of his introduction. Clearly, Neville dates Old Style, and Windet dates New Style. The careful allusion to February 16th is, as Edgerton reminds us, to the day of Sidney's funeral.

This demonstration of Windet's dating-habits may seem excessive in view of the articles previously cited, but Windet was, for a good while, official printer to the city of London, in which role, as when he printed Bills of Mortality, he might frequently have been called upon to set specific (Old Style) dates from the official copy before him.[57] There is also a title page from one of Barlowe's sermons (STC 1456) where the "1604" imprint tells us nothing, but where the title describes the Bishops' Conference as "at *Hampton Court,* Ianuary 14th, 1603." We know, of course, that this conference was held in 1604, and although the descriptive title page could easily have been produced by the compiler of the volume, not by its printer, the presence of this volume alone necessitates the foregoing argumentation.

We agree, then, that Daniel's volume could not have been printed after December 31st, 1607, and if we acquiesce in seeing the play as significantly influenced by Shakespeare's Roman drama, then a *terminus ad quem* for *Anthony and Cleopatra* can be moved back from May 20th, 1608 (S. R. entry) to December 31st, 1607, and Daniel would have had to see Shakespeare's play, or to read it, before the latter part of December. But this specific month is not a completely plausible one for a *terminus ad quem,* if we think of performances of Shakespeare's play, because, we will recall, there had been plague all fall until the hard frost set in on December 8th. The King's Men were not at Whitehall until St. Stephen's, when they performed on three consecutive days before the king, the only November court performance this year, being given before the king on the 19th by the Prince's Men. As for Globe performances, the city fathers would have observed on Thursday, December 10th, that 28 had died since the previous Thursday, and the drastically reduced death figure of seven for December 10th through 16th would, presumably, not have been compiled until the latter date.[58] Furthermore, the circumstances surrounding Daniel's 1607 edition as a whole cast doubt on December as a plausible date for Daniel seeing Shakespeare's play.

Daniel's 1607 edition of *Certaine Small Works* (1607W) which contains his *Cleopatra* is difficult to deal with, but we should observe that if we are to attempt to date Shakespeare's work by means of Daniel's closet drama we must reckon with the fact of Daniel's extensive revision of other pieces in the same volume.

In fact, there is a good possibility that Daniel was still revising *Philotas* in 1607, for in this year, too, Blount published a volume (1607P) containing a *Philotas* without any of the "sweeping changes" introduced into 1607W.[59] Thus, in 1607, Daniel had work appearing in two versions, the *Cleopatra* volume containing revisions of work in 1607P. Thus it is difficult to envision Daniel's viewing (or even reading) of Shakespeare's *Anthony and Cleopatra* in late December, 1607, with a consequent, but otherwise un-planned-for rewriting of the closet drama in time for publication before January. Finally, the possibility of two issues of 1607W would suggest that December, 1607, may, in fact, be untenable as a *terminus ad quem* for Shakespeare's play if it indeed influenced Daniel's work.[60]

W. W. Greg, if we read him correctly, revised his prior analysis of 1607W as follows. There were two issues, and, if we omit de-tails of foliation, Greg's concept of the ideal state of a first issue seems to be: 8⁰: ¶8 B-V8 A8, with ¶1 and A8 blank. The A quire is usually bound between ¶ and B, and it contains re-vised front matter for some individual pieces in the volume. Greg then distinguishes a second issue from the first by the fact that a cancel replaces 07,ʳ⁻ᵛ the cancellans having been printed on the formerly blank A8.ʳ⁻ᵛ [61]

There might, however, be other states of 1607W. Sellers ana-lyzes BM 644.a41 as follows: "¶1 and ¶2 wanting,* [¶5], [¶6], ¶3, [¶4], [¶7], [¶8]," the asterisk referring to the fact that "*a fragment of ¶2 has been pasted over the lower part of [¶5]." This confusion of order in the quire would seem to arise from error in the setting of pages for the top half of the inner forme of ¶, the mistake in ordering capable of producing the sequence described by Sellers.[62] At the same time, BM 644.a41 and Folger, copy 1, have in common the fact that they lack P2-V8, the missing portion representing two complete pieces, *The Queen's Arcadia* and the elegy on the Earl of Devonshire. Since all copies of 1607W have not been examined by this writer personally, it is difficult to be exact here, but it may be speculated that a history of the printing might take into account the following possible states or issues. There might, in the first place, have been some motivation for tentatively setting and even selling an edition of 1607W from which *Arcadia* and *Devonshire* might have been excised. If we deny this possibility, it is equally implausible to assume a common aversion to *Queen's Arcadia* and *Elegy* by the original owners of the Folger and British Museum copies. There might then be one stage mirrored by BM 644. a41 wherein there is an error in the order of pages for the inner forme of quire P, where *Elegy* and *Arcadia* are absent, and where there is the extra quire A with prefatory matter. Another stage might print the cancellans on A8, and, since the material in quire A is all prefatory supplement to matter up to P1 only, not applicable to *Arcadia* or *Devonshire,* these two works can have been added at any later time in such a hypothetical sequence.[63]

Probabilities which would account for such practice might be consonant with Daniel's own habits as well as with the commercial problems of his publisher Simon Waterson. Waterson owned *Queen's Arcadia* which was entered November 26th, 1605, and printed in 1606. And, at some point after April 3rd, 1606, when Devonshire died, the *Funeral Poem* appeared without imprint, but presumably it was owned by Waterson too since it is included in 1607W. It may possibly be the case that Waterson would thus have wished to await disposal of his remaining copies of these two works and therefore have issued a preliminary, and to our minds incomplete, version of 1607W. The printer, of course, would probably have printed the whole book from P2 through V, a simpler method than halting composition on P1. His or Waterson's effort to subtract P2ff. from the book would be no more illogical, at any rate, than an identical effort made by some private and hypothetical binder who, in two separate cases, was working for a book-owner who wished to rid himself of, or to set apart, this final material.

At the same time, an analogous but different set of possibilities might have dictated the setting of quire A, this time the agency being Daniel himself. Quire A contains new front matter for *Cleopatra* and *Musophilus,* with a sonnet to Lady Anne Clifford which, being on A7 (A7^v blank; A8-A8^v = *Musophilus* cancellans), was also presumably for *Musophilus* too. Therefore, quire A amounts to a general rewriting of several dedications. *Musophilus* traditionally "belonged" to Fulke Greville, and *Cleopatra,* of course, to the Countess of Pembroke.[64] Since *Musophilus* and *Cleopatra* appear within the body of 1607W without dedicatory poems, and since their prefatory matter in quire A represents expansion and revision of material traditionally accompanying those works, as well as a new title page for each poem, an obvious explanation is that Daniel had not finished his revisions until after Windet printed the body of the book.[65]

The general point here is to suggest that since all the possible states of the edition are dated "1607," and since all of them contained *Cleopatra,* it is difficult to see how Daniel could have revised his play following a December (1607) performance of Shakespeare's drama after the authorities concluded it would have been safe to open the playhouses. The first performance at court, we will recall, was December 26th. Since, also, the revised matter in quire A refers to changes in the *Cleopatra,* it would seem necessary to argue that whether the edition in fact appeared in December or not, Daniel himself may have needed time prior to December 31st, 1607 (the last possible date on which Windet's volume could have appeared), in which to accomplish the final state of 1607W as we have it today.[66]

If we then dismiss December, 1607, as a *terminus ad quem* for Shakespeare's play, several considerations arise. As we have noted, plague dominated the London theatrical scene most of the year 1607, the week after Easter being one possible interval of acting since the Lord Mayor was complaining about players at that point. It might therefore be possible to date *Anthony and Cleopatra* in the week after Easter of 1607, i.e. March 5th-12th; Daniel would have had sufficient time to see a performance, and Windet eventually to print the 1607 volume. We must, however, cope with the problem of Barnabe Barnes's *The Devil's Charter,* since this play too is adduced, by Chambers and others, as a mode of dating Shakespeare's *Anthony and Cleopatra,* Barnes's play being more confidently utilized in this respect than is Daniel's work.

In Barnes's drama, there is a scene in which two young Faventine princes coming in from tennis call for wine, sit on low chairs, and have their temples rubbed by barbers. Calling for music, they drink wine drugged by the Pope and to the strains of music fall asleep (sig. I3). Alexander enters in his cassock and nightcap, and with much emphasis on Morpheus, he draws out his instruments of murder while the boys murmer in their sleep about paradise. Drawing *"out of his boxes aspiks"* the Pope says:

Come out here now you *Cleopatraes* birds.
Fed fat and plump with proud Egiptian slime,
Of seauen mouth'd *Nylus* but now turn'd leane:
>   *He putteth to either of their*
>   *brests an* Aspike.
Take you repast vpon these Princely paps.
Now *Ptolamies* wife is highly magnified,
Ensigning these faire princely twins their death,
And you my louely boyes competitors,
With *Cleopatra* share in death and fate. . . .

What now proud wormes? howe tasts yon princes blood.
The slaues be plump and round; in to your nests,
Is there no token of the serpents draught,
All cleere and safe well now faire boyes good-night.

The Pope leaves, various characters exclaim over the sight of the
"princely boyes" upon "this bed" (sig. I4ᵛ), and the bodies are
carried out.

Certainly the sequence is suggestive, as much for the use of
the motif of sleep as for the employment of asps. It is clear too
that Barnes is not completely familiar with his Plutarch, or with
other versions of the Cleopatra story, or even with natural history
as known in his day, for he makes rather literal use of what in
Shakespeare is only a metaphor, the nursing image.[67] According
to Barnes's version, the asps have in the past been plump, have
been starved so that they will be ravenous, and are now expected
to suck blood. They are thus taken from the princes' breasts when
they have fed their fill: they are "plump" again from their
"draught", and emerge rather more like vampire bats than as the
snakes that Shakespeare and Daniel know. It could be, then, that
Barnes is rather literally following the salient, but figurative,
motif of Shakespeare's nursing imagery which may have proved
good theatre.

The Devil's Charter was entered October 16th, 1607, the Stationers' Register describing the drama as "played before his
Maiestie" and the title page of the edition (1607) mentioning
"Candlemas night last," presumably February 2nd, 1607.[68] But
if we assume for the moment that Barnes did indeed follow
Shakespeare, we have the problem of the subtitle to the edition of
the play: "But more exactly renewed, corrected, and augmented

since by the author, for the more pleasure and profit of the reader," a problem observed by Dover Wilson. This awareness of a reading public makes understandable the form of the contents, although it confuses the problem. There is, for instance, a dedication to Sir William Herbert and Sir William Pope, "Associates in the Noble Order of the Bath," [69] and a formal chorus, Guicciardini, is used not only in introduction, but also to comment at the end of each carefully delineated act. The acts themselves are formally divided into scenes, the play beginning with an elaborate dumb-show. The self-consciousness of the act-divisions alone might suggest caution as to assuming what would have been in the performance and what in the publication, but there are reasons for supposing that the death of the princes might have been part of the original production.

The scene in question would not necessarily add to the respectability of the work as much as might the philosophical and antiquated role of Guicciardini as chorus. It is worth noting too that Barnes's asp-sequence here is invention. What he had to work with was a passing allusion to Prince Astor of Faenza by Guicciardini who observes that Astor, after "some had satisfied their vile vnnatural lust on him, he was secretly put to death, together with his bastard brother." [70] Barnes uses this motif in connection with the same two brothers in III.i. where they are both presented as complaining about the homosexual demands made upon them, invoking the Destroyer of Sodom to deliver them from their soul-slaying prostitution. Barnes gives the unnamed brother, often called Giovanni in other sources, the name Phillippo, and, using the historian's remark about a secret murder, proceeds to invent the further activities for the young princes which we have already examined. In fact, Barnes represses some source material connected with the princes even while he does invent the asp-story about them, for though the siege of Faenza is presented as a major project of the Pope's by Guicciardini, Barnes goes to other sieges in the *Historie* for his war-scenes, Faenza merely existing as a way of identifying the "Fauentine" princes. The playwright followed his source more closely in spirit and more organically for his own purposes when he presented the allusions to homosexuality in III.i., for, though greatly expanded from source, these explicit statements are important for emphasizing a general depravity of the Papal court which is a major concern of Barnes's play.

The death of the princes does nothing to advance the plot of Barnes's play, nor does it add to the Pope's already well-established villainy, for the emphasis of the scene is on the picturesque quality of the princes and their relationship to sleep and death. If Barnes added this scene when rewriting his play for publication, he was being much less ostentatiously "intellectual" than when he produced a chorus, and act/scene divisions. Lying as it does outside of the plot emphasis, the scene would appear to be relevant theatrically, not logically—as relevant as a preceding Lucretia-scene in which a beautiful woman, a Cleopatra-like admirer of her own beauty, dies on stage from applying poisoned cosmetics to her face.

Granted that all the foregoing is only speculation, we must, however, cope with the fact that any dating of *Anthony and Cleopatra* by means of *The Devil's Charter* must not only deal with evidence of relationship but also with the consequences of any relationship that may be established. Entered as it was on October 16th, 1607, and printed in this year, going, in fact to two issues, the play offers two possibilities for the dating of *Anthony and Cleopatra*. If, for instance, Barnes changed his play for publication, after having seen Shakespeare's drama, and after *Charter* had already been acted, then the earliest point before October 16th, 1607, at which Barnes could have seen the play in London was in the holiday season before Lent, 1607. *The Devil's Charter* was acted February 2nd, 1607; Shakespeare's company played again on Thursday, February 5th, on Shrove Sunday, February 15th, and in Lent on Friday, the 27th. Thus, if Barnes changed his play *after* it was performed, he must have seen *Anthony and Cleopatra* at court on the previously mentioned dates, or in town on April 5th-12th, and these series of dates not only become possible *termini ad quem* for Shakespeare's play, but the possible dates for first performance.

If, however, as seems more likely, and, indeed, as is the assumption of Chambers and of other scholars who date *Anthony and Cleopatra* by Barnes's play, the asp-scene was in the original production of *The Devil's Charter* on February 2nd at court, the problem becomes more complex. Since the King's Men were paid for acting at court on Candlemas, they obviously did *The Devil's Charter* themselves. Previous to Candlemas, as we will note from our table of "Interims," there was probably no acting in town, but there were five performances at court, the first being on St. Stephen's, the second on the 29th of December, and three in Epiphany week, the 4th, 6th, and 8th of January. The Prince's Men act at court for the remainder of the month and Candlemas witnesses the next court performance of Shakespeare's company. On the assumption that Barnes saw *Anthony and Cleopatra,* writing his own scene in imitation at some time in the latter part of January, he would have had to see it in the last six days of December, 1606, or the first two weeks of January, 1607, or at some time even prior to all of these dates.

On the basis of Daniel's play alone, I would assign a first performance of *Anthony and Cleopatra* the *terminus ad quem* of February 27th, 1607. With a *terminus a quo* of (Interim IV) February 13th, 1605, this would mean that possible first-performance dates for *Anthony and Cleopatra* (always excluding provincial tours) would lie within Interims V, VI, or VII (the three months of the spring of 1605, the December to March period of 1605-06, Denmark's visit, or the court Christmas season of 1606-07).[71] The difficulty of the last of the foregoing dates is coupled with the implications of also using Barnes as a bench mark. If Barnes is "influenced" by *Anthony and Cleopatra* to the point where he put the asp-scene in the court performance of his play, then *Anthony* would occur before Candlemas, as we have seen, and possibly in the last week of December, 1606. But on December 26th, 1606, in this season, *King Lear* was performed. Whenever *Lear* was written, this first *recorded* performance could thus have occurred in the same season as *Anthony and Cleopatra* unless either of the plays was first performed much earlier, during the King of Denmark's visit, or in the spring previous. But Paul has argued, and later scholars have assumed, that *Macbeth* was first performed before the King of Denmark. If this is true, and the evidence for it is negligible, we have, in our progress backwards in time, now collected not only *Lear,* and *Anthony,* but also *Macbeth* to which the Roman play is often connected by reason of the "genius is rebuk'd" allusion (*Macbeth* III.i.56). A glance at the table of Interims will show, in fact, that this process of pushing backwards can be carried to the beginning of Interim V, the first interim in which we speculate that the King's Men might have new plays to present.

If we acknowledge the strong possibility that "stylistic evidence" and "topical allusion" are not really very definitive in chronology, we are thus left with any possible order of Shakespeare's tragedies after *Hamlet* and *Othello*. Our speculations, however, may be unacceptable because of traditional assumptions about the chronological interrelationship of *Macbeth, Lear,* and *Anthony,* an assumption which places the Roman play as last in the series. But the date of one *Lear* performance is really our only fact here, and it is puzzling that Chambers did not argue that this performance-date complicated his own estimate as to the dates of *Macbeth* and *Anthony,* especially since he himself uses *Devil's Charter* as a coordinate for the Roman play. We might therefore finally stress the point that the traditional order of the tragedies is not necessarily the accurate, or even the plausible one, at least in terms of external evidence. There is no reason why *Macbeth* might not have been written as late as 1611, in the same year that the *Tempest* was performed, and we cannot simply deny this because we wish to. Since, too, we know nothing about *Coriolanus,* we have no proof enabling us to deny such a hypothetical order as, *e. g., Othello, Anthony, Coriolanus, Lear, Macbeth,* with *Pericles* and *Cymbeline* sandwiched in anywhere. After all, Shakespeare's company must have been performing something before the king and the public in Interims V, VI, and VII.

Our review of these matters might serve finally to raise more general subjects for speculation, topics not necessarily confined to the problem of chronology. There is, for instance, the matter of the influence of the plague on our whole concept of London acting between 1603 and 1611. The facts, of course, are well known but not always taken into consideration. The large number of plays allowed by James at court from his accession to 1611 may not, for instance, have necessarily stemmed from the king's excessive love of entertainment; performance at court, in certain years, may have been a way of furnishing the actors with what was very often their only means of support.[72] Quite clearly, too, the beginning of the production of plays by the King's Men at Blackfriars some time after August 9th, 1608, would have been an event of first importance to the company if acting in that location could serve to exempt them from city plague restrictions. If we recall the brevity of Interims IX-XI together with the fact that Shakespeare's company was given money by James for "private practise in the time of infeccon" in April 1609, and again in March 1610 for practice "during the space of sixe weeks," Blackfriars would seem to be a likely location.[73]

Finally, there are aesthetic implications to consider. Whatever the order of the tragedies, it is clear that both *Othello* and *Lear* were performed at court in holiday seasons during or just following plague conditions in London. In the case of *Lear* especially, figures would have permitted no *public* performance after the preceding July, and it may be that we should revise our implicit assumptions that a number of Shakespeare's important tragedies were proven box-office successes before they were presented at court.[74] Private performances there might have been, or even performances in the provinces, but considering the endemic nature of plague in London during the five years after the accession of James, are we not faced with the possibility that court or other private performances were, for long periods of time, the only legitimate outlets for plays in or about London? If so, it is quite possible that Shakespeare may have been faced with an interesting artistic challenge, for in some autumns when plays were prohibited, he had to look forward to the holiday season at court as well as backward to the fact that one or more of his previous tragedies had been seen by the court in the previous season. Circumstances favored the possibility that at times he would have to contemplate writing drama specifically for presentation before the most (presumably) literate audience England had to offer and for acting areas, at Hampton Court or Whitehall, where staging expectations and opportunities might have exceeded or at least have been different from those at the Globe. His concept of the situation might therefore have influenced an increasing emphasis on artistic achievement and on complexity of effect. It is not a question of imagining Shakespeare laboring in vain before an unappreciative "popular" audience at the Globe; rather, it is a question of suggesting *a priori* justification for assuming that the tragedies may not, for Shakespeare, simply have been items in the casual commercialism of a

154

stage career, but vigorous and ambitious responses to the kinds of ideological and literary sophistication for which Jonson also wrote his masques.

University of Cincinnati

NOTES

[1] For the discussion of metrical criteria, see E. K. Chambers, *William Shakespeare* (Oxford, 1930), I, 266-269—hereafter cited as *WS*. For the table, see *WS*, II, Appendix H, Table V (Continued), p. 402. The small number of lines in *Per.* arise from Chambers' division of the play into Shakespearean and non-Shakespearean sections (see Table VIII from which this statistic is drawn).

[2] Chambers' justification for "pause" as criterion appears in *WS*, I, 262-266.

[3] For the dating of *Cor.*, *Cym.*, and *W.T.*, see *WS*, I, 479-480, 485, 489.

[4] For K. Muir, see *Macbeth*, ed. K. Muir (Cambridge, Mass., 1957), p. xviii. See also H. N. Paul, *The Royal Play of Macbeth* (New York, 1950), pp. 359-366.

[5] As for the passage itself, it can be argued that Malcolm is simply reaching the climax of his feigned self-deprecation, presenting himself not only as specifically sinful, but as a general enemy to that embracing principle of order invoked by Artegal in his sermon to the revolutionary giant. The conversation between Lorenzo and Jessica demonstrates Shakespeare's familiarity with this use of "concord," while Ulysses' speech on "degree" makes clear the poet's understanding of "unity." The traditional association of these terms is affirmed again by Spenser's use of Una in Book I and of Concord in Book IV. James' "unity" presumably implied a joining of Scotland and England—not necessarily that "unity" which, suggestive of musical harmony, denoted by analogy the Renaissance concept of order in which, for Ulysses, "degree" was a "string" which must not be untuned.

[6] See G. E. Bentley, "Lenten Performances in the Jacobean and Caroline Theaters," *Essays on Shakespeare and Elizabethan Drama*, ed. R. Hosley (Columbia, 1962), p. 353.

[7] In this article, all days falling between January 1st and March 25th will be dated New Style as far as the year-date is concerned.

[8] See E. K. Chambers, *The Elizabethan Stage* (Oxford, 1923), IV, 335—hereafter cited as *ES*. For the performances above, see *Malone Society Collections*, VI, 42-46. Malone Society publications will hereafter be cited as *MSC* or *MSR*.

[9] *ES*, I, 316.

[10] *MSC*, I, 87-88.

[11] See the copy of Bell's figures in J. T. Murray, *English Dramatic Companies* (London, 1910), II, 186 ff. Unless otherwise indicated, all death figures after Dec., 1605 come from here.

[12] See *The Christmas Prince, MSR,* XLVII, 228, 285. For Chambers, see *ES,* I, 316.

[13] Ommitted here is *Caesar,* the case for which, however, is weak when it is conjectured as appearing prior to 1603. For the evidence *pro,* see *WS,* I, 396 ff., but for a new translation of Platter's account and for a commentary on the weakness of this document as evidence, see Ernest Schanzer, "Thomas Platter's Observations on the Elizabethan Stage," *N & Q,* N.S. III (1956), 465-467.

[14] See John Stow, *The Annales* (London, 1615), sig. 3Z. I have not been able to consult Addl. MS 11402 from which Dasent's calendar gathers the March 19th restraint (for the reference, see *n.* 8—Chambers). It could have been a question of suppressing all amusements in anticipation of the queen's death or of so preventing, by anticipation, any resumption of acting after Lent ended. Possibly relevant here is the assumption by at least ten plague bills (11-20 of the Houghton Library collection and no. 41) that the plague began December 17th, 1602.

[15] For these matters, see *ES,* II, 185, 228, 208-209. We can assume that there was no playing on the two Sundays intervening, for a proclamation by the king on May 7th forbade it (*ES,* IV, 335). This prohibition was still in effect in 1606: see Nicholas Bownd, *The Doctrine of the Sabbath* (London, 1606), sig. S6ᵛ-S7, where there is not only Bownd's commentary but an accompanying gloss that mentions the specific proclamation. Cf. William Crashaw's sermon of Feb. 14th, 1608, which speaks of players profaning the Sabbath "which generally in the countrie is their play day" (*ES,* IV, 249).

[16] See F. P. Wilson, *The Plague in Shakespeare's London* (Oxford, 1927), p. 111 and *Henslowe's Diary,* ed. R. A. Foakes and R. T. Rickert (Cambridge, 1961), pp. 297-298. The intent of Joan's letter, which is clearly to persuade her husband to stop hawking and come home, may perhaps account for her optimistic picture of the plague situation. Alleyn's absence, if the rest of the company is indeed back in London, suggests no organized acting in the provinces at this time. Cf. a proclamation for the following summer, July 8th, 1604, forbidding Londoners to go to Bristol Fair— *A Booke of Proclamations* (London, 1609), sig. G2ᵛ.

[17] See *Proclamations,* sigs. D3ᵛ, E.

[18] See his will in Shakespeare, *Plays and Poems,* ed. Edmund Malone (London, 1821), III, 472-473.

[19] See *WS,* II, 329: "A play of Robin goode-fellow." I include *Fair Maid of Bristow,* entered Feb. 8th, 1605, as "played at Hampton Court by his Maiesties players," for between the season under discussion and the S.R. date, there is no other performance at Hampton Court.

[20] See *MSC,* VI, 39. The gift may have been stimulated by Burbage's acting ability, for neither Prince's nor Queen's, also at court this season, and also presumably in financial straits, is recorded as having received anything beyond normal payment. There may have been a play on the occa-

sion that Burbage was rewarded, and, if so, the reward was probably less than it appears. See *n.* 72.

[21] For these matters, see *ES*, II, 210, 328, 334-335.

[22] See his prorogations, *passim,* in *Proclamations.*

[23] See Wilson, pp. 116-117. See also *Cal. S.P. Venetian* (1603-1607), p. 190. Molin's dates must be adjusted (as they are throughout here) to English Old Style, except for year-date, since his own dating habits are (Continental) New Style: see *Venetian,* p. 288.

[24] Bartholomew Fair, for instance, was held in 1609, when plague figures were high. See Wilson, p. 121.

[25] See *ES*, II, 211, but cf. Murray, II, 378 and *n.* 5.

[26] For Somerset House, see *ES*, II, 211. Possibly relevant to the matter of plague at this time is the existence of a draft license for the Queen's Men conjecturally dated at some point in 1604. It has the proviso "when the infečon of the plague shall decrease to the Nomber of thirty weekly" (*MSC*, I, 266). As we can observe in Interim IV, such a qualification would be applicable only to January, and then, after Lent, to the spring or summer, there being little plague of note in the following fall. The proviso thus could perhaps apply to the spring of 1604.

[27] For the Bill of Mortality, see *MSS Sackville*, ed. A. P. Newton (London, 1942), I, 104; for the Lord Mayor's letter: *MSS Salisbury*, ed. M. S. Giuseppi (London, 1938), XVII, 206.

[28] For the prohibition, see *MSC*, I, 371. It is extremely significant for our general estimates here that in this fall we have Privy Council orders both to cease, and then to resume playing, because the death rate itself would seem relatively low. On October 12th, Chamberlain will refer to the "sodain rising of the sicknes to thirtie a weeke" and on the 24th he gives the figure of 22, but Molin, offering this latter figure on Oct. 16th, observes that the infection is not plague at all, but smallpox. See *Venetian,* p. 281, and John Chamberlain, *Letters,* ed. N. E. McClure, *Proc. Amer. Philos. Soc.,* XII (1939), I, 209-212. Molin's attitude and Chamberlain's figures suggest that, as Wilson speculated (p. 55), the authorities "usually closed the theatres long before plague-deaths rose to 30 or 40, and sometimes refused to take the risk of permitting them to reopen until some weeks after the mortality had fallen below that number." Apparently, too, plague was not the only medical condition closing theatres. Quite significant also, in these general respects, is the fact that the patent for the King's Men of May 19th, 1603, specifying that their acting may resume only after a decrease of plague, coincides with the weekly report of 22 plague deaths, figures for the three previous weeks being 10, 11, 18. See Wilson, p. 115, for a photograph of the bill for 1603.

[29] For the Privy Council order of December 15th, see *MSC*, I, 372. For the account of payment, see *MSC*, VI, 43-44.

[30] Wilson's reference here (p. 119 and *n.* 1) is to the Corporation of London Records—the *Repertories*, XXVII. 191 and the *Journals*, XXVII. 35b, 72, and 74b. Fol. 187^v of the *Repertories*, however, starts the recording year in April, 1606, and fol. 192 has an April 9th, 1606 entry; therefore

Wilson's reference would not seem to be operative much before April. Three of Wilson's references to the *Journals* refer to July, 1606, while 35b may not necessarily be pertinent: Item 7 in a list of public works to be undertaken is a new burial place which may be significant but not pertinent.

[81] See *MSC*, I, 270-271. For the problem of May games, see L. Hotson, "Maypoles and Puritans," *SQ*, I (1950), 205-207.

[32] *MSC*, VI, 44. In terms of repertory, there might have been a problem here, for ten plays had been presented before James in the previous Christmas season. If material presented both to Christian and James had to be new, at least to James, then plays performed this summer might well have been written in the previous spring. But if old material was presented, it is hardly likely that, as Paul suggests (p. 328), *Hamlet* would have been given, unless all of the pejorative remarks about Danish drunkenness and about Denmark in general had been excised.

[33] Giustinian dates Continental New Style (see *Venetian*, p. 430, a reference to the Gunpowder anniversary) and thus his remark about the cessation of plague is puzzling, unless he speaks in purely relative terms. If the figures came in on Thursday, Nov. 6th (Old Style), at the time Giustinian was writing, the death rate from plague for the previous week would have been 68. Furthermore, on Nov. 1st (Old Style), resort to court had been forbidden *(Proclamations*, sigs. M4-M4ᵛ). For the Lord Mayor's letter, see *Analytical Index to . . . the Remembrancia* (London, 1878), p. 337.

[84] Cf. also *n.* 28. Two puzzling title pages appear in the late spring and summer. *The Miseries of Enforced Marriage* (London, 1607): S.R. July 31st, 1607; subtitle: "As it is now playd by his Maiesties Seruants." *Three English Brothers* (London, 1607): S.R. June 29th, 1607; subtitle: "As it is now play'd by her Maiesties Seruants." The only plays entered in the first seven months of 1607 to have such subtitles, they seem to suggest an acting season. On June 29th, the previous weekly report would have been 21, but on July 31st, deaths would just have been reported at 43, figures never having been below 30 all July. Making all allowance for the distortions of publicity, it nevertheless seems difficult to assume, in such a context, that nothing had been staged all spring. But it may be that provincial performances are here alluded to; otherwise, these plays, at the soonest, would not have been sold until July and August respectively, times in which one does not expect city acting. Possibly the titles refer to winter performance: there would be some weeks in December, 1607, when such performance would be possible after the plague had eased. Whatever the case, it seems necessary to allude to evidence possibly contrary to our general contentions. See also Wilson, p. 187.

[85] See Stow, sig. 4F2.

[86] In the winter holidays since the accession of James court performances were as follows: 1603-04: 9 plays; 1604-05: 11 plays; 1605-06: 10 plays; 1606-07: 9 plays; 1607-08: 13 plays.

[87] For Lake, see *MSC*, II, 148-149; for La Boderie, see J. J. Jusserand, "Ambassador La Boderie and the 'Compositeur' of the Byron Plays," *MLR*, VI (1911), 203-205.

[38] See *Cal. S. P. Venetian* (1607-1610), pp. 76, 100, 116. There are also references to the mine for March 17th (English O.S.) and September 9th (New Style).

[39] See Cranfield's Cashbook: "January 10 [1611], for going into a play at Blackfriars, -7s." *Mss Sackville*, I, 232.

[40] See Sidney Race, "Simon Forman's 'Bocke of Plaies' Examined," *N & Q*, N.S. V (1958), 9-14. But cf. R. W. Hunt and J. Dover Wilson, "The Authenticity of Simon Forman's *Bocke of Plaies*," *RES*, XXIII (1947), 193-200, and D. A. Amnéus, "A Missing Scene in *Macbeth*," *JEGP*, LX (1961), 435-440.

[41] In a season which saw presented at court at least seven performances of Shakespeare's plays (1612-13), it seems perverse to reject "one playe called a badd begininge makes a good endinge" as an alternate title of *All's Well That Ends Well*. See *MSC*, VI, 56.

[42] For the documents, see *MSC*, I, 80-83. Cf. also *n.* 15 in this article. When a third playhouse was allowed, it was specified as an addition to the two named in the above-mentioned order, so the existence of another playhouse need not suggest a general disregard, during the early part of James's reign, for the Privy Council order. General references to "dailie" plays could refer to tandem performances by more than one playhouse.

[43] Edward Arber, *A Transcript of the Stationers' Register* (London, 1875-94), III, 378.

[44] *WS*, I, 477-478. For another résumé of the dating situation here and of other Shakespearean plays, see James G. McManaway, "Recent Studies in Shakespeare's Chronology," *SS*, III (1950), 22-33.

[45] For these matters, see *ES*, IV, 139-140, 172.

[46] This may have been so for Jonson too, since *Every Man In* and *Every Man Out* were performed during this same holiday, but were entered respectively Aug. 4th and April 8th, 1600.

[47] For *Othello*, see Marvin Rosenberg, "On the Dating of *Othello*," *ES*, XXXIX (1958), 72-74. For a different view of the date of *Measure*, see J. W. Lever, "The Date of *Measure for Measure*," *SQ*, X (1959), 381-388. Lever favors a date between April 9th and August 19th, 1604, but on the basis of topical allusions.

[48] See Arthur M. Z. Norman, "The *Tragedie of Cleopatra* and the date of *Antony and Cleopatra*, *MLR*, LIV (1959), 1-9.

[49] The parallels suggested by Case, in the old Arden edition, between *Antony* and *Bussy D'Ambois* as well as *Nobody and Somebody*, are not, as Chambers has argued, very valid. See *Antony and Cleopatra*, ed. R. H. Case (Indianapolis, 1906), pp. xii-xiii. As for Shakespeare's own recourse to Daniel, see Laurence Michel and C. C. Seronsy, "Shakespeare's History Plays and Daniel: An Assessment," *SP*, LII (1955), 549-577.

[50] References to Plutarch are from *Lives*, ed. George Wyndham (London, 1896), VI, 79.

[51] See Robert Garnier, *The Tragedie of Antonie*, tr. the Countess of Pembroke (London, 1595), sig. F5.

[52] See "Scarrus and the Scarred Soldier," *HLQ,* XXII (1958), 31-39.

[53] See Samuel Daniel, *Certaine Small Workes* (London, 1607), sig. G8.

[54] Later editions of *Cleopatra* do not change the readings of the lines here.

[55] See W. W. Greg, *A Bibliography of English Printed Drama* (London, 1939-59), IV, *Excursus* I, esp. p. xciv. See also W. L. Edgerton, "The Calendar Year in Sixteenth-Century Printing," *JEGP,* LIX (1960), 439-449; and E. H. Miller, "New Year's Day Gift Books in the 16th Century, *SB,* XV (1962), 233-243, alludes to Windet's STC 24117 and 24118 as such publications.

[56] For the cancelled entry, see Arber, III, 309; for the court records, W. A. Jackson, *Records of the Court of the Stationers' Company. 1602-1640* (London, 1957), p. 17.

[57] See, e.g., STC 10268, a Visitation Article which suggests an assumption of O.S. dating, Windet himself not specifically affixing the year of imprint. Edgerton's useful article mentions three of Windet's titles (STC 1137, 4473, 21226), but he sometimes assumes the validity of title page descriptions as well as speedy publication after the S.R. entry.

[58] There is always the possibility that on Thursday, Nov. 26th, when the weekly figure would have been observed as down from 46 to 21, the city fathers immediately allowed the theatres to open, but it seems unlikely. For the week ending Dec. 3rd, the figure is 19, and for the week ending Dec. 10th, as we have seen, the figure is back up to 28.

[59] See Samuel Daniel, *The Tragedy of Philotas,* ed. Laurence Michel (New Haven, 1949), Ch. V and *passim*. The verses "To the Prince," for instance, in 1607P, are the 1605 version, not the revised 1607W version.

[60] On the title page of 1607W, Daniel is for the first time described as "one of the Groomes of the Queenes Maiesties priuie Chamber" and is so designated in editions of 1609 and 1611. He is not among the "players" who, as "officers" to the queen were given red cloth for the coronation procession of March 15th, 1604 (*MSC,* II, 322-323), but his name is at the head of a comparable list for Anne's funeral, where he and Killegrew are listed as Grooms of the Queen's Privy Chamber in 1619 (*MSC,* II, 324). The omission from the former list is odd since, on Feb. 4th, 1604, in the patent for the Children of the Queen's Revels, he is specifically given the power of "approbacion and allowaunce" (*ES,* II, 49). In August, 1605, when James was at Oxford and Daniel's *Queen's Arcadia* was presented, letters from a "Mr. Daniel" are the authority for the reception of additional costumes by the university from Kendall, one of the men named in the 1604 patent (*MSC,* I, 256). F. A. Yates, *John Florio* (Cambridge, 1934), pp. 246-247, alludes to *Cal. S.P. Dom.* (1619-1623), p. 31, where Queen Anne's grooms are mentioned at the time of her death in 1619. Florio is listed as of 15 years' service, Daniel as only of 5. 1607W attests to the error of this figure which is probably a slip for "15." If so, we get a date of about 1604-05, a date embracing Daniel's period of highest apparent prestige with the queen, but we recall that the 1605 edition of the poems makes no mention of the writer as groom.

[61] See *Bibliography,* I, #132 (gI, gII); III, 1052-53; IV, 1669-70.

[62] For H. Sellers, see "A Bibliography of the Works of Samuel Daniel," *Proc. Oxford Bibl. Soc.*, II (1927), 40. The B.M. *Gen. Cat. of Printed Books* (London, 1951), XLVII, col. 835, describes this copy of 1607W by noting that *"Sig. ¶3, 4 are misbound after sig. ¶5, 6."* It is difficult to see how this would be possible in octavo unless Sellers' description is inaccurate. By misfolding, one can arrive at 5,6,3,4,1,2,7,8, however. Neither Sellers nor B.M. intimates that such is the case.

[63] Specifically, we might here suggest the following stages (not necessarily "issues") of 1607W:
I: ¶⁸ [¶1-¶2, ¶5-¶6, ¶3-¶4, ¶7-¶8], B⁸-¶1, A⁸ [A8 blank].
II: ¶⁸, B-V⁸, A⁸ [A8 blank]: Greg's "first issue."
III: ¶⁸, B-V⁸, A⁸ [A8 cancellans for 07]: Greg's "second issue."
For I, see B.M. (644.a.41); for II, see Huntington 60913; for III, see Folger, copy 1. Of course any variations and states, especially for I, are possible. Folger, copy 2, lacks P2-V8.

[64] A dedicatory sonnet to Greville prefaces *Musophilus* in the 1599, 1601, and 1602 editions, the last editions to contain the long poem before 1607W. An earlier version of the dedicatory poem to the Countess of Pembroke before *Cleopatra* appears in 1594, 1599, 1601, but not, strangely, in 1605, the last edition to contain *Cleopatra* before 1607W.

[65] Greg, *Bibliography*, p. 1053, notes that quire A is printed on different paper from that of the rest of the volume, and this fact may again argue for elapsed time in the preparation of the edition, even perhaps for a state of 1607W without A. Other methods of dating 1607W might be useful, if we accept the argument for Shakespeare's influence on it: perhaps a collation of Windet's type faces. As far as ornaments are concerned, 1607W has an ornament similar to McKerrow #379 (but without the "A H") on the title pages of *Ros.*, *Arc.*, *Mus.*, and *Phil.* This ornament often prints so that a flaw is discernible to the left of the image, on the lower ring. This flaw appears in Campion's *Masque*, given for Lord Hay on Jan. 6th, 1607, printed by Windet, and entered Jan. 26th, 1607. The flawing is erratic, however. None appears on this image for STC 1451 (1607), but the same flaw appeared in STC 1455, printed in 1606. McKerrow #282 also appears in 1607W, but it is not useful, for comparisons to its other appearances in Windet's printings reveal nothing beyond minor inking variations.

[66] Another possible delaying factor might be that Waterson would have wanted to wait until Blount's supply of 1607P was exhausted before issuing *Philotas* in 1607W. Foliation in 1607W begins on F5, *Philotas* having ended on F1ᵛ, dedicatory matter, title, and argument to "A Letter Sent from Octavia" occupying F2-F4, and the text of this latter beginning on F5. However, the oddity of beginning foliation within the forme might be explainable as a new compositor starting his stint.

[67] See "Shakespeare and Roman History," *MLR*, LIII (1958), 327 *n. 1*.

[68] See Arber, III, 361.

[69] They were so created July 24th, 1603. See Stow, sig. 3Z5ᵛ. For J. D. Wilson, see *Antony and Cleopatra* (Cambridge, 1950), pp. ix-x.

[70] Francesco Guicciardini, *The Historie*, tr. G. Fenton (London, 1599), sig. R6ᵛ.

[71] We can perhaps supplement F. D. Hoeniger's careful discussion of the date of *Pericles* (pp. xl ff. of the new Arden edition) by observing that this play, in the same Stationers' Entry as *Anthony*, might generally be subject to the same chronological considerations. Because Giustinian saw the play with La Boderie and his wife (*WS*, II, 335), a performance probably occurred in Interim VIII or IX. La Boderie's wife was with him "from at least April, 1607" (Chambers, *loc. cit.*), and Giustinian left England, by his own account, on Nov. 23rd, 1608 (*Continental* Style). By O. S. dating, the performance would then have fallen between April, 1607, and Nov. 13th, 1608.

[72] The rate of payment per play, it is true, seems to have been inflexible, disbursment being invariably twenty nobles (£6.13.4) per play, and "rewarde" being invariably five marks (£3.6.8) per play for the total of £10 per play in all. This does not change even when the King's Men entertain James and Christian in the summer of 1606 when, even though the occasion might have warranted a bit of princely largesse, three plays get the actors £30. On the other hand, after an anticlimax to accession generosity, the increase of plays presented at court had the following effect on the budget of Shakespeare's company. For the season of 1604: £110; of 1605: £100; of 1606: £30 (Denmark) + £90 = £120; of 1607: £130; of 1608: £120 + £40 (plague-reward) = £160; of 1609: £130 + £30 (plague-reward) = £160.

[73] I read the documents for pay in plague-time as both bearing on the same Christmas season, that of 1609-10 (see *MSC*, VI, 47-48). Chambers (*ES*, I, 331 *n.* 1) sees these payments as referring to the "Christmases of 1608-9 and 1609-10." Cf. F. P. Wilson, pp. 126-127. For the point generally, see the Dec. 20th, 1608, entry in the Gaol Delivery Register against William Claiton as an indication of attempts by certain companies to act during plague-time (*ES*, IV, 340). For the problem of Blackfriars occupancy by King's, see *ES*, II, 55, but cf. *ES*, I, 331 *n.* 1. Children do seem to have been prohibited from acting during plague-time, whatever adults might have been allowed in the private theatres. See Wilson, p. 126, the commitment of Pollard and Gwynn for a play at Whitefriars during plague-time. See also Mark Eccles, "Martin Peerson and the Blackfriars," *SS*, XI (1958), 105, *n.* 21. The qualification clause in the agreement between Kirkham and Daniel (April 28th, 1604) assumes that the boys might not at times be able to act their full six months "by reason of any prohibicion or pestilence in the citty." See H. N. Hillebrand, "The Child Actors," *Univ. of Ill. Stud.*, XI (1926), 335.

[74] See, e.g., *Macbeth*, ed. J. Dover Wilson (Cambridge, 1947), p. xxx.

ANTONY AND THE PROTESTING SOLDIERS: A RENAISSANCE TRADITION FOR THE STRUCTURE OF *ANTONY AND CLEOPATRA*

PAUL A. JORGENSEN

Antony and Cleopatra is commonly cited as the play in which Shakespeare followed with unusual closeness a single and obvious source.[1] This fidelity is seldom mentioned to Shakespeare's credit, for it is pointed out that his devotion to North's Plutarch led him to remote incidents and scenes. Nevertheless, a few interesting deviations in point of view and fact from the original have been discovered. These are attributed to a misreading of ambiguous passages (Octavius' reply to Antony's challenge) or a dramatist's need to condense a long narrative (combining of battles, abbreviation of Antony's long sojourn with Octavia, and elimination of the Parthian campaign). Less successful, on the whole, have been attempts to trace divergences to secondary sources.[2]

The present venture into this field will be guided by three limitations. It will concentrate on the first half of the play, principally the first two acts, for it is in this portion that Shakespeare differs most from his source.[3] Second, it will largely bypass the beaten province of most of its predecessors—the works dealing specifically with either of the two principals—and study mainly those treating a similar subject but different personages. And third, it will devote itself to form and stress more than to content and incident, and will assume that such structural influence may come not from one work alone but from the dramatic tradition governing a given subject.

I

A review of the first two acts will reveal the kind of dramatic pattern and conflict that Shakespeare, mainly in departure from Plutarch, is building. Shakespeare does not, as Willard Farnham observes, open the tragedy "with the colorful meeting of the lovers at the river Cydnus, as he might have done if he had wanted to construct it upon the frame of their love." [4] Instead he begins with a heartfelt denunciation of that love, spoken by the soldier Philo to his fellow Demetrius. This prominent and vigorous speech is not to be found in Plutarch. Its key expression, "this dotage of our general's," announces the dramatic theme of the first half of the play. As though to illustrate Philo's lament, Antony enters with the Queen and avows his grand indifference to Rome, which here and elsewhere stands for the appeal of duty. After the lovers leave the stage, Philo and Demetrius remain to comment on the spectacle, and their point of view is indicated by Demetrius' half-hearted hope for "better deeds to-morrow." The pattern of the scene, then, is this: two soldiers, on the stage throughout, making choric commentary at beginning and end on a tableau which depicts their general's dotage.

Scene two develops the soldier-idleness antithesis by showing the veteran Enobarbus in the company of Cleopatra's servants. Presently, after Cleopatra has appeared, first looking for Antony and then resolving not to see him, Antony enters with a bearer of war news: Labienus has shaken his "conquering banner" over Asia, while—the implied reproach is quickly felt by Antony, who now begins to reveal the struggle within himself which had been purely external during the first scene. He reflects, as did the two soldiers before, that he must break his Egyptian fetters or lose himself in dotage. News of the death of Fulvia, "a great spirit gone," evokes again the guilty sense of inaction and the resolve that he "must from this enchanting queen break off"; his "idleness" brings ten thousand harms. He tells Enobarbus his compulsion to leave "with haste." Enobarbus, as a soldier, agrees; but he lacks at this point Philo's earnestness. His intelligence presents him both the urgency and the irony of the situation. Hence, his warning to Antony is sarcastic rather than passionate; but through the sarcasm appears the soldierly conviction that between women and a great cause women should be esteemed as nothing. The scene closes with Antony's decision to inform Cleopatra of his "quick remove from hence." In scene three he so informs her, though not without great difficulty and not without the compromising assurance that he goes as her "soldier, servant," making peace or war as she affects.

Scene four takes us to Rome, but this new point of view, no less than that of the preceding scenes, is directed at Antony's basic tension. Now it is Octavius, rather than Philo or Enobarbus, who deplores his idleness and dissipation—his wasting a time

> That drums him from his sport and speaks as loud
> As his own state and ours.

Pompey's piratical successes require Antony's immediate action. And then, in as earnest terms as the simple soldier Philo's, Octavius prays that Antony will resume the warlike nature shown at Modena, the hardihood which wounds his honor to be recalled now. But the act ends ominously with Cleopatra in fretful idleness, remembering her former conquests.

Act II begins with the pirate Pompey's point of view. This, like that of the previous male characters, is a soldier's, but it differs from the others in its mixture of derision and hostility. As an enemy, he rejoices that Antony will make "no wars without doors," and, apostrophizing Cleopatra, asks that her witchcraft and lust continue to master Antony's honor "even till a Lethe'd dulness." But at the amazing news that Antony is expected in Rome, he prides himself that his "stirring"

> Can from the lap of Egypt's widow pluck
> The ne'er-lust wearied Antony.

This synopsis has been carried far enough to indicate the kind of stress Shakespeare is building and the ways in which he assembles his scenes and characters to produce that stress. Every scene has focused, often at the beginning and end, upon one major question asked by protesting soldiers and by himself: Will Antony renounce his idleness, regain his lost soldiership, and become once more formidable in empire and in war? Well into

165

the third act this question is important, though not central in every scene. Later it takes a somewhat different form. It is then no more a question of his going to war, but of his being able to cast off Cleopatra's baneful influence on his tactics. Here still the choric warnings and laments of his soldiers are prominent. Not until the last two acts, after Antony's downfall, does the stress change in Cleopatra's favor to make possible the final drama of growing heroism and love in defeat.

No detailed comparison with Plutarch is necessary to show how different the structure—notably the quality of tension—is in Shakespeare's opening acts. Plutarch never asks Shakespeare's basic question; it is scarcely implicit in the narrative. And it is not found in Plutarch for a good reason: There is never any hope of Antony's shaking off his charm, because, unlike Shakespeare's Antony, his life has been with a few exceptions one long debauchery which the historian denounces from beginning to end. As a youth, he was "given to love" and was instructed by the dissolute Curio in "great follies, and vaine expences upon women, in rioting and banketing." For this libertine, Cleopatra is merely, but inevitably, "the last and extreamest mischief of all other." [5] Hence, as O. J. Campbell remarks, "by lightening this emphasis on Antony's grosser vices," Shakespeare "makes his hero's libertinage entirely due to Cleopatra's power of seduction." [6] Plutarch does not build his narrative upon the assumption that Antony may regain his soldiership. Antony's story is told without tension, because there is no hope to make tension possible. With one exception there are no pleading soldiers, and there is virtually no struggle within Antony himself.

To support this departure from Plutarch, Shakespeare was obliged to alter radically his Cleopatra. Since she is to be the single enchantress, she must be a deadly one, her sexual charm unadulterated by political acumen or culture. That Shakespeare partially supplied these Plutarchan traits in the last two acts is evidence of a split in the play. There are, in terms of character and dramatic stress, two plays rather than one. The first is concluded when Antony fails tragically to conquer his dotage. The second, involving an entirely different conflict, ends triumphantly when both lovers prove their loyalty. The second is indebted to both Plutarch and Samuel Daniel. The first owes its incidents and characters basically to Plutarch, and its arrangement of incident, alteration of character, and creation of stress largely to an important dramatic tradition involving a soldier in relationship to a woman.

II

There were three dramatic patterns available to the Elizabethan playwright who would present, with fullest popular understanding, a noble warrior in tragic, or nearly tragic, struggle. The warrior might be (1) unable to adjust himself to the complexities, intrigues, or decorums of a peacetime state (Coriolanus, Othello);[7] (2) ungratefully used by sovereign, court, or populace (Titus Andronicus, Alcibiades, Coriolanus); or (3) dishonorably diverted from his proper business by amorous dotage. The third type, of which *Antony and Cleopatra* is a complex development, was the most popular of the three; it is found abundantly and variously from Lyly through Fletcher; and it was applied, with more or less historical warrant, to almost every known conqueror. Its primary theme is suggested by Othello when he assures the Senate that Desdemona's presence in Cyprus will not impair his generalship:

> No, when light-wing'd toys
> Of feather'd Cupid seel with wanton dullness
> My speculative and offic'd instruments
> That my disports corrupt and taint my business,
> Let housewives make a skillet of my helm,
> And all indign and base adversities
> Make head against my estimation.
>
> (I.iii.269)

If an Elizabethan stage conqueror is to prove triumphant, he almost invariably announces his superiority to weakening passions. Thus Tamburlaine, whose wars not even Zenocrate can impede, assures his audience:

167

> I will not spare those proud Egyptians
> Nor change my martial observations
> For all the wealth of Gihon's golden waves,
> Or for the love of Venus, would she leave
> The angry god of arms and lie with me.[8]

The statuesque conquering hero of *The Wars of Cyrus* refuses even to see the captive princess Panthea, for

> by the eie love slips into the heart,
> Making men idle, negligent.
> Nothing can more dishonour warriours,
> Then to be conquered with a womans looke.[9]

In *The Virtuous Octavia*, one of the early plays based on Plutarch's *Antonius*, Octavius Caesar surprisingly appears as the ideal conqueror:

> To manage steele our nature dooth encline,
> Of womens wanton toyes we are ashamed.[10]

As there are none of Antony's protesting lieutenants in this work, Octavius' warlike example is possibly invented to supply their conventional function.

Since these three conquerors are ideal, there is no struggle apparent or necessary in their rejection of love, and only in *The Wars of Cyrus* is the issue significantly raised. But other plays helped to prepare for the conflict consummately expressed by Shakespeare. Especially influential was Lyly's *Campaspe*, the story of the maiden loved by both Alexander and Apelles. Lyly shapes the drama so as to subordinate the struggle between Alexander and Apelles to that between Alexander as a lover and Alexander as a conqueror. The latter conflict is expressed not within Alexander himself, but in the opposition between his idleness and his warriors, for whom Hephestion is the principal spokesman. Hephestion's reproaches are expressed in a patterned manner that influenced future soldierly protests in the drama, including that of Shakespeare's Philo. He asks:

shall it not seeme monstrous to wisemen, that the hearte of the greatest conquerour of the worlde, should be found in the hands of the weakest creature of nature? of a woman? of a captive? . . . Remember *Alexander* thou hast a campe to governe, not a chamber; fall not from the armour of *Mars* to the armes of *Venus*, from the fiery assaults of war, to the maidenly skirmishes of love. . . .[11]

Hephestion is not, however, blind to Campaspe's beauty; and, as with Enobarbus, it is paradoxically this rough soldier who describes her "partes" and seductiveness most felicitously. But, he asks, "what of this?" and proceeds to rebuke Alexander for succumbing to such charms.[12] In the earnestness of his rebuke, he is closer to Philo and Scarus than to Enobarbus, whose sense of irony leads him to denounce by means of praise. Alexander listens sympathetically to Hephestion's protests, but finally stops him: "No more *Hephestion* . . . thou maist be a good soldier, but never good lover" (II.ii.112-114), a warning which resembles Antony's silencing of Enobarbus: "Thou art a soldier only. Speak no more" (II.ii.108). Lyly employs other protesting lieutenants, including Permenio and Clytus, to give variety to the groupings; and, like Shakespeare, he represents certain soldiers entering into the spirit of the general idleness by conversing with a courtesan and resolving that "this peace shall bring us some pleasure" (V.iii.1).

Structurally, then, *Campaspe* offered Shakespeare suggestions for the grouping of characters into patterns of conflict. It necessarily disregarded, however, one important direction of stress in that Campaspe is no Cleopatra and does not even try to win Alexander. A second neglected source of stress is within the conqueror himself. Alexander is in no danger of succumbing to his prolonged idleness. Halfway through the play he makes his position clear. When Hephestion tells him (III.iv.33) of "all Persia swelling in the pride of their own power: the Scithians carelesse what courage or fortune can do: the Aegiptians dreaming in the soothsayings of their Augures," Alexander confesses conquering to be his proper work, but pleads that recreation is "necessary among so many assaults, bloudye wounds, intollerable troubles." Doubt not, he declares, but that he can, at the

169

necessary time, "throw affections as farre from him as he can cowardice." The reassurance is later repeated (V.iv.3-4) and is realized when he gives orders to prepare for immediate conquest in Persia. "The conquering of Thebes," rejoices Hephestion (V.iv.148-149), "was not so honourable as the subdueing of these thoughts." The structure of the play bears him out, for Lyly considered the decision of enough dramatic importance to serve as the conclusion to the drama.

When the author of *Caesar's Revenge* wished to dramatize Julius Caesar's famous affair with Cleopatra, he chose his major incidents from Plutarch, but his dramatic pattern from *Campaspe* or similar works. This Roman play was produced as early as 1595 but published in 1607, a date significant for Shakespeare's drama. In *Caesar's Revenge* we find a conqueror in the hands of a real, though not fully mature or infinitely various seductress, who offers the Roman warriors such "Aegiptian pleasures" as "a Royall goulden bowre." [13] Both Caesar and Antony are stricken, the former resolving:

> And now hang up these Idle instruments.
> My warlike speare and uncontrouled crest:
> My mortall wounding sword and silver shield,
> And under thy sweete banners beare the brunt,
> Of peacefull warres and amorous alarmes.
>
> (Sig. D 1ᵛ)

Here, in substance, is the Hephestion type of protest, but now uttered shamelessly by the fettered conqueror himself, who cites his illustrious predecessors in dotage; even Mars, he recalls, was wont to allay his "bloudy rage" in Venus' bed. But the real agent of protest is Dolobella, who conventionally regrets (sig. D 2) the baneful effects of enchanting love upon a conqueror. No protest, however, is really needed, for Caesar suddenly announces himself free of Egypt—

> Now that I have shaked of these womanish linkes,
> In which my captive thoughts were chayned a fore—
>
> (Sig. E 2)

and like Lyly's Alexander contemplates world conquest, to the applause of Dolobella.[14] So effortless is the escape, that the painfully stricken Antony refers (sig. E 3ᵛ) to Caesar's affection as "lip-love, that never touched his heart." Indeed, the only real erotic conflict in the play is that which is now disclosed "in the marble of [Antony's] brest," so deep that "time nor Fortune ere can raze it out." This conflict is interestingly depicted by means of a rebuke, not by another soldier, but by Antony's "bonus genius." The struggle is thus more or less internal. Shakespeare, it will be recalled, converts Plutarch's early narrative of Antony's warlike hardihood into a soldierly lament by Octavius. The speech of the "bonus genius" in *Caesar's Revenge* likewise gives to Plutarch's matter-of-fact narrative the emotional stress of recollection:

> Hast thou so soone forgot the discipline,
> And welcome taskes thy youth was trayned to,
> Thy soft downe Pillow was a helme of steele:
> The could damp earth, a bed to ease thy toyle,
> Afrighted slumbers were thy golden sleepes:
> Hunger and thirst thy sweetest delicates. . . .
> (Sig. E 3ᵛ)

But, the genius assures him (sig. E 4), the gods will not let him drown his fame in idleness:

> Yet must Philippi see thy high exploytes,
> And all the world ring of thy Victories.

The scene closes, like similar scenes in Shakespeare, with Antony demanding of himself:

> Cast off these base effeminate passions:
> Which melt the courrage of thy manlike minde,
> And with thy sword receive thy sleeping praise.
> (Sig. E 4ᵛ)

Antony does so, but the play now turns its attention to Caesar's assassination and the resultant civil war. Though crude in workmanship, this drama goes significantly beyond *Campaspe* as a structural model for *Antony and Cleopatra,* for it adds a compelling woman, an internal struggle, the poignancy of recollected soldiership, and a scene constructed so as to highlight the strain in Antony's breaking away from Egypt.[15]

Hercules is represented as a loitering conqueror in Thomas Heywood's *The Brazen Age,* a play published in 1613 but possibly presented before 1596.[16] Whether it influenced or was influenced by *Antony and Cleopatra* is of less concern here than the fact that in dealing with a warlike demigod, Heywood followed the approved dramatic pattern for conquerors. Hercules is shown doting effeminately on the "strumpet" Omphale, Queen of Lydia. Jason, Nestor, Castor, Telamon, Atreus, and Pollux come from Greece, at Dejaneira's request, to reclaim him. These heroes then form a group of protesting soldiers at the sight of "the *Libian* Conqueror, now a slaves slave." [17] Hercules, however, quickly becomes himself again when Dejaneira's presents are given him:

> What strumpets this, that hath detain'd my soule? . . .
> Hence with these womanish tyres,
> And let me once more be my selfe againe.[18]

III

Omphale is a formidable seductress, and like Cleopatra she boasts reminiscently of her conquests; but neither she nor the other female characters so far mentioned provide the closest parallel to Shakespeare's queen in relationship to a warrior. Let us first recall that Shakespeare's heroine of the opening acts is not Plutarch's. As Case observes,[19] her "arts of irritating perverseness employed in Act I, sc. iii" are not indicated by Plutarch, whose Cleopatra weeps when she is sad. Schücking's description of Shakespeare's early Cleopatra brings out in bold relief her contrast with the original:

Love seems to be her only aim in life. If the object of her passion is absent we must imagine her (I, v; II, v) reclining drowsily on her couch, yawning and wishing to sleep away the time until her lover returns. . . . Her laziness is equalled by her sensuality. . . . This side of her character is brought to our notice by the contemptuous expressions—'a gipsy's lust' and 'a strumpet'—which Philo uses in the first scene of the first act. . . . Her whole behavior toward Antony is dominated by an element of calculation. [She always has at her disposal the] power of falling ill at the right time, of being seized by swoons and fits . . . and in every case her cleverness puts him in the wrong.[20]

Now there is a personage whose typical portrayal in Elizabethan literature is far closer to that described by Schücking than is the picture of Cleopatra which Shakespeare found in Plutarch. I refer to Venus, who is commonly presented not as a goddess of regal dignity but as a purely erotic woman, infinitely various, calculating, and lazy.[21] Nevertheless, I should not urge the importance of the model she offered Shakespeare—any more than, say, that of the Dark Lady sponsored by many critics—were it not for the context in which she most frequently appears. While Tudor poets were fascinated by her pursuits of Adonis and her humiliation with Mars in Vulcan's net, these classical stories are less prominent in Elizabethan literature than that of Mars's subjection to the goddess.

In *Venus and Adonis,* Venus boasts of her conquest of "the stern and direful god of war . . . Who conquers where he comes in every jar":

> Over my altars hath he hung his lance,
> His batt'rd shield, his uncontrolled crest,
> And for my sake hath learn'd to sport and dance,
> To toy, to wanton, dally, smile, and jest. . . .[22]

She is thus consciously superior to the passion which has enslaved her warrior, as is the Cleopatra of the first half, but not the second, of Shakespeare's tragedy. One of Greene's poems[23] depicts her, quite typically, converting Mars's jealous wrath into a meek plea of repentance. Whereas he had come armed for ven-

173

geance "gainst Loves brightest Queene," he remains to receive Venus' gracious forgiveness. This poem appears in a novella "setting out in lively portratures," as its title page announces, "how young Gentlemen that ayme at honour should levell the end of their affections, holding the love of countrie and friends in more esteeme then those fading blossoms of beautie that onely feede the curious survey of the eye." A Roman warrior, Lentulus, comes to grief because he abandons his Parthian campaign in favor of love.

Mars's subjection to the goddess became for Tudor soldier-alarmists a favorite symbol of the deterioration of England as a warlike state and of the folly of soldiers dallying in love.[24] Barnaby Rich not only warns conventionally of Venus and love in his tract *Allarme to England,* but illustrates fictionally his favorite theme in *A Right Exelent and Pleasaunt Dialogue, Betweene Mercury and an English Souldier* (1574). The English soldier goes on behalf of his fellow soldiers to petition Mars for greater respect and more employment. Mercury conducts the soldier (sig. M 1^v), inauspiciously, to Venus' court, "where Mars was layed in Venus lap." The soldier presents his grievance, but is interrupted (sig. M 2^v) when "the Goddess Venus sodainely arose in a great rage, as it semed, turning her selfe toward me." She rebukes the soldier for following war and for contemning her "creatures." Were not, she asks (sig. M 3), Hercules, Alexander, and other worthy warriors conquered by love? Venus' reproach daunts the soldier, but a reconciliation is achieved when Venus recognizes that she and the soldiers have much in common.

This is of course not drama, but it contains elements—such as Mars in Venus' lap and the petitioning soldier reconciled with Venus—which are given interesting dramatic arrangement in Robert Wilson's *The Cobbler's Prophecy.* Here Mars is not merely resting in Venus' lap; the symbol is enlarged to represent him as a conqueror shamefully tarrying in dotage. Following the alarmist model of the soldier-authors, Wilson shows Mercury deploring the security that has weakened the kingdom of Boeotia and pointing out Mars in the court of Venus:

> His Harnesse is converted to soft silke,
> His wares are onely wantonings with her.[25]

Mars has come down to see his love because he had just listened delightedly to Newfangle, her man, discussing Venus' vagaries with Nicenes, her maid. These two attendants, in caring for their inconstant lady, suggest the idleness of Cleopatra and her court. Newfangle had told Nicenes:

> That following of my Ladies humor thou dost make hir coy,
> For once a day for fashion sake my Lady must be sicke,
> No meat but mutton or at most the pinion of a chicke,
> To day hir owne haire best becomes which yellow is as gold,
> A perriwigs better for tomorrow, blacker to behold.
>
> (Sig. D 3)

Mars, thus arriving in sportive mood, finds Venus lonely and "half sickly by ill hap." Two visitors from earth then come to see Mars as he lies with his head on Venus' lap: Sateros, the conventional protesting soldier, and the Cobbler, charged by Mercury to awaken Mars and warn him of Venus' infidelity. Sateros promptly berates Mars for his effeminacy, complaining that he can scarcely recognize him with his "bodie lapt in soft silke which was wont to be clad in hard steele." Venus turns angrily upon this "rough shaped souldier enemie to love"; but reconciled by his entreaty for peace, she gives him a favor. The Cobbler, however, now comes forward with Mercury's message, which concludes:

> Then rouse thy selfe, then reach thy sword,
>   and win thy wonted fame.
>
> (Sig. D 4ᵛ)

Mars, rising "in a rage" while Venus "offers to staie him," exclaims at the thought of his love's abusing him for a person of no account:

> A dunghill cocke to tread my hen?
> Breake forth yee hangrie powers,
> And fill the world with bloodshed and with rage.

His reaction crudely suggests Antony's fury at Cleopatra's several misdemeanors, particularly when he detects her honoring Thyreus. But Venus, like Cleopatra, knows how to pacify her furious warrior with indulgent irony.[26] At his threat of revenge, she sighs:

> Aye me!
> Revenge true Lovers wrongs immortall powers,
> And nere let Lady trust a souldier.
> *Make as if shee swounds.*

At this point Mars is reduced to frightened penitence, especially when Venus assures him that he has slaine "her whome your honny words cannot recure againe." But she fortunately recovers and takes him on her lap again, while Nicenes, Newfangle, Dalliance, and Jealozie entertain with music. Presently, however, Mars wakes to find that Venus has deserted him for the base Contempt. All Venus' attendants run away, while Mars resolves to make war and regain his manhood:

> Gainst wantonnes proclaime I open warre. . . .
> These wanton ornaments for maskers fit
> Will Mars leave off, and sute him selfe in steele,
> And strumpet Venus with that vile Contempt
> I will pursue unto the depth of hell.
>
> (Sig. E 2)

We appropriately see him finally on the battlefield helping Sateros with his wars.

The play is of course an allegorical dramatization of an "alarm" tractate, and the characters are constructed to show the debilitating effect on kingdom and warriors of security, luxury, and love. Hence, although Venus is not without the charms of evil women, these charms are necessarily destined for a bad end. She is deprived of godhood and condemned (Sig. E 4ᵛ) to be called only "the detested name of lust, or strumpet Venus."

Venus, then, is a purely erotic character: love is her only occupation and her charms are solely those of idleness. She is various and contrary in mood and has, like Cleopatra, "a celerity in dying." She can check the temper of her warrior, but not ultimately keep him from breaking away to his rightful business. Most important for our purpose, she is confronted by angry soldiers who try to reclaim their conquering general. In the opprobrium heaped on her, she resembles Cleopatra seen through the eyes of Philo, Scarus, and Enobarbus or the angry eyes of Antony. Just as she is branded "lust" and "strumpet," so in Philo's denunciatory lines Antony is likened to a "plated Mars" now become a "strumpet's fool" and subject to a "gipsy's lust." There is also an interesting parallel between the ways in which the two women treat the "rough shaped souldier enemie to love." Mac-Callum aptly observes the "little touch of irony, apt to be overlooked," in the fact that Scarus, "who has cursed Cleopatra's magic and raged because kingdoms were kissed away, should now as grand reward have his merits commended to 'this great fairy,' and as highest honour have leave to raise her hand—the hand that cost Thyreus so dear—to his own lips." [27] In Plutarch, Scarus is featureless and had never abused Cleopatra.

IV

One can, therefore, consistently find most of the structural elements for the opening acts of Shakespeare's tragedy—the elements wanting in Plutarch's narrative—in Elizabethan plays which depict the struggle, internal and external, of the conqueror impeded by love. There were the protesting soldiers, their traditional form of lament for the idle conqueror, the unsympathetic attitude toward the seductress, and the question affording the primary tension: Will the conqueror regain his lost manhood and resume his warlike work? Antony does not successfully break away, and for an Elizabethan audience that fact would have constituted the end of a complete drama told within the first two or three acts. His soldiers, signaling his defeat, gradually leave him.

Did Shakespeare acquire the structure for this drama from the plays, *novelle,* and alarmist tracts dealing with conquerors and

177

their soldiers, or did the structure come to him directly from a dramatic reading of Plutarch? Neither alternative is really necessary. Without denying his ability independently to reshape prose narrative for the theater, one may nevertheless suppose that he turned, more or less consciously, to a dramatic pattern which not only was ready-made for his subject but had proved itself both successful and necessary on the stage. Certainly it seems safe to say that some ideas for the stress created by the repeated rebuke from the soldiers came from the convention which placed them in opposition to a seductress, whether or not she was Venus.

University of California, Los Angeles

NOTES

[1] A. W. Ward's statement (*A History of English Dramatic Literature* [London, 1899], II, 186) typifies conservative opinion: *"The Life of Antonius* in North's version of Plutarch is, so far as is known, the solitary source of Shakespeare's tragedy." George Wyndham, in his enthusiastic Introduction to North in the Tudor Translations, affirms (VII, xciv) that "throughout the first three acts all the colour and the incident, throughout the last two all the incident and the passion," are from North. J. W. Draper, studying "The Realism of Shakespeare's Roman Plays" (*SP*, XXX [1933], 225-242), notes that whereas in *Julius Caesar* Shakespeare paid little attention to classical authenticity, in *Antony and Cleopatra* he followed Plutarch "so closely that Coleridge called it a chronicle history." Though suggesting a few other influences, Kenneth Muir agrees with the closeness of Shakespeare's dependence upon North. See *Shakespeare's Sources*, I (London, 1957), 201-219.

[2] In this respect only Samuel Daniel and, to a lesser extent, Appian, have proved rewarding. R. H. Case found "resemblances more or less slight" between Shakespeare's play and Daniel's *Cleopatra* (Introduction to his English Arden Edition of the Play, Eighth Edition, p. x). For indebtedness to Daniel's *Letter from Octavia to Marcus Antonius*, see R. C. Bald, "Shakespeare and Daniel," *T.L.S.*, Nov. 20, 1924, p. 776; Willard Farnham, *Shakespeare's Tragic Frontier* (Berkeley, 1950), pp. 172-173; and Joan Rees, "Shakespeare's Use of Daniel," *MLR*, LV (1960), 79-82.

[3] M. W. MacCallum believes that the obligations to Plutarch "become conspicious a little before the middle of the third act" (*Shakespeare's Roman Plays and Their Background* [London, 1925], p. 327). But it is this first part that has received the least attention from critics, possibly because of the greater emotional appeal of the finale.

178

4 Farnham, p. 175.

5 *The life of Marcus Antonius, Plutarch's Lives,* Englished by Sir Thomas North, The Tudor Translations, ed. W. E. Henley, XII, 2, 4, 24.

6 *The Living Shakespeare* (New York, 1949), p. 981.

7 I discuss this kind of conflict in "Shakespeare's Coriolanus: Elizabethan Soldier," *PMLA,* LXIV (1949), 221-235.

8 *1 Tamburlaine,* V.i.58, ed. U. M. Ellis-Fermor (London, 1930).

9 *The Warres of Cyrus King of Persia* (London, 1594), Tudor Facsimile Texts, sig. B 3. "They that would be conquerors," Cyrus later reaffirms (sig. F 1$^\text{v}$), "Should chiefly learne to conquer their desire."

10 Samuel Brandon, *The Tragicomoedi of the vertuous Octavia* (London, 1598), Tudor Facsimile Texts, sig. E 5$^\text{v}$.

11 *Campaspe,* II. ii. 52, *The Complete Works of John Lyly,* ed. R. Warwick Bond (Oxford, 1902). The resemblance to Philo's speech is noted by Bond, but not by editors of Shakespeare. This type of protest is not original with Lyly, although he gave it its most significant expression for the Elizabethan drama. Ovid's Briseis protests similarly to Achilles (*Heroides,* III), as does his Dejanira to Hercules (*Heroides,* IX). A comparable lament by Dejanira is found in Seneca's *Hercules Œtæus,* Act II. Lyly was especially influential in the dramatic convention which assigned the protest to either a soldier or a chorus of soldiers.

12 *Campaspe,* II. ii. 62-76.

13 *The Tragedie of Caesar and Pompey. Or Caesars Revenge* (London, 1607), Tudor Facsimile Texts, sig. D 1.

14 Caesar's struggle is not found in Plutarch's *Life of Julius Caesar,* which devotes only two or three pages to Cleopatra (*ed. cit.,* XI, 50-52) and which gives no hint of dotage.

15 Fletcher's *The False One* (*c.* 1620), in dealing with much the same segment of history as this drama, likewise employs the conventional dramatic pattern. Influenced no doubt by Shakespeare's play, it employs in addition to Dollobella, the comic "free Speaker" Sceva as a protesting captain. Sceva has some of Enobarbus' irony, a quality which I do not find in drama earlier than Shakespeare's. Sceva follows the tradition which makes a rough soldier present the seductress' beauties to his general, but he does so in an ingenious manner. It is he, unwittingly and unhistorically, who carries Cleopatra to Caesar in a "packet" and ever after abuses himself as "a Bawd grown in mine old days."

16 See R. B. Sharpe, *The Real War of the Theaters* (Boston, 1935), p. 198. A. M. Clark would date it later than 1609; see his *Thomas Heywood* (Oxford, 1931), p. 63. The Herculean tradition behind Shakespeare's Antony is ably described by Eugene M. Waith, *The Herculean Hero in Marlowe, Chapman, Shakespeare and Dryden* (New York, 1962), pp. 113-121.

17 *The Brazen Age* (London, 1613), sig. K 1$^\text{v}$.

179

[18] *Ibid.,* sig. K 2ᵛ. R. H. Case notes the resemblance of these lines to Cleopatra's boast in *Antony and Cleopatra,* II.v.21:

> I drunk him to his bed,
> Then put my tires and mantles on him. . . .

Hercules was of course Antony's supposed ancestor.

[19] Case, Introduction, p. xvii.

[20] L. L. Schücking, *Character Problems in Shakespeare's Plays* (New York, 1922), pp. 121-125.

[21] Certain resemblances between Cleopatra and Shakespeare's Venus have been suggested by Adrien Bonjour, "From Shakespeare's Venus to Cleopatra's Cupids," *Shakespeare Survey 15* (Cambridge, 1962), 73-80, and by J. W. Lever, "Venus and the Second Chance," *Ibid.,* 81-88. See also, for another probable influence, Michael Lloyd "Cleopatra as Isis," *Shakespeare Survey 12* (Cambridge, 1955), 88-94. For an interesting article, showing Antony's enslavement not only to lust but to gluttony and sloth, see J. Leeds Barroll, "Antony and Pleasure," *JEGP,* LVII (1958), 708-720. In the same author's "Enobarbus' Description of Cleopatra," *Texas Studies in English,* XXXVII (1958), 61-78, an article which I did not see before composing the present study, Venus is studied as an example of the *voluptas* figure, enticing the Herculean Antony who is at the crossroads. Mr. Barroll thus stresses, as do I, the conflict within Antony. None of the foregoing, however, concentrates upon the important dramatic tradition of the *soldier* in love and the role of the protesting soldiers.

[22] *Venus and Adonis,* lines 97-106.

[23] Song from *Ciceronis Amor, Tullies Love* (ed. 1589), in *The Life and Complete Works . . . of Robert Greene,* ed. Grosart (London, 1881-86), VII, 133-134.

[24] In his translation, *The Preceptes of Warre* (1544), Peter Bentham warns (sig. B 3) that when captains "doo applye suche wanton pleasures, and gyve them to Venus Daliaunce, then they forsake the feates of Armes, and despice the manlye wrestlynges of Mars. For hys goddas doth destroy the courage of the minde and wasteth the strength of the bodye." Dudley Digges, in *Foure Paradoxes* (1604), pp. 84-85, protests that "the folly of some souldiers in time of Idlenesse hath given some colour to the fable of Mars and Venus," but he "cannot see how the profession can deserve that imputation." Poets, lawyers, and other idlers, Digges reasons, are more subject to Venus than are active warriors. Lodowick Flood, in commendatory verses to Rich's *Allarme to England* (1578), tells his countrymen to "March forth with Mars, clap corslets on, ring larum loud apace," and "Let Venus be." For, he points out,

> What worthie Cyrus gaynd by warres, what noble Ninus wanne,
> That Sardanapalus lost by sloth, even from thassyrians then.

The homely lines of these soldier-authors may have partially suggested the role of the protesting soldiers in the conqueror dramas.

[25] Robert Wilson, *The Coblers Prophesie* (London, 1594), Malone Society Reprints, sig. A 3. This scene follows the tableau pattern noted in the first scene of *Antony and Cleopatra.*

[26] Astrology supported Venus' mollifying influence on Mars. According to Ficino, a man born under Mars has "greatness of soul" and "a temper." If the influence of Venus follows, "she does not check that virtue of a great soul given him by Mars, but she does suppress the vice of temper. Hence she seems to master and appease Mars, 'but Mars never masters Venus.' " *(Marsilio Ficino's Commentary on Plato's "Symposium,"* translated by Sears Jayne, *The Univ. of Missouri Studies,* v. XIX, no. 1, p. 177.) See also Robert Greene's *Planetomachia* (London, 1585), Second Part, fol. 9ᵛ.

[27] MacCallum, p. 360.

BAROQUE ASPECTS
OF *ANTONY AND CLEOPATRA*

EDITH M. ROERECKE

Much has been written to prove or to disprove that Shakespeare's plays are examples of the baroque style in dramatic poetry.[1] Some of this literary criticism based upon art analogy, it seems to me, is confused and often silly because first, the definitions of the term *baroque* which are usually offered are too inclusive; and second, Shakespeare's dramas are too often treated as if they were all of a piece. German critics from the 1930's had been calling Shakespeare's plays either baroque or mannerist—often without much definition of those terms or recognition of their national and chronological phases. These difficulties were noted briefly by Roy Daniels as far back as 1945 when he pointed out not only that the literary styles of the Renaissance had several stages only one of which was baroque, but also that Shakespeare reflected these various stages. Said Daniels:

> Anxious as one might be to keep off the knotty problem of the connection, if any, between the art of Shakespeare and baroque, it is impossible not to suspect a relation between the progression from high renaissance to baroque and the evolution of form from the symmetrical arrangements of *A Comedy of Errors* to the looser structure of, say, *Lear* in which the demands of the tragic theme are satisfied by a preoccupation with the total effect of the play—with its shape as a unified whole.[2]

Although Daniels' treatment of the art periods failed to be specific as to developments which lay between the high renaissance and the late baroque,[3] he did recognize that as far as structure was concerned, there was not merely one Shakespeare; there were several.

182

In 1955 Prof. Wylie Sypher attempted to clarify the evolution of sixteenth and seventeenth century style from high renaissance through mannerism and baroque to late baroque and to trace Shakespeare's dramatic development through the first three of these stages.[4] Although occasional critics have neglected Sypher's book, perhaps out of a conservative preference for time-honored confusions,[5] it may be that Prof. Sypher has made a certain orderliness via oversimplification, and the need is for further refinements. For example, Prof. Briganti distinguishes three consecutive forms of Italian mannerism, all of which are distinct from the French mannerism discussed by Sir Anthony Blunt, and Prof. Wittkower distinguishes four phases of Roman baroque, plus those of Venice and Piedmont, all of which are different from baroque as it was developed in Germany or France.[6] Notwithstanding these difficulties, we seem for the most part to be on our way to a better understanding of Shakespeare in terms of the esthetic climate of his time. I therefore venture to examine one of Shakespeare's great plays from his last, half-holiday period. If Shakespeare is baroque anywhere he is baroque in *Antony and Cleopatra*.

The first task is, of course, to define baroque. I would agree with René Wellek that baroque should not be thought of "in purely stylistic terms" (which, he shows us, recur throughout literary history), but rather "in more general terms of a philosophy or a world-view or even merely an emotional attitude toward the world," [7] such as occurred between the late 1500's to the mid-1700's. Most critics seem to agree with this "world-view" notion, which Sypher wisely qualifies, however, by reminding us that we must allow for individual differences in temperament operating within this larger historical scope.

E. B. O. Borgerhoff, who sees baroque as a fusion of the classic renaissance tradition and the "expressive" reaction against this tradition, also concurs with this *Weltanschauung* notion of baroque. He attempts to narrow down the period to a more specific time. He says:

That something happened to Europe around the year 1580 is pretty clear; the evidence is in the literature and in the arts. Precisely *what* happened we ought to try to discover. [Other writers can be more specific here.[8]] That it did happen needs no demonstration. That for one reason or another this wave of disturbed expressiveness which is called mannerism was followed, even in Spain, by a certain calming down is equally evident.[9]

I think I would not have chosen the words "calming down" (in spite of Mr. Borgerhoff's qualifications), but the baroque reaction to mannerism indicated a much greater certainty about life than had been prevalent before. Let me cite Wylie Sypher again:

> In general, then, baroque art has an effect of decision, release, and fulfillment; and resonantly declares the glories of heaven and earth. After the crisis in mannerist conscience, with its repressions, defections, complexities, and double evasive answers, its dissonant, involved contours, baroque performs a mighty katharsis by spectacle, by an expressive power. The baroque canon of style does not depend upon mannerist contingencies, but upon assurances and certainties —certainties lacking the mannerist sublety and discrimination. These certainties, confidently affirmed, are exhilarating to the eye even if they are not wholly convincing to the mind. But then, baroque is able to win assent from the spirit through its power over the sensorium alone.[10]

And how is this "certainty" manifested in the arts? By the artists' use of spectacle, robustness, paradox, bombast, color, light, motion, massiveness, spaciousness, sensuousness. By the portrayal of passion, horror, and self-determination. These are the lifeblood which quickens the ceaseless activity of the sculpture; the vivid color, the *chiaroscuro* and the restless, off-balanced accent of the paintings; the curved, undulating lines of the massive architecture; the *tuttis* and the intricate counterpoint of the newly born *concerto grosso;* the soaring and restless garden fountains; the elaborate operas on revolving stages.[11]

"After the bloodless and shrunken mannerist forms, the baroque is a style of plenitude, capable of absorbing, and robustly transforming to grandeur, every sort of realism. It is an art given to superlatives." [12] And it was in this spiritual setting that Shakespeare wrote *Antony and Cleopatra.* It is the last of the great tragedies, yet Shakespeare's treatment is wholly baroque when one compares it to a distressed, harsh, and bizarre mannerist tragedy

such as *Hamlet,* or the bitter comedy *Troilus and Cressida.* Yet
it is also a far cry from the serene, rather naïve, carefully measured
high-renaissance tragedy that *Romeo and Juliet* represents.[13]

How can one escape the aptness for *Antony and Cleopatra* of
such terms as "katharsis by spectacle," "epic hero," "pageantry,"
"mutability," "overstatement," "paradox," "the transfiguration
to grandeur of realism," "decision," "release," "fulfillment,"
"color," "energy," and "mass"? This play has all these elements.
Shakespeare immerses us in the panorama of the ancient world
where we, as spectators, are hurriedly shifted back and forth between Egypt, the land of fruitfulness and decay, and Rome, the
land of honor and treachery; where, when we are in Egypt, our
thoughts are turned to Rome, when in Rome, our senses are
pulled back to Egypt; and where the vastness of the setting (constantly reinforced by the imagery) promises us, finally, that beyond this huge world there lies yet another.[14]

If the vast setting and the hurried action do not leave us
breathless, then certainly the two protagonists do. As Sir Arthur
Quiller-Couch has it, Antony and Cleopatra are great "as the gods
are great, high-heartedly, carelessly, . . . indifferent to consist-
ency." [15] The paradoxical Queen of Egypt is arrogant, volatile,
unscrupulous, witty, sensual, and grand. Her passions are enor-
mous and splendid—she is indeed "a wonderfull peece of worke."
Enobarbus says of her:

> Age cannot wither her, nor custom stale
> Her infinite variety: other women cloy
> The appetites they feede, but she makes hungry,
> Where most she satisfies. For vildest things
> Become themselves in her, that the holy Priests
> Blesse her, when she is Riggish.
>
> (II.ii.274-79)[16]

To her lover she is the "foul Egyptian," but also the "day o'
th' world." And when she weeps, her sighs and tears are like
wind and water—"they are greater stormes and Tempests than
Almanackes can report."

Counterpart to Cleopatra is the Herculean Antony—a man
valiant, audacious, self-indulgent, unprincipled and passionate.

185

Antony is "the Crowne o' th' earth," a "triple Pillar of the
world," "the demy *Atlas* of this Earth." "In his Livery / Walk'd
Crownes and Crownets: Realms and Islands were / As plates
dropt from his pocket." Alexas refers to his moods in terms of
the seasons; Lepidus to his goodness and his faults in celestial
terms; Euphronius to his affairs as like a "grand Sea" compared
to which the objectives of other men seem like drops of dew.
Cleopatra gives us this picture:

> His legges bestrid the Ocean, his rear'd arme
> Crested the world: His voyce was propertied
> As all the tuned Spheres, and that to Friends:
> But when he meant to quaile, and shake the Orbe,
> He was as ratling thunder. For his Bounty,
> There was no winter in't. An *Anthony* it was,
> That grew the more by reaping: His delights
> Were Dolphin-like, they shew'd his backe above
> The Element they liv'd in.
>
> (V.ii.101-109)

And when Antony died, even his opponent, Caesar, reacted with
thought of universal repercussion:

> The breaking of so great a thing, should make
> A greater cracke. The round World
> Should have shooke Lyons into civill streets,
> And Cittizens to their dennes. The death of *Anthony*
> Is not a single doome, in the name lay
> A moity of the world.
>
> (V.i.19-24)

We are here indeed dealing with mass, energy, spectacle and
paradox; and as I mentioned earlier, the imagery and the tempo
of the verse reëcho the baroque flavor of the characterization and
the setting.

Shakespeare gives mass to his swift dialogue by the repetition
of words and phrases, of which I offer only a random sampling.

O madam, madam, madam!
I am dying, Egypt, dying.
O, come, come, come.
He words me, girls, he words me.
Husband win, win brother.
Well, is it? is it?
But why? why? why?

Or witness Charmian's opening speech of the second scene in the first act: *"Alexas,* sweet *Alexas,* most anything *Alexas,* almost most absolute *Alexas. . . ."* And further on in Act I we see these echo devices being used to add mass to the dialogue between Antony and Enobarbus—a perfect example of functioning redundancy:

> *Ant.* Fulvia is dead.
> *Eno.* Sir.
> *Ant.* Fulvia is dead.
> *Eno.* Fulvia?
> *Ant.* Dead.
>
> (79-83)

In the third scene also we have Cleopatra speaking these moving lines:

> Sir, you and I must part, but that's not it:
> Sir, you and I have lov'd, but there's not it.
>
> (109-110)

For the most part, of course, this *Worthäufung* is dramatically effective, and rarely does it intrude to the point of seeming unnatural or disturbing.

On the other hand, Shakespeare's mastery of enjambment by the use of light and weak endings, his rejection of conventional syntax, his ability to place the mid-line pause at any point in the line—all these devices contribute toward infusing mass with movement. The passages spoken by Caesar in Act III are examples. Shakespeare's cataloguing of the glittering place names found in North is quite as grandiloquent as are the lists of Milton. Consider:

> Great Media, Parthia, and Armenia
> He gave to *Alexander*. To Ptolomy he assign'd,
> Syria, Silicia, and Phoenetia
>
> (vi.15-17)

And:

> He hath assembled,
> *Bochus* the king of Lybia, *Archilaus*
> Of Cappadocia, *Philadelphos* King
> Of Paphlagonia: the Thracian King *Adullas*,
> King *Mauchus* of Arabia, King of Pont,
> *Herod* of Jewry, *Mithridates* King
> Of Comageat, *Polemen* and *Amintas*,
> The Kings of Mede, and Licoania,
> With a more larger Lift of Scepters.
>
> (vi.75-83)

Enjambment, of course, is not the poet's only device to keep his masses in motion. He uses imagery and counterpoint as well. One critic points to Cleopatra's invocation in Act IV as an example of thin sounds and feminine endings being set against richer, masculine cadences so that "the result is a certain lilting, rippling, melody curiously countering the tragic passion beneath." [17] The lines he has reference to are:

> Oh Sunne,
> Burne the great Sphere thou mou'st in, darkling stand
> The varrying shore o' th' world.
>
> (IV.xv.16-18)

F. E. Halliday also examines extensively the use of counterpoint by Shakespeare, and he cites the famous description of Cleopatra on the river Cydnus as a perfect example. Halliday says,

North secures his effect without the aid of imagery, yet, as Mr. Middleton Murray has shown, it is Shakespeare's imagery that articulates and gives a new significance to North's description, by representing the winds, the water, and the air as overcome with love for Cleopatra. . . .

North makes no mention of "water," but Shakespeare contrives *water . . . follow faster . . . fancy outwork nature,* all of them words which by their position in the line induce a counterrhythm, so that the verse is interpenetrated and harmonized by assonance and a secondary measure, each of which is dependent on the other for its full emphasis and extension. It is only in *Anthony and Cleopatra* that Shakespeare brings this counterpoint to perfection, by the full exploitation of the redundant syllable and mid-line pause.[18]

Thus, the addition of the moving elements and the counterpoint give the "mass" of the passage (both literally and figuratively) impetus and energy.

The employment of imagery to add movement appears elsewhere in the play too. G. Wilson Knight has noted the preponderance of "melting" imagery: "Let Rome in Tyber melt," and its companion thought, "Melt Egypt into Nyle." There is also the melting that is death in "The Crowne o' th' earth doth melt." [19]

Caroline Spurgeon notes use of verbs and adjectives of motion in the play ("the visiting moon," Antony's dophin-like delights); she also pointed out the movement of Antony's disturbed stars (III.xiii.174-76) and the motion imagery throughout Caesar's "instability of fame" speech in Act I:

> It hath bin taught vs from the primall state
> That he which is was wisht, untill he were:
> And the ebb'd man,
> Ne're lou'd, till ne're worth loue,
> Comes fear'd, by being lack'd. This common bodie,
> Like to a Vagabond Flagge upon the Streame,
> Goes too, and backe, lacking the varrying tyde
> To rot it selfe with motion.
>
> (I.iv.47-54)[20]

189

The imagery, moreover, not only adds motion and mass, but also reëchoes the paradox to be found in the shifting values of the play. The wind kindles but also cools—"the Bellowes and the Fan . . . / coole a Gypsies Lust"; the "diuers coulour'd Fannes whose winde did seeme, / To gloue the delicate cheekes which they did coole, / And what they vndid did." The asp both suckles and kills. The Nile is both a grave and a source of life. The priests are holy, but they also bless the riggishness in Cleopatra. And, finally, Cleopatra herself "makes hungry, / Where most she satisfies."

The style also reflects the baroque element of theatricality which is so overpowering in the setting. The often fustian speeches uttered by the characters, some portions of which I have already quoted, can certainly be labeled as examples of baroque elaboration. The extravagant "apostrophes to the sun, the heavens, the elements, virtues, vices, and gods; [the] exaggerated wishes, the ranted resolutions" [21]—all are examples of the excess which the play is full of. Then, too, there is to be found what Imbrie Buffum calls "the predilection for horrifying subjects vividly portrayed" [22] which, though most typical of mannerist art, still occurs quite often in baroque. It appears here too, but the impulse to employ it is hardly as strong in Shakespeare during this period of his production as it was in his previous mannerist phase. Antony, when in his prime as a warrior, could drink "the stale of Horses" and "eate strange flesh, / Which some did dye to looke on"—a fairly innocent example of horror. So too is Cleopatra's speech in Act III:

> . . . the next Caesarian smile [smite?]
> Till by degrees the memory of my wombe,
> Together with my braue Egyptians all,
> By the discandering of this pelleted storme,
> Lye grauelesse, till the Flies and Gnats of Nyle
> Have buried them for prey.
>
> (xiii.194-99)

So much, then, for the form of *Antony and Cleopatra* as it conforms to the general style of the baroque period. But if, as Wellek pointed out, the baroque had a particular world view as well as a particular style, then the next task is to consider the theme of the play.

190

That there is controversy about the meaning of the play is a well-known fact. Lord David Cecil puts his finger on the problem nicely:

> *Antony and Cleopatra* has been discussed by all sorts of eminent persons from Coleridge downwards. And some of its most important features have been examined exhaustively. It would be a waste of your time and mine should I force you to listen to yet another application of the varied splendour of its poetic style, or the iridescent brilliance with which Shakespeare has portrayed . . . Cleopatra. . . . [yet] in spite of all the praise that has been lavished upon it, its position among Shakespeare's work has remained ambiguous. . . .[23]

Is *Antony and Cleopatra* basically a hymn to transcendental love, or is it really a morality play? As Franklin M. Dickey, who takes the latter view, points out:

> Like Dante, Shakespeare presents a moral universe. If he did not sit down to write plays to illustrate ethical doctrine, his work is informed by a system of morality. Shakespeare's ethics are part of his art. . . . Elizabethan didacticism, however, is less formidable than it sounds. By "didacticism" we should understand something a great deal more exciting than sermonizing. Renaissance poets habitually designed sensuous description to persuade rather than merely to ornament; poets strove to delight, but in delighting they aimed to move the soul in order to convince it of conceptual truth.[24]

Hence Dickey can rationalize the impact of Cleopatra's "iridescent brilliance" by reminding us that although she is magnificent she is also destructive. And he concludes, "Were sin not alluring, who would sin?"[25]

But, somehow, few can share Mr. Dickey's concern about "sin" when reading the play. Most reactions seem to fall closer to those of G. Wilson Knight, who belongs to the love-is-a-purifying-flame school. Yet Knight, in spite of his rhapsodic style, does state the case rather well in this passage:

> Without shirking any ugly facts or colourings of "realism" the poet expresses the finest delights of his vision. Within this whole dualisms so starkly divergent in the sombre plays

191

are all resolved, dissolved, melted into a sublime unity. We must be prepared to see all elements herein of sordidness resolved in a total beauty. . . . The whole structure is like a wide window: look at it obtusely—from the strictly ethical and didactic view—and you see little beyond it; draw nearer . . . and you stare full in the face of the sun-kissed expanse outside.[26]

That most critics are so ready to give assent to the grandness of the passion in this play is rather perplexing, particularly in our rather Apollonian world. But, if we think back to Wylie Sypher's definition of baroque (cited above), some of this perplexity might vanish:

In general, then, baroque art has an effect of decision, release, and fulfillment; and resonantly declares the glories of heaven and earth. . . . [It] performs a mighty katharsis by spectacle, by an expressive power. . . . [Baroque certainties are] confidently affirmed, are *exhilarating to the eye even if they are not wholly convincing to the mind. But then, baroque is able to win assent from the spirit through its power over the sensorium alone.* [Italics mine.]

Yes, generally we do approve of what Antony does, in spite of what our rational judgment may tell us. Perhaps this approval is, in Freudian terms, merely projection. But, more likely, our reaction is in response to the sheer magnificence of the play and of the two towering people who move in it. Though Antony falls, and though his downfall is a product of his own willfulness, Shakespeare makes of that will (to live, to love, and to die) a *grand* folly.

Antony is, therefore (if we use Sypher's criteria), the true baroque hero. His internal conflict is as severe as that of Hamlet. But consider Sypher's statement in which he compares to Hamlet another baroque literary hero:

. . . the scale of passion is heroic and impersonal; he is a mythical, archetypal Captive, Sufferer, and Contestant. His psychological vocabulary is not the fastidious, evasive language of Hamlet, who gives himself over, sicklied with thought, to the intrigue of the metaphysical mind with its own responses, random, exploratory, indecisive. . . . The baroque psychology has reduced and simplified . . . emotions, which are magnified to epic pain. . . . [And the] baroque action is "total" in gesture and energy, ruinous and final as is the fall of Satan or the exile from the Garden.[27]

This, of course, is Sypher describing Milton's Samson, a typical baroque hero. But is this not also Antony?

In conclusion, then, we can say that Shakespeare was baroque in his last stage of development, and *Antony and Cleopatra* serves as a fine example of baroque art. What closer literary analogy can we have to the art, the music, and the architecture of this period? Some critics will still reject the use of analogy between the arts as useful in literary criticism, others may subscribe to Roy Daniels' remark, "There is excellent fun to be had in the slightly disreputable pursuit of poaching across the boundaries which separate the arts." [28] Mr. Daniels is perhaps a bit naïve here. The boundaries of which he speaks are an aspect of modern intellectual fragmentation. Sixteenth and seventeenth century quadratura painting deliberately blended the arts so thoroughly that at times, as in Cortona's Barberini ceiling, it is impossible for the uninitiated viewer to tell what is painting and what is sculpture. Poets and philosophers commonly wrote the programs for important frescoes in palaces and churches. Certainly Verrocchio, Leonardo, Raphael, or Michelangelo would have been surprised or amused to learn that if one's chief concern is sculpture, he should neglect painting, or that if one does spread over those two, that he therefore should not dabble in poetry, architecture, politics, or science. Their surprise would have been shared in the seventeenth century by Bernini, Cortona, and Rubens. If contemporaneous intellectual history is relevant to a dramatic work, so is contemporaneous esthetics. Both have much to tell us about those stage directions which we do not inherit and therefore must supply to mount a modern production.

The Pennsylvania State University

NOTES

1   René Wellek gives a most thorough treatment of the subject in his "The Concept of Baroque in Literary Scholarship," *JAAC*, v (December 1946), 77-109.

2   "Baroque Form in English Literature," *University of Toronto Quarterly*, xiv (1945), 399.

3   He does not mention mannerism as such, but he does see baroque as a fusion of the "high renaissance accompanied by a reaction against it." (p. 396) This "reaction" is what is now so commonly called mannerism.

4   *Four Stages of Renaissance Style* (Garden City, N.Y., 1955). Sypher wisely cautions us that we must not assume that every artist necessarily follows this evolution. He points out that "in any period as fertile as the renaissance two or more different styles can be current at not only the same moment in different artists but even in the same artist." (pp. 17-18)

5   Patrick Cruttwell is an example. In his "Shakespeare and the Baroque," *SJ* (1961), pp. 100-108, he is still confusing baroque and mannerist, and he is still treating Shakespeare's work as a homogeneous entity. In all fairness to Mr. Cruttwell, however, one must point out that he is working across national lines, and Odette de Mourgues has shown that ". . . European terminology is a battlefield. In France the baroque and the précieux do not yield much ground to each other. In England baroque and, recently, its offspring mannerism, have slipped in as a menace to the well-defined word metaphysical. . . . Germans use baroque chiefly. When specialists get together there is confusion." (*Metaphysical, Baroque, and Précieux Poetry* [Oxford, 1953], pp. 3-4.) The situation is not quite as chaotic as Miss de Mourgues would have it, however, for since the fifties there seems to be greater agreement about the definition of the term *baroque*.

6   Giuliano Briganti, *Italian Mannerism* (London, 1962), pp. 5-56; Anthony Blunt, *Art and Architecture in France, 1500-1700* (London, 1957), pp. 33-110; Rudolf Wittkower, *Art and Architecture in Italy, 1600-1750* (London, 1958).

7   *Op. cit.*, pp. 92-93.

8   Sypher, for example, cites the Council of Trent which having "convened in a climate of mannerist doubt, laid the foundations for a settlement of theology and a reintegration of style in the arts. . . ." (*op. cit.*, p. 180)

9   " 'Mannerism' and 'Baroque': A Simple Plea," *CL*, v (1953), 327.

10 *Op. cit.*, p. 185.

11 William Fleming, "The Element of Motion in Baroque Art and Music," *JAAC*, v (December 1946), 121-128.

12 Sypher, p. 181.

13 Sypher gives a brief analysis of the structure and content of *Romeo and Juliet* in terms of its high-renaissance qualities. (*op. cit.*, p. 80)

14 A favorite trick of the baroque artist, according to Sypher. He explains that "authentic baroque space arises from a contradiction: first, setting

monumental limits by melodramatically opening a vista beyond them, thus seeming to perform a heroic feat of liberation. Infinity is the boldest baroque spatial illusion." (*op. cit.*, p. 214)

[15] *Studies in Literature* (New York, 1922), p. 204.

[16] William Shakespeare, *The Tragedie of Anthonie and Cleopatra*, ed. Horace Howard Furness. New Variorum Edition (Philadelphia, 1907). All references to the play will cite this edition.

[17] G. Wilson Knight, *The Imperial Theme*, p. 202.

[18] *The Poetry of Shakespeare's Plays* (London, 1954), p. 162.

[19] *Op. cit.*, pp. 235-239.

[20] *Shakespeare's Imagery* (New York, 1936), pp. 22-52.

[21] Richard David, *The Janus of Poets* (London, 1935), p. 97. This is from his definition of bombast.

[22] *Agrippa d'Aubigné's "Les Tragiques": A Study of the Baroque Style in Poetry* (New Haven, 1951), p. 153.

[23] *Antony and Cleopatra* (Glasgow, 1944), pp. 6-7.

[24] *Not Wisely But Too Well* (San Marino, California, 1957), pp. 9, 12.

[25] *Ibid.*, p. 187.

[26] *Op. cit.*, pp. 255-256.

[27] *Op. cit.*, p. 229. Strangely enough, Sypher, with his clear understanding of baroque art, singles out *Othello* rather than *Antony and Cleopatra* as the example of the baroque in Shakespeare. Yet by Sypher's own definition, the baroque hero's battle with the world is self-determined. It seems to me that Antony who, in Enobarbus's words, makes "his will Lord of his Reason," would serve as a much better example. In *Antony and Cleopatra* we have none of the evil machinations of an Iago. Antony makes his decision quite of his own accord: "Heere is my space, / Kingdomes are clay: Our dungie earth alike / Feeds Beast as Man; the Noblenesse of life / Is to do thus. . . ." (I.i.47-50)

[28] *Op. cit.*, p. 408.

"EXCELLENT DUMB DISCOURSE": THE LIMITS OF LANGUAGE IN *THE TEMPEST*

W. T. JEWKES

Sentimental it may be, as many critics charge, to consider *The Tempest* as Shakespeare's "last word." Yet, fashions of criticism to the contrary, it is only by closing the ears to one whole level of the structure of this shortest of his mature plays that we could congratulate ourselves on being appropriately "unsentimental" about it. Not that Shakespeare was sentimental, at least not in this pejorative critical sense; he can never be accused of that. Nor is it fair to equate Prospero with Shakespeare himself and place all the weight of the evidence on Prospero's "lie there, my art," and breaking his staff, and drowning his book, tempting as the association may be. But the fact is, *The Tempest* is Shakespeare's play about language in a way that no other is, not even *Love's Labour's Lost*, or *Hamlet*, or *Macbeth*, or *Lear*. While those plays touch more heavily than others on certain aspects of language (in a sense, of course, one could inanely argue that all the plays are to one degree or another about language), none of them is really *about* language in the way that *The Tempest* is. In this what I must call Shakespeare's last word, we find all the former concerns about language gathered together. We discover the puns and wit of *Love's Labour's Lost* in the brittle scene between Gonzalo, Antonio, and Sebastian (II.i); the paralyzing effect of thought in *Hamlet* in the distracting Act IV; the equivocation of the fiend in the murder plot between Antonio and Sebastian; and the handy-dandy of *Lear* in the ironic, parodic antics of Stephano, Trinculo, and Caliban. We find all these gathered together—and so much more.

Shakespeare seems always to have been fascinated by the problems of two major modes of communication—sight and speech.

196

If *King Lear* can be called Shakespeare's most passionate and final disclosure of the difference between sight and insight, then *The Tempest* can be called his most delicate and final disclosure of the essential difference between speech and communication, for one very resonant level of the language of this play reverberates with the changes upon this theme. And besides, these resonances are echoed at other levels of the play.

The trouble with language is that it becomes almost powerless when confronted by miracle. There is no stinting of miracles in *The Tempest*, nor of directing our attention to them. Miranda, as her name signifies, "will outstrip all praise, / And make it halt behind her," and she herself tells Ferdinand:

> Nor can imagination form a shape
> Besides yourself to like of.
> (III.i.56-7)

and concludes that in saying so she "prattles too wildly." The events likewise beggar description and confound reason. Gonzalo comments on this most frequently:

> But for the miracle,
> I mean our preservation, few in millions
> Can speak like us.
> (II.i.6-8)

and later he speaks again of the "rarity" of their garments being dry. At the final disclosure of Prospero's power, it is again he who calls for it to be "set down with gold on lasting pillars." (V.i.207) And Gonzalo, like Polonius, is a man never at loss for words, a "spendthrift of his tongue," as Antonio maliciously characterizes him. (II.i.24) The Boatswain, another man not at a loss for words is also caught short before the final revelation:

> *Gonz.*   Now, blasphemy,
> That swear'st grace o'erboard, not an oath on shore?
> Hast thou no mouth on land?
> (V.i.218-20)

197

The "high miracle" of the ending, of course, taxes language (and therefore reason) most heavily:

> *Gonz.*   Whether this be
> Or not be, I'll not swear. . . .
> *Prosp.*   I perceive these lords
> At this encounter do as much admire
> That they devour their reason, and scarce think
> Their eyes do offices of truth, their words
> Are natural breath.
>
>   (V.i.122-3, 153-7)

Alonso can think of only one kind of pronouncement which could adequately encompass the marvel:

> This is as strange a maze as e'er man trod,
> And there is in this business more than nature
> Was ever conduct of. Some oracle
> Must rectify our knowledge.
>
>   (V.i.242-5)

and although Prospero advises him not to "infect his mind with beating on / The strangeness of the business" and promises him that all will shortly be explained and "seem probable," he never fulfils his promise, at least within the compass of the play.

The irony of language, the product and instrument of reason, in the face of miracle, touches bottom at several places in the play, most amusingly in Gonzalo's description of his Utopian kingdom, which betrays even to his unsympathetic critics the inability of language to encompass the paradoxes of ideality: "The latter end of his commonwealth," laughs Antonio, "forgets the beginning." (II.i.154) And with a characteristically clever touch, Shakespeare deflates with a douche of common sense the idea of language as a miracle. As Miranda speaks, Ferdinand exclaims:

>   My language? Heavens!
> I am the best of them that speak this speech
> Were I but where 'tis spoken.
>
>   (I.ii.429-31)

But this is just after Miranda has insisted that she is "No wonder" (428), just as Prospero's retort to her " 'Tis a spirit" is:

> No wench, it eats and sleeps, and hath such senses
> As we have, such.
>
> (I.ii.413-4)

That "wench"! To drive the limits of language home, the scene just mentioned receives a parodic treatment in Stephano's first encounter with Caliban:

> This is some monster of the isle with four legs, who hath got, as I take it, an ague. Where the devil should he learn our language?
>
> (II.ii.64-7)

Later he is properly disillusioned:

> He's in his fit now and does not talk after the wisest. He shall taste of my bottle. . . . Come on your ways; open your mouth; here's that which will give language to you, cat.
>
> (II.ii.72-3, 81-2)

There are many miraculous things in the play—but language, *ipso facto,* is not one of them.

In fact, in *The Tempest* there are many instances in which language quite deliberately fails to perform what is required of it. It cannot command. In the storm at the beginning, the commands of the Master are not heard, let alone obeyed, by the passengers, much to the Boatswain's disgust, and that worthy makes short work of Gonzalo's protests:

> . . . if you can command these elements
> to silence and work the peace of the present, we will
> not hand a rope more; use your authority. . . .
>
> (I.i.20-2))

Nor can it educate. Miranda taught Caliban language:

> . . . would'st gabble like
> A thing most brutish. I endowed thy purposes
> With words to make them known.
> (I.ii.356-8)

but he finds words of little profit:

> You taught me language, and my profit on't
> Is, I know how to curse. The red plague rid you
> For learning me your language.
> (I.ii.363-5)

It is not allowed to plead. Prospero warns Miranda about Ferdinand, "Speak you not for him; he's a traitor," (I.ii.461) and when she disobeys him commands:

> Silence. One word more
> Shall make me chide thee, if not hate thee.
> (I.ii.476-7)

and drives his point home at the end of the scene with the final repeated "Speak not for him." Most strikingly, words cannot console. Unlike Sebastian, whose malicious nature will not comfort Alonso, and whose "truth doth lack some gentleness, / And time to speak it in," (II.i.132-3) Gonzalo tries valiantly to fill the void with words, to "shut up the thoughts" of the King. But the response is brutal:

> You cram these words into mine ears against
> The stomach of my sense.
> (II.i.102-3)

and "Thou dost talk nothing to me." (II.i.166) Words *can* narrate, but curiously enough, cannot keep the listeners awake. Miranda falls asleep despite her protest that her father's tale "would cure deafness"; Gonzalo falls asleep to the sound of his own fiction and Alonso follows him at once; Prospero falls asleep every afternoon over his books, and the final story he promises to tell to Alonso is never told. So all remains like the tale Prospero had never told Miranda, "rather like a dream than an assurance."

All the deceptions of language with which Shakespeare has concerned himself over and over again in previous plays reappear in this last play. The power of words to deceive either oneself or others receives mention time and again. Perhaps the most charming and innocuous of these is Ferdinand's:

> Full many a lady
> I have ey'd with best regard and many a time
> The harmony of their tongues hath into bondage
> Brought my too diligent ear.
>
> (III.i.39-42)

but even this is given a serious perspective by Prospero's "the strongest oaths are straw / To the fire i' th' blood." (IV.i.52-3) The ambiguity of language is forced most strongly on our attention in II.ii, where Antonio and Sebastian plot to murder Alonso and Gonzalo, and especially in Antonio's equivocation over sleep and death:

> Say this were death
> That now hath seized them, why, they were no worse
> Than now they are. . . . What a sleep were this
> For your advancement. . . . Here lies your brother,
> No better than the earth he lies upon
> If he were that which now he's like—that's dead;
> Whom I with this obedient steel (three inches of it)
> Can lay to bed for ever; whiles you, doing thus,
> To the perpetual wink for aye might put
> This ancient morsel, this Sir Prudence, who
> Should not upbraid our course. For all the rest,
> They'll take suggestion as the cat laps milk.
>
> (II.i.254 ff.)

Here the imagination is also corrupt and self-deceived:

> *Ant.*   The occasion speaks thee and
> My strong imagination sees a crown
> Dropping upon your head.
>
> (II.i.201-3)

The whole scene is cast in a grotesquely impotent attitude with some of Shakespeare's most curious macabre:

> *Seb.* What? Art thou waking?
> *Ant.* Do you not hear me speak?
> *Seb.*   I do; and surely
> It is a sleepy language, and thou speak'st
> Out of thy sleep. What is it thou didst say?
> This is a strange repose, to be asleep
> With eyes wide open; standing, speaking, moving,
> And yet so fast asleep.
> *Ant.*   Noble Sebastian,
> Thou let'st thy fortune sleep—die, rather; wink'st
> Whiles thou art waking.
> *Seb.*   Thou dost snore distinctly;
> There's meaning in thy snores.
>
> (II.i.204-12)

This scene also finds its parody in the subplot, where characteristically the theme receives its norm:

> *Steph.* [*Gives Caliban drink.*] You cannot tell who's your friend.
> Open your chaps again.
> *Trinc.* I should know that voice. It should be—but he is drowned;
> and these are devils. O, defend me!
> *Steph.* Four legs and two voices—a most delicate monster! His
> forward voice now is to speak well of his friend; his
> backward voice is to utter foul speeches and to detract.
>
> (II.ii.84-91)

Prospero himself is reflected in this comic-profound statement, as he acts the heavy father with Ferdinand, so that even Miranda, who has never known deception, must apologize:

My father's of a better nature, sir,
Than he appears by speech.

(I.ii.497-8)

In the witty scene between Gonzalo, Adrian, Antonio, and
Sebastian, even the language of the poet comes under a rigorous
objective scrutiny:

Adrian. Though this island seem to be desert—
Ant. Ha! Ha! Ha!
Seb. So, you're paid.
Adrian. Uninhabitable and almost inaccessible—
Seb. Yet—
Adrian. Yet—
Ant. He could not miss't.
Adrian. It must needs be of a subtle, tender, and delicate
    temperance.
Ant. Temperance was a delicate wench.
Seb. Ay, and a subtle, as he most learnedly delivered.
Adrian. The air breathes upon us here most sweetly.
Seb. As if it had lungs, and rotten ones.
Ant. Or as if 'twere perfumed by a fen.
Gonz. Here is everything advantageous to life.
Ant. True; save means to live.
Seb. Of that there's none, or little.
Gonz. How lush and lusty the grass looks! how green!
Ant. The ground indeed is tawny.
Seb. With an eye of green in it.
Ant. He misses not much.
Seb. No; he doth but mistake the truth totally.
Gonz. But the rarity of it is—which indeed is almost beyond
    credit—
Seb. As many vouched rarities are.
Gonz. That our garments, being, as they were, drenched in the
    sea, hold, notwithstanding, their freshness and gloss, being
    rather new-dyed than stained with salt water.
Seb. If but one of his pockets could speak, would it not say he lies?

Here the ruthless 'realism' of Antonio and Sebastian has a more
bitter, sardonic undercurrent than, say, a similar scene between

Romeo and Mercutio. But while we cannot side wholeheartedly with the unsympathetic pair, we are struck by the similarity between their view of the imagination and that of Plato, and recollect Shakespeare's earlier description of the poet as one who gave "to airy nothing / A local habitation and a name." The art of Prospero consists indeed in deliberate deception; a feature perhaps most striking in the scene in which Ariel provokes a quarrel between Stephano and Trinculo by interjecting (ironically enough) "Thou liest" into their conversation at certain points.

Language is made to fail in *The Tempest,* fail as a vehicle for meaningful communication. Even the language of a man of imagination is made fun of; and the language of action and decision is felt as "sleepy," sleep-producing, like a dream, with as much meaning as a snore.

But other kinds of communication prevail in the play; other forms of language seem to have more force than the language of speech. The power of paralanguage in *The Tempest* is in fact quite remarkable. The play opens with a cry—in fact the whole first scene is full of cries, so loud that they threaten to drown the other noises of this noisy passage:

> *Boatswain.* . . . A plague upon their howling. They are
> louder than the weather or our office.
>
> (I.i.33-5)

And cries continue throughout the play—cries of pity, fear, sorrow, anger, and finally of wonderment in a series of "O's!" We note that the emphasis of these cries is on their power to move:

> *Mir.*   O, the cry did knock
> Against my very heart.
>
> (I.ii.89)

> *Mir.*   Alack, for pity!
> I, not remembering how I cried out then,
> Will cry it o'er again.
>
> (I.ii.133-4)

> *Prosp.*   . . . There they hoist us,
> To cry to th' sea that roared to us; to sigh

To th' winds, whose pity, sighing back again,
Did us but little wrong.

(I.ii.149-52)

In reminding Ariel of the torment from which he had been delivered, Prospero notes:

> . . . thy groans
> Did make wolves howl and penetrate the breasts
> Of ever angry bears.

(I.ii.287-9)

The responses take the form mostly of gestures, and especially of tears. Miranda's eyes, like Cordelia's, are frequently washed with tears ("Wipe thou thine eyes," says Prospero, almost embarrassed). But her smiling tears take the place of speech, and did so even when, her "crying self," she was "not out of three years old," too young to speak:

Prosp.   . . . thou didst smile
Inspir'd with a fortitude from heaven,
When I have decked the sea with drops full salt,
Under my burden groaned.

(I.ii.153-6)

Ferdinand too is found "cooling the air with sighs":

> He does hear me;
> And that he does I weep. Myself am Naples,
> Who with mine eyes, never since at ebb, beheld
> The King my father wracked.

(I.ii.433-7)

Noise too fills the play, from the "dreadful thunderclaps" and "cracks of sulphurous roaring" of the opening scene, on which Ariel so prides himself, to his "Hark, they roar," as the sounds of the hunt die away at the end of the fourth act. Again, the emphasis is on the power of noise. It is used by Prospero as a threatened instrument of punishment. He informs Caliban that he will "make thee roar / That beasts shall tremble at thy din," (I.ii. 370-1) and the salvage tells us:

> His spirits hear me,
> And yet I must needs curse. . . . but
> For every trifle are they set upon me;
> Sometime like apes that mow and chatter at me,
> And after bite me; . . . sometime am I
> All wound with adders, who with cloven tongues
> Do hiss me into madness.
>
> (II.ii.3-14)

Prospero's comment on the tempest that he has raised is:

> Who was so firm, so constant, that this coil
> Would not infect his reason?
>
> (I.ii.207-8)

Yet the noise, though it is associated mostly with pain and punishment, with tempest and anger, has also a strange power to awaken men to reality. The Boatswain makes quite a point of this when telling what happens to him:

> We were dead of sleep
> And (how we know not) all clapped under hatches;
> Where, but even now, with strange and several noises
> Of roaring, shrieking, howling, jingling chains,
> And moe diversity of sounds, all horrible,
> We were awaked; straightway at liberty;
>
> (V.i.230-5)

And it is the noise of the elements that serves as conscience for Alonso:

> O, it is monstrous, monstrous!
> Methought the billows spoke and told me of it;
> The winds did sing it to me; and the thunder,
> That deep and dreadful organ pipe, pronounced
> The name of Prosper; it did bass my trespass.
>
> (III.iii.95-99)

But noise does not run the range of associations that cries do. Instead, it operates as a kind of polarity against the effect of music. The music of *The Tempest* has been written about before and only two aspects of it need be dwelt on here. First, even in the songs of *The Tempest* we remark that they turn away, especially in the refrains, from logical or lexical words, to onomatopoeic ones: "Bowgh, waugh," "Cock-a-diddle-dowe," "Ding, dong, dell," and so on, as though music best carries cries and calls as it dies upon the ear, or drifts us into dream. The other noteworthy thing is the power of music. Caliban's speech is, of course, famous:

> Be not afeard; the isle is full of noises,
> Sounds and sweet airs that give delight and hurt not.
> Sometimes a thousand twangling instruments
> Will hum about mine ears; and sometimes voices
> That if I then had waked after long sleep,
> Will make me sleep again; and then, in dreaming,
> The clouds methought would open and show riches
> Ready to drop upon me, that, when I waked,
> I cried to dream again.
>
> (III.ii.132-140)

The power of music to work on Caliban is perhaps the most noteworthy of all, but it also hath charms on others; its magical and curative power is remarked on more than once. Ferdinand's first speech remarks upon the music in the island:

> Sitting upon a bank,
> Weeping again the King my fathers wrack,
> This music crept by me upon the waters,
> Allaying both their fury and my passion
> With its sweet air.
>
> (I.ii.390-4)

At the end, Prospero requires "some heavenly music" and commands:

> A solemn air, and the best comforter
> To an unsettled fancy, cure thy brains
> Now useless, boiled within thy skull.
>
> (V.i.58-60)

It is a passage full of the overtones of Lear's return to sanity.

The power, the force of these metalinguistic levels of the play finds its most concentrated focus in III.iii., and the only thing to do is to include the most notable section of that scene here. It makes a striking contrast with the earlier exchange between Gonzalo, Adrian, Antonio, and Sebastian, quoted previously:

Solemn and strange music; and Prospero on the top (invisible). *Enter several strange Shapes, bringing in a banquet; and dance about it with gentle actions of salutations; and, inviting the King &c. to eat, they depart.*

Alonso. What harmony is this? My good friends, hark!
Gonz.   Marvellous sweet music!
Alonso. Give us kind keepers, heavens! What were these?
Seb.   A living drollery. Now I will believe
          That there are unicorns; that in Arabia
          There is one tree, the phoenix' throne; one phoenix
          At this hour reigning there.
Ant.   I'll believe both;
          And what does else want credit, come to me,
          And I'll be sworn 'tis true. Travellers ne'er did lie,
          Though fools at home condemn 'em.
Gonz.   If in Naples
          I should report this now, would they believe me
          If I should say I saw such islanders?
          (For certes these are people of the island)
          Who, though they are of monstrous shape, yet note,
          Their manners are more gentle, kind, than of
          Our human generation you shall find
          Many, nay, almost any,
Prosp.   [aside] Honest lord,
          Thou hast said well; for some of you here present
          Are worse than devils.
Alonso.   I cannot too much muse
          Such shapes, such gesture, and such sound, expressing
          (Although they want the use of tongue) a kind
          Of excellent dumb discourse.

                                    (III.iii.18-39)

The whole purpose of Prospero's "rough magic," "airy charms," music, and shows has been "To work mine end upon their senses" (V.i.53), to "justle them from their senses," (V.i.158) and when he has done so:

> The charm dissolves apace
> And as the morning steals upon the night,
> Melting the darkness, so their rising senses
> Begin to chase the ignorant fumes that mantle
> Their clearer reason.
>
> (V.i.64-8)

It is, of course, something of a paradox, to write a play about the limits of language. In fact, some special words in the play do seem still to have power. Not the traditional power words, of course. "What care these roarers for the name of King?" thunders the Boatswain at the beginning of the play. But Prospero's book is his most treasured possession, until he lays it aside; it embodies moral purpose, and symbolizes effective art, and *his* words of command are obeyed:

> *Prosp.*   . . . but exactly do
>   All points of my command.
> *Ariel.*   To th' syllable.
>
> (I.ii.500-1)

And a single word it is that delays the execution of Antonio's murder plot until Ariel can give the warning. But even the book is eventually drowned; the charms "dissolve," if they do not "crack"; the staff is broken; the magic *is* only rough. What is left? Prayer, it seems. The play begins with a call to prayer; in the middle of the play, Ferdinand wishes to set Miranda's name in his prayers, and the Epilogue passes most movingly beyond praise and blame to a simple plea:

> Now I want
> Spirits to enforce, art to enchant;
> And my ending is despair
> Unless I be relieved by prayer,

> Which pierces so that it assaults
> Mercy itself and frees all faults.

No formulas are given for prayer; it seems to be more a gesture, a posture, than something recited or spoken. For at the core of this last play is a silence more still than any of the silences in the late plays. In the first scene, the Boatswain calls for silence that he may carry out his duty; the spell which the audience casts upon the players at the end is silence; and Prospero's play within the play is brought to life by silence:

> No tongue! All eyes! Be silent.
> (IV.i.59)

Speech breaks the spell; there is therefore no more to be said. After the poetry, which is as like music as words can become, has gone, music and show remain behind, "best comforters / To an unsettled fancy" such as ours:

> Such shapes, such gesture, and such sound, expressing
> (Although they want the use of tongue) a kind
> Of excellent dumb discourse.

If no voices wake us, unlike Caliban we will not cry to dream again.

The Pennsylvania State University

METRE AND EMPHASIS:
A CONSERVATIVE NOTE

HERBERT HOWARTH

"All unnecessary emphasis must be bad emphasis." Kemble's rule[1] came to my mind during an amateur *Hamlet*: an excellent performance by members of two famous colleges, in which half-a-dozen misplaced emphases were the more noticeable because the general standard of playing and speaking was high. Hamlet put aside Horatio's deference with "Sir, my good friend; I'll change *that* name with you"—an emphasis which can be justified but is not really necessary. He remembered his father with "I shall not look upon *his* like again"—whereas "his *like*" conveys the meaning. Claudius shuddered at the news of Polonius' death: "It had been so with us had we *been* there." Claudius succumbed to the lure of the royal "we" and invited Laertes "Be you content to lend your patience to *us*," and so diverted attention from the "patience," recommended by the King in place of that impulsive, mindless drive to action that characterizes Laertes and differs significantly from Hamlet's reflective patience and over-patience.[2]

How did Kemble decide when emphasis was "necessary"? He was celebrated in his time for his articulation of the "poetry" of Shakespeare, and his sister, a champion of his practice, mocked the great rival, Macready, for a naturalistic delivery tantamount, she said, to reducing Shakespeare to prose. William Archer has written that "The Kemble tendency was to take care of the measure and let the sense take care of itself." This remark, not quite self-explanatory, I take to mean that Kemble's first preference, in the study of a Shakespearean passage, was to conserve the regular iambic rhythm; to elicit the beat by shading, with the various subtleties of which an expertly-managed voice is capable, the significant syllables placed where the iambic stress must normally fall; to reverse some feet, of course, practically without noticing it, because the common usage of the language

211

requires it; but otherwise to allow any extra variation of the iambic pattern only where trial convinced him that he would otherwise miss the point.

If the *Hamlet* performers had adopted this procedure, they would not have wrested the emphases in the four lines I have quoted. In all four cases they disturbed the normal iambic pattern. In all four they could have kept the pattern without loss of sense.

In these notes I shall apply the "Kemble approach" to a number of passages: some of them the clearer if the actor respects the iambic stress, one or two of them clearer if the actor supposes that Shakespeare wished a variation, even a wrenching, of the norm.

First, a case where the modern player may be embarrassed if he follows the metre faithfully, yet should. *Richard the Third* is a play which involves, side by side with effects brazenly gratifying to the noisiest taste, other scenes embellished with the "Arcadian rhetoric" and furnished for the admiration of the poetasters in the audience, to whom they demonstrated the author's craft. To a modern audience the virtuoso display sounds as "artificial" in an adverse sense as it was meant to sound "artificial" in a welcome sense to an Essex. But if we are right nowadays to reproduce Shakespeare's stage conditions, we may also be right to try to reproduce his verbal effects, including this. When the sick King Edward rebukes his relations because none of them pleaded for Clarence:[3]

> The proudest of you all
> Have been beholding to him *in* his life;
> Yet none of you would once plead *for* his life.
> (II.i.128-130)

the actor was expected to bring out the antithesis between the prepositions: "*in* his life" and "*for* his life." The temptation to a modern speaker is to avoid stress on prepositions; and while he will be puzzled by line 129 and think it lame, he will find a fatally easy way-out in line 130, that of throwing the stress back to "plead." But Shakespeare often demands a stress on prepositions; here certainly he is attempting a rhetorical grace in the contrast of the two phrases. Approach the lines in Kemble's way, keeping the measure, and the effect is obtained.

"How camest thou hither . . . ?" Juliet asks when she finds Romeo under her balcony. And he, answering her point by point with something, but a less strained something, of the rhetorical organization of *Richard the Third*, tells her

> With love's light wings did I o'erperch
>   these walls;
> For stony limits cannot hold love out,
> And what love *can* do, *that* dares love attempt;
> Therefore thy kinsmen are no let to me.
>
> (II.ii.66-69)

The passage is Romeo's first declaration of love, and "love" is the main word of the passage, the repeated word. It has taken its passionate emphasis in line 66, and rings through the lines. The unhabituated reader may go on emphasising it in line 68. Which will wreck the rhythm. The habituated reader follows the metrics, lightly stresses "can" and "that," and speaks the aphorism as Shakespeare intended it—perhaps with an over-lilting "music," but that is in the nature of *Romeo and Juliet,* and it is better not to better Shakespeare.

The modern eye, rapid-reading, runs over Shakespeare's lines like a muscular schoolboy covering miles of rough ground, jumping from tuft to tuft. The tufts, those apparently firm points on which we momentarily rest, are usually the nouns and main verbs, rather than prepositions and auxiliaries. Sometimes we pause longest, breathe and take pleasure, on words that strike us as colourful, words with strong visual associations, or words that, having become obsolete or changed character, have acquired an interest of which the Elizabethans never dreamed. Often these are not the words that Shakespeare intended to be emphasised. So in *The Winter's Tale*:

> Nor night nor day no rest: it is but weakness
> To bear the matter thus; mere weakness. If
> The cause were not in being,—part o' the cause,
> She the adulteress; for the harlot king
> Is quite beyond mine arm, out of the blank

> And level of my brain, plot-proof; but she
> I can hook to me: say that she were gone,
> Given to the fire, a moiety of my rest
> Might come to me again.

(II.iii.1-9)

In line 7 the eye of the modern reader rests on "hook." But for the speaking voice the preceding word, "can," matters much more. The actor will give "can" its force if he listens to the metrics. He must listen to the metrics if he is to understand the sequence of broken phrases which register Leontes' madness. Leontes is whipping himself up to order Hermione's execution in the belief that vengeance will restore his lost repose. He can't get total vengeance, for Polixenes is beyond his reach; but she who is in his power, she can be slain. The actor must decline the attraction of "hook" and let it do anything it has to do without the help of emphasis, and he must keep the iambic stresses:

> but *she*
> I *can* hook *to* me: say that she were gone . . .

He must also notice that the colon works like a dash and that "she I can hook to me" is not a sentence but a noun: "the-one-I-can-hook-to-me."

At the end of the same scene Leontes is informed that Cleomenes and Dion have returned from Delphos. Returned with most remarkable speed, observes one of the faithful lords:

> So please you, sir, their speed
> Hath been beyond account.

(II.iii.197-198)

Leontes evidently makes an inward reckoning to check that and finds it true:

> Twenty three days
> They have been absent: *'tis* good speed: foretells
> The great Apollo suddenly will have
> The truth of this appear.

(II.iii.199-201)

214

Here again the eye may deceive the reader, skipping the familiar and apparently colourless " 'tis." But the ear will find the force in it: the king's enthusiastic corroboration: "You are right! It *is* good speed."

"Crave" is a word that charms the modern eye with an antique quality. For Shakespeare it is simply the right verb for obedience supplicating power. In *Measure for Measure* when the Duke tells Mariana: "Never crave him, we are definitive" the pressure—all the pressure of that Law of which Angelo professed himself the instrument—is on "him." The emphasis is knell-like. It has already been heard at the moment when the Duke has thrown back his cowl and made himself known. To Escalus he has said

> What you have spoke I pardon: sit you down

but then has turned to Angelo:

> We'll borrow place of *him*
>
> (V.i.366-367)

Angelo hears his fate in the menace of the pronoun. A few moments later the Duke has married him to Mariana, and pronounced his death, and promised her a better husband. She sinks to her knees:

> O my dear lord,
> I crave no other, nor no better man.

and the Duke gives that answer:

> Never crave *him*, we are definitive
> (V.i.430-432)

All this is plain as soon as we attend to it. But when we study with the eye alone we don't always attend. Do we always attend when we read the familiar opening scene of *Othello*? After Iago's neat hit, "You are—a senator," Brabantio says "This thou shalt answer." In a quick reading we probably direct the remark back at Iago. But to do so we put the emphasis on "This." If, however,

215

we read the words metrically, we put the emphasis on "thou" and address the whole line to Roderigo; which is the way to read it, as the next line proves:

> *Brab.* Thou art a villain.
> *Iago.*   You are—a senator
> *Brab.* This *thou* shalt answer; I know *thee,*
> Roderigo.
> *Rod.* Sir, I will answer any thing.
>
> (I.i.119-121)

Brabantio has not recognized his taunter, but is determined some-one shall pay, and turns to Roderigo, whom he has recognized.

At the end of the same scene Brabantio speaks to Roderigo again with a comparable emphasis on the pronoun, but a very different tone (I.i.176). To a servant he says, mobilising kinsmen and friends to hunt Othello, "Call up my brother." Then to Roderigo: "O, would *you* had had her." The actor who is faithful to the metre will get at the force in this exclamation, the lament-able preference—when we come to the test of marriage—for the third-rate local man over the heroic alien.

Of many obvious cases of insistent emphasis on the pronoun I choose one from *The Tempest*. Caliban rages against Prospero:

> I say, by sorcery he got this isle:
> From *me* he got it . . .
>
> (III.ii.60-61)

Even the eye cannot miss this: the inversion brings "from me" to the head of the line and compels the attention. A case where the Kemble method is needed to help out the eye is the following from *Henry the Eighth*. Queen Katharine repudiates her judges, appeals to the Pope, and begins to leave the court-room. Con-fusion: Cardinal Campeius complains to Henry; Henry orders the crier to call her again; the crier's voice rings out, as it has at the pompous opening of the trial-scene. But still she seeks her path. Griffith, her gentleman-usher, warns her "Madam, you are call'd back." To which she says

216

What need you note it? pray you, keep your way:
When *you* are call'd, return.

(II.iv.128-129)

No emphasis on either of the two "you's" in line 128. Emphasis on "you" in 129. A cutting emphasis, which she at once regrets, and utters a prayer and self-reproach:

> Now, the lord help.
> They vex me past my patience.

(II.iv.129-130)

—for she has transgressed the code of patience with which Shakespeare, adopting the Griselda tradition that grew among Katharine's friends and Henry's opponents, invests her. Yet she will not go back: "Pray you, pass on."

Often in drama the dialogue is heightened by a shifting of the emphasis from one point to another, and actor and director may perceive the resources of a passage, or confirm their sense of its dynamic, if they use Kemble's test. In the pivotal scene of *Coriolanus,* that mid-point at which Martius is condemned to exile, there is a shift of stress from abstract noun to personal pronoun, which typifies Martius' habit of rushing from public principle to personal outrage. The tribunes, speaking with the authority of a supreme court, say that Martius ought to be put to death, but—

Brutus   But since he hath
          Served well for Rome—
Martius   What do you prate of service?

(III.iii.82-83)

The actor may want to hurl scorn into that "you"; but it would be premature. The accent is on "service," and there is scorn in the word "prate," since it is the habit of demagogy to entertain and manage the people with words, cheap and deedless. The switch from the general to the personal rage comes a moment later. Brutus draws it upon himself. Angered by "prate," he alters it to "talk," and claims that he knows what he's talking about.

217

> *Brutus* I *talk* of *that,* that *know* it.
> *Martius*   *You?*
> (III.iii.84)

That is a tile-rattling "You" of contempt. And following that shift and soar of rage actor and director will prepare the audience for the same unarrestable upstorm of temper in the last scene at Antium when Martius brushes aside a lord's conciliation and precipitates his own death.

The pivotal mid-point of *Othello* is the extended scene in which Iago drives the events forward with the compulsion of the Pontic Sea, so that, still a servant at the outset, he is the master by its close. He is able to take his essential step on the opportunity of Othello's anger, betrayed by an insistent pronoun (III.iii.35-95). Cassio petitions Desdemona, then at Othello's approach slips away in shame (one of the fatal mistakes in a play in which not merely the protagonist but all his flanking characters exhibit fatal flaws and commit fatal mistakes). Iago, the tactician, promptly exploits the "guilty-like" withdrawal. "I do believe 'twas *he*," says Othello, with the anger of the previous night audible in his emphasis on the last word. Then Desdemona pleads for Cassio. That confirms Othello's observation, and, confirming it, doubles his anger: "Went *he* hence now?" It is the tendency of Desdemona's purity to call Othello back from error to reason—even later when he is far gone into the mad neverland of jealousy her presence almost draws him back to the real world—and the conversation with her gradually transports him; but the very act of obedience to his request for solitude, that very act which transports him, leaves him with Iago and without her saving grace, and Iago, who has tenaciously borne in mind their glimpse of Cassio and the vulnerability implied in his chief's anger, is able—not easily, but with lunges that for a moment or two swing in empty air, baffled, till they suddenly gain purchase—to proceed with the attack.

One of the most marvellous scenes for a Shakespearean actress is that in which Desdemona is treated as a whore by her maddened husband; and more marvellous is its sequel in which she complains of her treatment to the man who, unknown to her, incited it.[4] She tells Iago, and herself, that she cannot even say "whore," still less do the act that would deserve the name. The accents we put on "say" and "do" if we read that prose sentence aloud, Shakespeare assures through his metrical arrangement, positing "say" against "do," "word" against "act," giving each word a stress:

> Unkindness may do much
> And his unkindness may defeat my life,
> But never taint my love. I cannot *say* 'Whore':
> It doth abhor me now I *speak* the *word;*
> To *do* the *act* that might the addition earn
> Not the world's mass of vanity could make me.
>
> (IV.ii.159-164)

At the same time, by a striking experiment, which may spring out of the vehement pleasure of thrusting forward his study of jealousy, a study sparing neither himself nor us, he threads a contrapuntal effect across his emphases: the pun of disgust: "Whore" and "abhor." "Whore" is the eleventh syllable of line 161. A light, "feminine" eleventh syllable is a textbook common place of the Shakespearean drama. But an eleventh syllable carrying a word of this significance! A word the speaker loathes! The key word of the scene! "Whore" stands on the eleventh syllable, a monster on a promontory. Yet it does not take so strong an accent as the preceding "say." It may take a more thrilling tone. The actress must sustain the metre and the faultless innocence of her role by giving full play to "say"; yet she may also exploit the dramatic and metrical riches of the unusual eleventh syllable, wresting from it by the timbre of aversion, or by a whisper, or whatever her virtuosity advises, another guarantee of her purity, and another tribute to the nature of a pure love.

A subsequent speech in the same play shows Shakespeare again exploring the resources of a weighty eleventh syllable—and again a weighty eleventh syllable which is preceded by an emphatically-stressed tenth. One must kill in the dark, one must confine evil to the dark, and when Othello enters the bedchamber to strangle Desdemona, he advances his hand to snuff the taper. But before the light is out, it has spoken to him, almost healed him, another and the last of those moments of near-escape, near-salvation, which occur throughout the play and kindle and then thwart the spectator. He perceives the contrast between the two lights, the one faint, common, extinguishable and renewable, the other lustrous, unique, and mortal:

> Put out the light and then put out the light:
> If I quench *thee*, thou flaming minister,
> I can again thy former light restore,
> Should I repent me. But once put out *thy* light,
> Thou cunning'st pattern of excelling nature,
> I know not where is that Promethean heat
> That can thy light re-lume.
>
> (V.ii.7-13)

In line 8 there is an accent on "thee," as he plays his hand near the flame. In line 10 as he turns to Desdemona the antithesis is heavily scored: "but" is a stressed word, "thy" is stressed. "Thy" is the tenth syllable. After it comes another word "light." Too important a word in the sentence, far too important in a drama that reiterates "light" and "dark," a drama whose light is Desdemona, to be a "feminine" eleventh syllable. Like the other example just observed, it resonates bizarrely between two lines. And yet, in spoken practice, it is the loveliest completion of the curve of the line. This speech is constructed on a system of exquisite vocal curves, triply repeated curves—repeated but modulated: the triple "It is the cause"; the triple "Put out the light"; and the triple "One more." Which curve did Shakespeare intend for "Put out the light" in line 7? Did he say to himself "Pŭt oút thĕ líght," or "Pút oút thĕ líght," or "Pút oŭt thĕ líght"? In line 10 I think he intended "bŭt ońce pút oút *thỳ* light." Did he, in that case, intend "pŭt oút thĕ líght" for line 7? I do not know, but I can say the passage that way with ecstasy. Similarly I do not know whether "It is the cause" should be spoken with the dipping curve, "Ít ĭs thĕ caúse" or with the iambic emphasis "Ĭt ís thĕ caúse." The argument for the dipping curve is the significance of the word "it." The English language loves to adopt a neutral word—"it" or "thing"—and fill its blankness with brimming horror. Othello so loathes adultery—as Desdemona loathes the act and name of "whore"—that he cannot name it. She can, although she says she can't and does it with aversion. He in his mad subjection really cannot. If I were challenged to act the part tomorrow, I would plunge for "It is the cause," in the first line, and would modulate to "It *is* the cause" in line 3; then would follow the dipping curve with "put out the light / and then / put out the light."

But in doing so I should be breaking the Kemble rule.[5] Kemble too might break it. There are moments, every actor knows by instinct and every reader by instinct or teaching, when the rules go by the board. Everything said in this paper can be made to seem absurd by the citation of supreme lines:

> Fortune, good night: smile once more; turn thy wheel!
> (*Lear*, II.ii.180)

But though the *reductio ad absurdum* argument might appear at first sight to demolish my paper, it actually cooperates with the Kemble method. Kent's line, and others which exalt us by their difference from the iambic measure, illustrate Ezra Pound's note that felicity in art lies in a departure from fixed positions: unforeseen, unforeseeable, suddenly-realised departures from the norm.[6] These exceptional felicities, however, are only possible when the position has indeed been fixed, the norm repeatedly struck. A beauty only a little below the greatest lies in the constant plying of the norm. In fact, when the norm is plied with skill to the accomplishment of many varied ends, the beauty a little below the greatest is so satisfying that the classically-disposed mind may prefer it to the greatest.

I promised at the outset to glance at one or two passages in which the actor will decide that the measure cannot be kept. I shall, however, pass over the familiar variations which everyone who has grown up in the English language recognizes and assimilates—and some instances of which, like Katharine's "Now, the Lord help," have already appeared in the quotations above. But it may be worth looking at a case where the measure might be kept without ruining the line, yet I cannot think that Kemble would keep it, since the drama becomes the sharper for a variation. During the storm in *Lear*, the King thinks he has not deserved the general chastisement, which the gods, as the thunder tells, prepare for the perjured, the incestuous, the covert murderer. These with their "close pent-up guilts should

cry

> These dreadful summoners grace. *I* am a man
> More sinned against than sinning.
>
> (III.ii.58-60)

"I" in line 59 means "I am not as guilty as they are. I need not sue for mercy as they must. Or if, as a mortal touched with the faults of all mortals, I must sue, I can expect readier mercy." "I" requires the stress of antithesis. And the actor must bring out the stress the more clearly because Lear's claim is false. He is not more sinned against than sinning. The claim shows that he is still deceiving himself. He is still the egoist dominated by his "I." Men are deluded by their "I"—and by their "eyes," as the play says, exploiting three-dimensionally a homophone which Shakespeare had already briefly used in *Romeo and Juliet*,[7] and Wyatt before him.[8] For once the actor may elect "bad emphasis," and roar or groan the "I" of Lear's mortal error.

The foot in which the Elizabethan blank-verse poets were generally least willing to reverse the stress was the second. Evidently it was felt to be the most sensitive. But when Aufidius denounces Coriolanus to the Volscians—

> He has betray'd your business, and given up
> For certain drops of salt, your city Rome,
> I say '*your* city,' to his wife and mother
>
> (V.vi.92-94)

—the second foot of line 94 is reversed and the measure wrenched: Aufidius wants to rouse the Volscians and justify himself to them, and work himself into the heat of killing.

Coriolanus is a late play, and this liberty with the second foot may seem typical of a liberty with the medium which is often said to have increased as Shakespeare aged and as the Jacobeans took over from their predecessors. But I am not sure that the evolution of Shakespeare's metrics was quite so simple. It was not a movement from a rigid conformity to the norm to an easy negligence. A passage from *King John* shows that the early Shakespeare could be high-handed with his stresses. The King is adjudicating Robert Faulconbridge's suit against the Bastard:

> Your father's wife did after wedlock bear him,
> And if she did play false, the fault was hers;
> Which fault lies on the hazards of all husbands
> That marry wives. Tell me, how if my brother,
> Who, as you say, took pains to get this son,
> Had of your father claim'd this son for his?
> In sooth, good friend, your father might have kept
> This calf bred from his cow for all the world.
>
> (I.i.117-124)

Some variety energises the lines. Not an enchanting variety. Not always purposeful—for the reversed second foot in line 124 is scarcely purposeful, certainly not as in Aufidius' line. But robust. And perhaps the reversal of the third and fourth feet in line 120 is purposeful. John is going to put an irresistible legal argument. "*Tell* me, *how* if . . ." is dramatically right for the assurance of the arbitrator who sees his way clear, and right as a cue from dramatist to audience: it alerts the litigation-mad Elizabethan audience, which took as much pleasure in legal chess as in the Hamlet-Laertes fencing, and invites them "Watch this."

And for an early-middle passage in which lines of a standard metrical pattern mingle with lines of highly dramatic metrical shifts, we can turn to *The Merchant of Venice*, to Shylock's dangerous bargaining with the Gentiles:

> Well then, it now appears you need my help:
> Go to, then; you come to me, and you say
> 'Shylock, we would have moneys': you say so;
> You, that did void your rheum upon my beard

> And foot me as you spurn a stranger cur
> Over your threshold: moneys is your suit.
> What should I say to you? Should I not say
> 'Hath a dog money? . . .'
>
> (I.iii.115-122)

The reversal of the second foot in line 122 is violent. But it is not only to that reversal I am listening, but to the unexpected metrics, the hiatuses and emphases, of 116 and 117, and to the shifting of the word "you" throughout the passage. Whenever Shakespeare forces the metrics across a whole passage as he does here, a dissonant music, unprecedented, awesome, is won. It is possible that in this scene in which Shakespeare first presents Shylock and has the task of registering him for the audience, he is seeking to imitate "Jewish English." But this would lead us into a difficult debate, involving the question whether Shakespeare had ever met anyone Jewish at all, never mind anyone who spoke "Jewish English"; and it had better be left for another time. Yet this is to be said: that Shylock's poetry in this first scene as he stands up against the arrogant Venetians and asserts himself as enemy-victim, is unlike anything else in Shakespeare: dissonant indeed; grand with its glimpse of the shepherd tents of Biblical history, frightening with its sense of the mediaeval ghetto; bleak with suffering and energy.

So Shakespeare was already very free with metre at an early date. He did subsequently acquire additional rights over his medium; between 1604 and 1608 we see them abundantly exercised: two skipping syllables for one short syllable; that occasional vibrant eleventh syllable. But, by and large, he was towards the end more conservative in his treatment of the beat rather than freer. The very real late freedom shows itself in the rush of words from line to line; in the break-up of clauses within the line; in an apparent syntactical obscurity that comes from what is truly the naturalistic pursuit of the thought-processes as they manifest themselves in interrupted speech. This freedom is achieved within the "fetters of form," as people say about the late work of Beethoven. The fetters of the iambic pentameter are willingly accepted, and sometimes carefully-guarded. To the eye certain passages in the late plays are disorderly—exhilaratingly energetic, but disorderly—but to the ear they are subtle and ordered. In that speech of Leontes, quoted above, the sequence that looks so obscure to the eye need not be obscure to the actor if he holds on to the carefully-guarded metrics.

We have come to know too much about blank verse. Familiarity has bred a damaging contempt. As a result of the work of the verse dramatists, then of the continuing and converting work of Milton, and then of the nineteenth-century revival of blank verse for both narration and introspection, we, who are heirs of that popularising success, can all turn out sounds that mimic the masters. We cannot hear Elizabethan blank verse as a revelation. The Elizabethan audience could. Surrey had introduced it only half a century earlier; and his innovation had taken root and proliferated. Blank verse seemed right for the theatre because its absence of rhyme appealed to the Latinist *laudatores temporis acti* and proved right for the theatre by its "naturalness" and its adaptability to the shapes of passionate English. The poets and the audiences of 1590 and 1600 were in love with the unrhymed pentameters. To us familiar; to them a Newfoundland. They ran riot with the discovery, as an age does when a new creative medium falls to its portion. They heard the beat with rapture. Even when the poets and players subtilised the beat, it must have been still a more powerful presence and a greater source of positive, conscious enjoyment than we in our sophistication will usually let it be.

I recollect moments in the theatre when the Shakespearean emphases have been magnificently recovered. At Stratford, Ontario, for example, when *Coriolanus* was presented in 1961. In the third act the tribunes frustrate Martius' election by goading him to an outburst of feeling and betrayal of his real mind:

> *Sicinius*   It is a mind
> That shall remain a poison where it is,
> Not poison any further.
>
> (III.i.86-88)

Sicinius, an equaliser, at once pompous and insecure, prudent and sly, accents "shall," "remain" and "poison" equally, but the exasperated Martius notices the verb "shall," which means "must," a word only to be uttered by authority, and it tells him how the tribunes have appropiated the power from his own class. He seizes on it, echoes it with fulminating emphasis:

Coriolanus   *Shall* remain!
    Hear you this Triton of the minnows? Mark you
    His absolute 'shall'?
Cominius   'Twas from the canon.
Coriolanus   'Shall'!
    O good but most unwise patricians! why,
    You grave but reckless senators, have you thus
    Given Hydra here to choose an officer,
    That with his peremptory *'shall,'* being but
    The horn and noise o' the monster's, wants not spirit
    To say he'll turn your current in a ditch,
    And make your channel his?

                        (III.i.88-97)

The actor reiterates the telltale "shall" and sets it ringing in the ears of the audience. It rings again when Martius is banished:

                  in the name of the people
    And in the power of us the tribunes, we
    Even from this instant banish him our city,
    In peril of precipitation
    From off the rock Tarpeian, never more
    To enter our Roman gates: i'the people's name
    I say it *shall* be so.

                        (III.iii.99-105)

and Hydra yells endorsement

            Iĭ *shǎll* bĕ só, iĭ *shǎll* bĕ só.

Then again Brutus intones "It *shall* be so" and again the people chorus their double assent. In Michael Langham's thrilling version the citizens shouted in unison with swinging hammer-strokes on "shall." Shakespeare put twenty years of stagecraft into the scene, remembering what he knew of the weight of the collective demonstration in Church or at public executions, imagining what the chorus may have done in Athens, forethinking the mass effects of opera or symphony; and he exploited as a means towards the result his twenty years' work with metrics and the taste of his public for the emphatic beat.

University of Pennsylvania

NOTES

[1] The first stimulus to this paper came from a passage in "Some Phases of the Changing Interpretation of William Shakespeare's Plays," an M.A. thesis (Pittsburgh, 1959) by Edward A. Teichert Jr. Mr. Teichert quotes "All unnecessary emphasis must be bad emphasis" from James Boaden, *Memoirs of Kemble* (London, 1825), Vol. II, p. 522, and "The Kemble tendency was to take care of the measure . . ." from William Archer, *Macready* (London, 1890), p. 197.

[2] It is an irony of *Hamlet* that patience, wise and virtuous, works to the advantage of crime (if it be an advantage to the criminal to continue in the possession of the fruits of his crime).

[3] The Shakespearean passages in this paper mainly follow Hardin Craig's text: *The Complete Plays of Shakespeare* (Chicago: Scott, Foresman and Co., 1951).

[4] Othello, IV, ii. This plea to Iago begins at 148.

[5] And I should be ignoring the argument of the stress on "out" in the famous comparable phrase, "Out, out, brief candle!" (*Macbeth*, V. v. 23).

[6] "Art is a departure from fixed positions; felicitous departure from a norm." Quoted from Pound by T. S. Eliot, *Ezra Pound: his Metric and Poetry* (New York, 1917), p. 15.

[7] *Romeo and Juliet,* III, ii, 54-50.

[8] Consider the refrain in the lovely poem "And if an Iye . . .", *Collected Poems of Sir Thomas Wyatt*, ed. K. Muir (London, 1949), pp. 75-76.

SHAKESPEARE IN NEW YORK, 1823-24: THE *MIRROR*, MORALS, AND THE *MERRY WIVES OF WINDSOR*

HARRISON T. MESEROLE

In the early years of the nineteenth century, American popular interest in Shakespeare was at a high pitch. A century of acting his plays on the stage, beginning with an amateur presentation of *Romeo and Juliet* in New York in 1730, had brought all but six of the plays to public notice and had, by the decade of the 1820s, established a round dozen of them as basic repertory for theatre companies in Philadelphia, New York, Boston, Baltimore, Washington, and Charleston, South Carolina. In Philadelphia, for example, as R. D. James has shown in his study of that city's *Old Drury*, audiences in the first quarter of the century could have seen twenty-one of Shakespeare's plays, including 60 performances of *Richard III*, 43 of *Hamlet*, 42 of *Macbeth*, and 33 of *Romeo and Juliet*. In Boston the visiting English tragedian George Frederick Cooke delighted capacity crowds in January 1811, appearing fourteen times during that month as Richard III, Henry IV, Shylock, Othello, and Macbeth and receiving more than $3,600 for his engagement. New York City was no less hospitable to Thomas A. Cooper, Edmund Kean, Junius Brutus Booth, and Charles and Fanny Kemble, principally in Shakespearian roles, at the Park and Chatham Garden theatres in the 1820s and '30s.

For more than a century Americans had owned copies of Shakespeare's works and had discussed, quoted from, and written about them in private diaries and correspondence and in the public press. By 1795-96, the first American edition of the plays and poems had been issued in Philadelphia. Its success and attendant publicity in turn encouraged publishers in New York and Boston to undertake multivolume editions of their own, and had stimulated booksellers in every city and town as far west as Cincinnati and Lexington, Kentucky, to import cheap sets from England which they could advertise for sale in the weekly papers along with the latest novel "by the author of *Waverley*" and the perennial bestseller, Richard Baxter's *Saint's Everlasting Rest.* Individual plays were reprinted also, with the phrase "As performed at the Theatre in Boston" or "At the Dramatic Repository, Shakespeare Gallery" on the title page as sales boosters. Plays and poems were produced in paper-covered "parts" which when cumulated provided for subscribers to the series a complete set of the *Works* at reasonable price (cloth- and leather-bound copies were expensive in terms of 1830 book prices). Dramatic series were published, under titles such as *New York Theatre* or *English and American Stage,* in which Shakespeare plays were featured, and anthologies of the "Beauties of Shakespeare" variety, often handsomely bound in half-calf with extra gilt tooling, were compiled by the score.

For the periodical press, the early nineteenth century was the era of rapid growth—the era Frank Luther Mott calls "epochal" in his *History of American Magazines.* New magazines were founded at an astonishing rate. No matter that most were short-lived: when one expired, another rose to take its place—and its list of subscribers. And Shakespeare appeared as prominently in the columns of the new weeklies and monthlies as in those of the earlier Philadelphia *Port Folio* and *New-York Magazine.* Lines from *As You Like It* and *Macbeth* served as mottoes for *Spectator*-like essay serials. Portions of *Hamlet* underlay episodes in current fiction: in *Whig and Tory: A Tale of the Revolution,* serialized in 1823, the tragedy of the Danish prince was played out by protagonist Charles Jansen and his Ophelia in an American setting. Memorable passages from *Richard III* and *Henry IV, Part I* were offered as examples of the "purest patriotism." Act II, Scene ii of *Romeo and Juliet* was named exemplar of the "noblest and most exalted feelings" between man and woman. Lyrics from *Midsummer Night's Dream* and *Twelfth Night* encouraged myriad imitations from the host of occasional poets who jostled one another for space in the "Apollo's Corner" or

"Seat of the Muses" of their favorite weekly. The story of Lear and his daughters was called up again and again in the moral tales and sketches on "Filial Piety" that were staple fare in even the best of the general and literary periodicals. And of course, in the drama columns that were an important and regular feature of Boston, New York, and Philadelphia magazines, Shakespeare's dramatic art was the touchstone not only for serious playwrights of this and earlier eras but also for the actors and actresses seeking star status at the Federal Street, Park, and Chestnut Street theatres.

In numberless other ways, too, Americans of the era demonstrated their adoration of England's greatest playwright. Manuals of oratory and declamation mined the tragedies and history plays for appropriate passages to serve as forensic models. Literary annuals and gift books, which began their brief moment in American literary history in the 1820s, "selected" lines from *Henry V*, *Julius Caesar,* and *The Taming of the Shrew* to be illustrated by "engravings from the world's principal artists." Itinerant booksellers like Mason Weems of "George Washington and the Cherry Tree" fame found room in their carts for cheap reproductions of the Chandos portrait of the bard, and enthusiastic shipbuilders christened new packet ships the *Romeo* or the *Shakespeare.* Busts of Shakespeare graced theatre lobbies and the foyers of private homes; Puck began a long reign as prince of the public water fountain; and Shakespeare discussion and luncheon clubs by the dozens swelled the numbers of cultural societies that were being established in every city and county in the young nation.

In short, Shakespeare was, if not all things to all men, then certainly premier playwright and poet, teacher and philosopher, master of the heart, limner of Nature, and name to conjure with for Americans of the early nineteenth century. Columbia had added its voices to Albion's choir of worshippers.

Rampant though this Shakespeare idolatry was, it had not completely silenced adverse criticism. Shakespeare was still reproved for his punning, despite Maurice Morgann's rebuttal of 1777. The old cry that the plays did not observe the unities of time, place, and action had been reduced to a whimper by the counterarguments of Dr. Johnson and Lord Kames in England and of Joseph Dennie in America, but the whimper was extraordinarily persistent and was still audible in articles printed in the 1840s. That Shakespeare was a "plagiarist" is the startling indictment to be read in some literary magazines of the 1820s: "It is well known that the bard of Avon made very free with the literary property of his predecessors and contemporaries," announced an essayist in September 1823. However, he continued, "he always made such an excellent use of these pilfered gems, that the theft was easily forgiven; that is, when the exquisite style in which he set them did not so disguise them as to prevent detection." Yet probably the strongest critical voice that remained to be heard over the general chorus of praise was that which objected to Shakespeare's violation of decorum, specifically his "scenes of ribaldry and low humour," and his "monstrous coarseness." Nowhere was this voice more strident than in the pages of the *New-York Mirror* and in the words of its publisher and principal editor, George Pope Morris.

The *Mirror*, which published its first weekly issue on August 2, 1823, and did not expire until 1842, was one of the longest-lived magazines of the era and the most influential literary periodical in New York City during the 1820s. Specialists in early nineteenth-century American literature will recognize George Pope Morris, but for most of us today Morris belongs to that not inconsiderable gallery of figures whose names are forgotten but whose places in the canon of American letters are assured because of a single memorable piece of writing: in Morris's case, the famous poem "Woodman, Spare That Tree." Morris's associate in founding the *Mirror* also belongs to this gallery: Samuel Woodworth we have forgotten, but his song "The Old Oaken Bucket" still echoes in the popular memory.

From the beginning the *Mirror* carried a regular column on "The Drama" in New York, principally at the Park Theatre but after May 1824, at both the Park and Chatham Garden theatres. Usually the column reported programs of the past week, gave news of coming events, reviewed one or two performances with particular emphasis on the merits and faults of the leading actors in them, and concluded with a few sentences of advice for the *Mirror*'s "dramatic followers," the audiences at the playhouse, or the theatre managers. Often the column contained brief essays on matters of taste in drama. On October 11, 1823, after a busy theatrical month marked by what Morris and Woodworth felt was an inordinate amount of third-rate stuff, they complained:

> If the "play-going people," those who are the main support of the establishment, will only patronize *trash,* and permit the muse of Shakespeare to plead in vain—if they will yawn over the Hamlet of Cooper and cry *bravo!* to the buffoonery of [Charles] Mathews—. . . The good old *legitimate* drama is laid on the shelf; not from any wilful fault or whimsical caprice in the managers, but because the public *will* have it so. The same monstrous perversion of taste has consigned to (we hope only temporary) oblivion, the poetry of Dryden, Pope, Parnell, Goldsmith, Thomson, Beattie, Campbell, and a host of others, while the maniac ravings of a Byron are listened to with (generally *affected*) rapture.

Such remarks were sure to bring—perhaps, indeed, were baldly designed to bring—replies from the actors criticized or from local essayists hungry to take active part in "literary" argument, for the volumes of the *Mirror* from beginning to end are full of this sort of bickering, much of it inconsequential and most of it short-lived. But early in 1824, Morris began frequently to find fault with the managers of the Park Theatre and an argument arose that was to last a year and have its most violent moments concerned with Shakespeare's *Merry Wives of Windsor.*

In February Morris complained that the managers were not providing adequate seating for patrons and were regularly overselling the house, so that conditions were unsuitable for proper enjoyment of the plays: "Nothing but the *unusual* attractions of the stage [*Othello,* with Conway and Cooper starring] could have induced us to suffer the uncomfortable *squeezing. . . .*" March and April issues carried notes about insufficient lighting and complaints about the way some of "New York's favourite actors" were being treated. On April 24, for example, in a long review of *Macbeth,* Morris took up the cudgel for R. C. Maywood, whose starring roles, he said, had been handed over to actors of less ability. Maywood was disgruntled and was ready to leave New York, warned Morris, unless something were done. Thomas Hilson, one of the stars of the Park company, replied to Morris's criticism in a long letter which Morris printed in the May 1 issue, adding a paragraph of his own stating that it was not his intention to offend anyone but that "as critics we are bound to point out every thing that may strike us as improper, either in the performers or the managers."

In May, Morris complained briefly about poor stage effects, particularly the ringing of bells in Beaumont and Fletcher's *"Little Thief; or, the Night Walker,* as altered by J. F. Foote, Esq.,"* but apparently mollified by assurances from manager Edmund Simpson that improvements were being made, changed his tune in the issue for May 22 in which he wrote a long article praising Simpson and the Park and deploring recent slender attendance. At the end of the article Morris wrote:

> We should not forget to mention that on Monday evening the comedy of the Merry Wives of Windsor, the Miller's Maid, and other entertainments . . . will be brought forward for the benefit of Mr. Hilson. This gentleman has long been a favourite with the public, and we confidently trust a full house will, in some measure, reward him for the pleasure he has given them during his present engagement.

But the fire had only been banked, not extinguished. In a complete reversal of position Morris sharply attacked the Park in his review the following week. The play *The Merry Wives* was "indelicate," and although portions of it were "calculated to please," it was not the sort of play to be staged in New York. Indeed, "no performance should be produced on our boards that will cause the cheek of modesty to mantle with a blush, and no chord should ever be touched that vibrates unpleasantly on the ears of our fair country women." This objection has been raised a number of times before, Morris added; "I am really astonished that no notice has been taken of it." And he concluded with the admonition, "Look sharp, Mr. Manager, or we shall look sharp after you."

The Chatham Garden Theatre meanwhile had begun its first season in mid-May, and though Samuel Woodworth had written the early notices of that theatre for the *Mirror,* Morris took over that job beginning with the June 5 issue and wrote articles praising the new house, its company, and its managers. The Park was virtually ignored by Morris during June, though he found room for brief notices of each week's programs. On June 26 he wrote:

"Since the publication of our last number, we have not witnessed any performance at this theatre which we think it necessary to criticize." But in reviewing the Park's next-to-last program of the season in the July 3 *Mirror,* Morris was as acid as ever. The principal drama of the evening, the *Fortunes of Nigel,* was "puny" despite "the full exertions of the performers in its favour, and passed off in that sing-song style which similar effusions have generally done." The interlude, however, bore the brunt of Morris's attack: "The indecent entertainment between the play and the farce, we regret to say, was received with peals of unbounded admiration. What must we think of the taste of an audience who would endure, much more relish, such tainted trash?" The Park was to close for the season the following Monday evening, concluded Morris; "we hope, when it opens again, some alteration will be made."

Preparations for the fall season began at the Park in early August, and in the issues of the *Mirror* for that month Morris took occasion several times to remark that individual players, managers, and playhouses had always been treated in the drama columns "with candour and impartiality," and that "if at any time the feelings of any member of the *dramatis personae* have been wounded, it has been unintentional." The Park was still his target, however. On August 28, the *Mirror* printed the usual card announcing that "The public is respectfully informed that The Theatre will open for the season on Monday, August 30, 1824 . . . ," and Morris resumed his attack in a paragraph printed below the notice:

> Now this notice is very well, save the spirit it seems to breathe of monopoly. "The Theatre will open." What Theatre?—Why, the Park Theatre, of course—but there are two establishments of this kind in our city—the above notice would infer [sic] that there was but *one,* which is "The Theatre"—it is very modest, to say the least of it. No, Mr. Manager, your house *shall be* called the "Park Theatre;" and you have no more right to the patronage of the New-York public, than has Mr. Barrere, who comes from the land of Lafayette, "though by your advertisement you seem to say so."

In his notices of programs at the Park during September and October Morris repeated his gibes at "The Theatre," complained that the costumes were dirty, and reiterated his point about inadequate seating and "squeezing," though he praised Lydia Kelly for her performance in *Much Ado*, Mr. Stanley in the *Merchant of Venice*, Cooper in *Macbeth*, and Woodhull in *Cymbeline*. On November 8, however, the Park again staged the *Merry Wives of Windsor*, again starring Thomas Hilson as Falstaff, and in his review of the performance printed in the *Mirror* for November 13, Morris let fire all batteries. To summarize his tirade would be to lose its flavor, so I include it in full.

> The house, this evening, was very thin, and we were happy that it was so, for there is no play in the English language of so exceptionable a character as this indelicate production of Shakespeare. There were very few ladies present, which is an evidence that the females of our city avoid the theatre when this piece is to be represented. The manager ought to be ashamed of *himself,* after the many public objections that have been made to such compositions, to permit them again to be brought forward. When we go to the "temple of the muses," we wish to be instructed as well as amused—we go to learn virtue, and not vice—we go to indulge "useful mirth and salutary wo"—and are we to have our understanding insulted with the buffoonery of the circus, or the slang of Billingsgate?—"Shame on it! oh shame!" Where is the being, possessed of the least refinement, who can sit patiently, and hear expressions from the stage that would disgrace a brothel? Every uncontaminated mind revolts with indignation when they are offered, and the situation of a female of the least sensibility is of the most unpleasant nature, for she is compelled to listen to language and witness scenes from which she turns with disgust and displeasure. Does the manager (for he alone is accountable for this prostitution of the boards) suppose that the American women are destitute of morals and feeling? or does he wish to corrupt their minds by the representation of infamous scenes and low ribaldry? If he does, he is not qualified to superintend an establishment, where, if vice is displayed for hatred, it should never be joined with obscenity, and

some other individual should be selected, who is better ac-
quainted with what is due to that sex whom it is our privi-
lege to protect from insult. We are complaining of a serious
injury to society, and we confidently hope that an enlightened community will assist us to hiss from the stage all
future attempts to destroy the morals of our mothers, our
wives, and our daughters. We heard the coarse laugh, it is
true, of the *groundlings*—they were *delighted,* but it was at
the expense of *decency.* If such pieces as the "Merry Wives
of Windsor" are to be frequently brought before the audience, the theatre will soon become a *public nuisance,* and
we should ardently hope that the *police* might interfere,
and close the detested mansion of *sin and infamy.* The
manager cannot plead, as his excuse, that the public call for
such offensive trash, and his own good sense, if he has any,
we trust, will deter him from offering us another "dish of
this sort." We hope that this will be the last time we shall
have cause to complain of grievances too palpable to pass
unnoticed.

Scarcely pausing for breath, Morris went on to give his estimate
of the actors' performances in the various roles, and though here
his regard for the abilities of Hilson and Henry Placide worked
to temper his fury somewhat in their behalf, it did not protect
others in the cast.

Perhaps there is no man living who could perform the part
of Sir John Fallstaff [sic] better than Mr. Hilson; but this
gentleman's fine talents are entirely lost when employed for
so vile a purpose. The Justice Shallow of Mr. [James] Wat-
kinson was rather too *shallow* to merit comment. Master
Slender had but a *slender* representation in Mr. [John]
Barnes. Mr. [J. F.] Foote's Page was more than a *page* of
errors. Mr. [W.] Ritching's Pistol *went off* with little effect.
Mr. [Gilbert] Nexsen, as Simple, was *simple* enough; and
this is praise sufficient for this murderer of Las Casas. The
rest of the performers were *below par,* with the exception
of Mr. Clarke and Mr. Placide. The ladies of the company
were *not* in their proper stations—they received a good share
of *pity,* but *no applause.*

As a parting volley, to make absolutely clear who bore the responsibility for this extreme violation of the rules of taste and propriety, Morris exclaimed:

> We are either surfeited or displeased almost every evening [at the Park]—and thus goes the season away. Oh, for the days when Cooper managed this theatre!

Morris's vitriol brought no reply from the managers or actors at the Park, but in the issue of the *Mirror* the following week, Morris printed a long essay signed "Z. A. K." with the remark: "On the receipt of the following communication, we were in doubt whether to substitute it for our usual remarks upon the performances at the Theatres or not, but courtesy for the author, whom we esteem as a liberal-minded gentleman, and one who holds a most distinguished rank in society, has induced us to give it the preference."

In its opening sentences addressed to those who would deny actors full social rights in the "present enlightened and refined age," the essay is in sum a full-scale assault on the "ancient bigotry and groundless prejudice" that remain in the minds of those who "assume the character of wisdom and liberality." To convince doubters of the value of theatre, the essayist appeals to authorities from Solon to Napoleon Bonaparte, invokes man's conscience and social responsibility, and analyzes the qualities of the human understanding and imagination. Attention is called to the instruction in morality the stage offers when Shakespeare's plays are performed, and hortatory paragraphs deplore the "absurd antipathy" displayed by some Americans to rewarding "merit and genius, whether called into action upon the stage, on the racecourse, or on the tented field." Those who presume to scoff at actors or playwrights are warned that they do so at great peril, for in so doing they insult "the Creator, by treating with contempt the beings of his make." It concludes: "The wise, the feeling, the high-minded, and the great man, will be above the narrow prejudices that prevail."

After November 20, Morris wrote no more drama criticism for the *Mirror* of 1824. In the remaining issues for November and December the familiar signature "G. P. M." disappears from "The Drama" column, and instead, notices of the Park are signed "B"

237

and those of the Chatham Garden, "A." And beginning with the first issue for 1825, Theodore Sedgwick Fay took over the commentary.

Nor did Morris's indictment of the *Merry Wives* cause it to be withdrawn from New York stages, for it was performed at least six times at the Park Theatre during the next two years and more frequently thereafter, thus continuing its record begun in 1773, of successful production by New York theatre companies.

The Pennsylvania State University

AKIMOV STAGES *HAMLET*

EDGAR H. LEHRMAN

Perhaps the most unusual version of Hamlet ever staged anywhere had its premiere at the Vakhtangov Theater on the Arbat in Moscow on May 19, 1932. The director was a thirty-one year old iconoclast named Nikolai Pavlovich Akimov. He was "responsible for every detail," including the new order of the scenes, the stage properties, the costuming, the entrances, the exits, and the general interpretation.

Akimov's career in the theater had begun in 1922 at the Children's Theater in Kharkov. He then moved to Leningrad where he designed the sets for a 1927 semi-Shakespearean production called *Sir John Falstaff*. A. Piotrovskii and N. Nikitin had created this work from the two parts of *King Henry IV*, but they had added ingredients of their own to make Prince Hal into a degenerate villain and Falstaff into an "idealized, broad-minded democrat." Cuts were made, the sequence of scenes was revised, and the battle scenes were changed into a circus.[1]

The following New Year's Day, a *Twelfth Night* in which Akimov participated had its premiere. Shortly afterwards, he received an invitation to join the Vakhtangov Theater and he moved to Moscow.

Hamlet has long had a special place in the hearts of many Russians. Mikhail Lermontov considered it Shakespeare's best play and Ivan Turgenev once asked whether Russians could not understand the Prince of Denmark better than Danes could, or Englishmen.[2] Thomas G. Winner has shown Anton Chekhov's great interest in *Hamlet,* particularly in the *Sea Gull*.[3] Indeed, *Hamlet* is the only Shakespearean play to have given the Russian language a common noun: *gamletizm* [Hamletism], defined in Ushakov's dictionary as "indecisiveness, suppression of the will by reflection."

It now remained to put *Hamlet* and Akimov together: this was done when Akimov decided to stage the play in 1931. All the ex-

239

tensive resources of the Vakhtangov organization were now his, and he used them lavishly. The actors were given lectures on the English Renaissance, the costumes of the Elizabethan age, the meanings of obscure allusions, and on famous interpretations of *Hamlet* in the past. Mikhail Lozinskii furnished a new translation of the play—the first to be done in Soviet times. Dmitrii Shosta-kovich wrote music for it.[4] An American critic observed that all this was presented on a stage as large as that at the Metropolitan Opera, and that the resources of the production exceeded those of Broadway during its "most prosperous times." No money, no effort, no enthusiasm was spared in the drive for a brilliant pro-duction of Akimov's new conception.

Akimov's approach to the classics was to translate them into "the language of the present-day [1932] theater." Any play ought to be relevant to its audience, but Akimov's own involvement in *Sir John Falstaff* did not augur well for *Hamlet*.

As for the Vakhtangov Theater, it had a certain empathy for a director who would drastically revise the text of classical plays. At about that time, it mounted an altogether extraordinary pro-duction of Schiller's *Kabale und Liebe*. The date of this play was advanced from 1786 to 1803 to show the influence of the French Revolution, and a love song written by the young Robespierre was inserted.

Akimov decided that much existing criticism was not Eliza-bethan at all, but coated with Goethe's nineteenth-century, Ger-man, bourgeois thinking—which had to be removed.[5] All the re-actionary interpretations had to be eliminated, and the Eliza-bethan element was to be restored, in the director's opinion. However, there seemed to be some confusion in his mind between the Elizabethan outlook on life and his own unique interpreta-tion of Soviet Marxism-Leninism.

One can examine Akimov's idea of "translation" in part by his treatment of madness. Relying on Geoffrey H. Crump's idea that madness was comic to the Elizabethans, Akimov sought some twentieth-century Soviet equivalent which would also be funny. He followed Elmer Edgar Stoll's conception that *Hamlet* was a play of intrigue; for the Russian, the play was full of tense dra-matic conflict between the Prince and the King. In sympathy with Lorenz Morsbach's idea that Hamlet was an active character,

Akimov considered the main motif of the play to be "a struggle for the return of the throne which has been illegally taken away" from the Prince.[6] Apparently no one pointed out to him Shakespeare's clear indication that the throne of Hamlet's Denmark was not hereditary but elective (V, ii, 65, 366-367).

Hamlet for Akimov was a play with a message. After all, he considered himself a Marxist-Leninist and such people always stress the didactic element in art. "Hamlet's fate," he wrote, "is the artistic reflection of the fate of sixteenth-century humanists," caught between and humiliated by the clash of the outgoing feudal system with the rising capitalist system. The Prince was both a feudal lord and a humanist, and these elements in him were in constant conflict. At times Akimov seems to be trying to make Hamlet into an Elizabethan facsimile of the conscience-stricken landowner so common in nineteenth-century Russian literature.

Akimov saw the philosophical content of *Hamlet* as a combination of the "poetic expression of Erasmus' thoughts" and quotations from the same author.[7] He therefore changed the text of the play to strengthen his point. A prologue explained Akimov's ideas, told how decadent critics had perverted *Hamlet*, and declared:

> We are showing you today a Hamlet full of the will to fight for the throne [and] his passionate struggle with Claudius; we are showing comic liveliness instead of a tragic carcass; we are showing the triumphant activity of Fortinbras. Through our co-ordination of all the phenomena of the tragedy, we attain our clear-cut objective—the fight for the throne.[8]

Hamlet's advice to the players was removed and replaced by advice for Soviet actors. The ending of the production was as non-Shakespearean as the prologue; Horatio delivered a new curtain line: "How gay it is to live, ladies and gentlemen!" [9]

The essence of various characters was also changed. Having noticed that one dialogue in Erasmus' *Colloquies* dealt with a person who dressed up as a ghost to frighten a priest, Akimov decided to eliminate the Ghost in the tragedy and to play the scene for comedy by having Hamlet speak the Ghost's lines into an earthen jar, *à la* Erasmus.[10]

Akimov minimized the importance of the soliloquies. He considered that they had very little philosophy to begin with, and what there was had been borrowed. So, "O, that this too, too solid flesh would melt . . ." was delivered "in the spirit of a vaudeville buffonade." "To be or not to be" was set in a tavern as Hamlet sits on a table, bottle in hand, and a papier-mâché crown in evidence; some of the lines in that soliloquy are given to Horatio, and the resultant dialogue emerges as a discussion about whether Hamlet is to be or not to be King of Denmark.

Transpositions and extraordinary stage settings were used freely. After the first confrontation between the Prince and what should have been the Ghost, the action shifts to Hamlet's book-lined study. Here he sits reading Erasmus and talking lightly with Horatio, when a gravedigger enters with the skull of Yorick. "Alas, poor Yorick," says Hamlet, and he recites that speech in full at this point. A conversation between Claudius and Gertrude is held in bed. Some of Hamlet's advice to Soviet actors is set in a bath, complete with shower curtain. When Claudius first receives Rosencrantz and Guildenstern, he is wearing his most lavish robes of state for a formal portrait. At one point, the King steps forward and leaves his magnificent costume behind, thus revealing himself, in Alexander Woollcott's phrase, as the "poor little spindle-shanked thing he really is."

Extra scenes were inserted, including a market place and a stag hunt. The Queen knits and servants beat rugs onstage— apparently to show how provincial the court was at Elsinore.

The second performance of the "mousetrap" seems to have been a highlight of the production. The King appears at the top of a staircase (the main setting) and races headlong downstairs followed by a forlorn page boy.[11]

Just as Akimov had removed the Ghost, so he changed the treatment of Ophelia. Declaring that the text nowhere indicates "directly or indirectly" that Hamlet has ever loved her, Akimov sees her relieved of restraint when her brother is away and her father is dead. She attends a ball inserted by the director, drinks too much, and staggers off to drown in a nearby brook.[12] One wonders why no one ever told Akimov before the play was staged that Shakespeare repeatedly states Hamlet's love for Ophelia. (See II, ii, 109-124; III, i, 116-121, and V, i, 292-294.)

The costuming was also quite unusual. At one point, Hamlet appears in a nightshirt with a vegetable in his hand and a skillet on his head. In another, he wears a veil and top hat. Claudius, after Polonius' death, runs around in his underwear.[13] Almost anything was done for a laugh. The only taboos affected sex and heretical politics.

Such a well-publicized production of *Hamlet* attracted considerable international attention. Western critics hastened to Moscow to see it and were on the whole rather generous in their reactions. One German visitor was ready to forgive almost everything on the grounds that Akimov had captured Shakespeare's humor. Of the Americans, Ernest J. Simmons found it a highly successful effort in adapting Shakespeare to Soviet demands, Richard Watts called it "stupendous" and "the best show in Europe," Mordecai Gorelik felt that Akimov had achieved many memorable moments but had tried to do too much, while William Henry Chamberlin termed it "startling, brilliant, thought-provoking and controversial." Chamberlin added that it was "scarcely recognizable as a philosophic tragedy." The English-born wife of Maksim Litvinov also called it brilliant and wrote, in an English-language Moscow periodical, that it was an "extremely respectful and scientific" production. Only one Westerner stated point-blank that he did not like it.[14]

Chamberlin did point out a logical inconsistency in Akimov's approach. If, he said, Hamlet is in no way connected with Ophelia's death, there is no reason for Laertes to seek vengeance against him.

Other *non sequiturs* were pointed out by Soviet critics; on the whole, they were much more incensed by this production than were the Western visitors. For one thing, Shakespeare in Russian is no more novel to a Muscovite than Chekhov in English to a New Yorker; hence the Russian critics were less apt to be distracted by side issues. Furthermore, the Moscow critics were working in the same philosophical framework as Akimov was trying to, and tolerance under such circumstances was both a sign of weakness and a vice.

To change Ophelia's mad scene into a drunken delirium, said one Russian, impairs the effectiveness of Shakespeare's writing by turning an innocent young girl into a giddy courtesan. A second pointed out that Hamlet's desire for vengeance is inspired from beyond the grave in Shakespeare, but that the Ghost has been turned into a fraud by Akimov—a fraud which genuine humanists such as Shakespeare would not have tolerated. Akimov was accused of negating Goethe blindly. Instead of Goethe's tragic, passive and pessimistic Hamlet, Akimov produced a comic, active, and optimistic Prince.[15]

Iuzuf Iuzovskii called the Vakhtangov Hamlet "the most 'incorporeal' Hamlet of all the Hamlets ever to appear on the stage," and compared Akimov to one of Lenin's favorite *bête-noires* of antiquity—Herostratus. A. A. Bartoshevich accused Akimov of staging an episodic production which lacked any infusing idea; the brilliance of individual scenes could not compensate for this basic shortcoming.[16] Akimov was repeatedly condemned for tampering with the text of *Hamlet* beyond permissible limits. The past should not be rewritten, said Karl Radek; it should rather be reinterpreted in the light of Marxism.[17]

Akimov was attacked for the gaps in his own knowledge. I. S. Grossman-Roshchin asked why the influence of Montaigne and others on Shakespeare had been neglected. Emil'ian Beskin deplored Akimov's belief that cultured Elizabethans did not believe in ghosts; he stated that the educated French Pléiade of the same period did. S. Podol'skii observed that Horatio's lines show that he too believed in spirits from another world (I, i, 113-125, 148-156).[18]

S. Petropavlovskii declared that the director had used a bag of formalistic tricks, without content. P. A. Markov too commented on the "inner emptiness" of this *Hamlet,* whereas A. S. Bulgakov stated that the former set-designer had wavered between a passion for unproductive formalism and another for equally unproductive estheticism. Radek belittled the idea that a mere struggle for power ages ago in a distant country could be of any interest *per se* to Soviet playgoers; he felt that the production should have shown how the play was rooted in its times.[19]

The *Vserosskomdrama* (the All-Russian Committee on the Drama) held at least two discussions of the production. At each of them, several critics attacked Akimov for formalism, eclecticism, lack of historical perspective and destruction of the play.[20]

Even the Fricheans were heard from. Their leader, Vladimir

Maksimilianovich Friche, had died in 1929, but the Rutlandite nonsense which he had begun propounding even before the revolutions of 1917 was not yet dead in the Soviet Union, even though it soon would be. His disciples were still at work. S. Amaglobeli believed that to make Hamlet an optimist was "not justified by Hamlet's class nature." V. Vishnevskii charged Akimov with insufficient boldness (!) and still believed the play to be reactionary.[21] Vishnevskii even attempted to analyze Danish politics under King Christian II (1481-1559, reigned 1513-1523) in a missed connection with Shakespeare's play.

All this commotion did succeed in bringing the spotlight back to the play itself. One important question now raised was the reason for Hamlet's procrastination. For Podol'skii, the answer was that the Prince was a feudal lord who, despite his democratic tendencies, feared the masses and distrusted the bourgeoisie. Iuzovskii disagreed, declaring that Hamlet simply had no desire to put the times back into joint. Levidov supported Iuzovskii, but Petropavlovskii seconded Podol'skii; for Petropavlovskii, the Prince was caught in a transitional stage, paralyzed by the fact that he had rejected the old but had not yet managed to accept the new.[22] Hence, as a result of Akimov's production, some very important questions were raised in Soviet Shakespeare criticism —questions that had not really been dealt with in the fifteen-year history of the Soviet regime.

But Akimov's own moment on the stage was over. Even the actor who played the title role later admitted that the profundity, the lyricism, and the suffering in the play had been needlessly sacrificed in Akimov's production.[23]

From now on, the chief importance of this production of *Hamlet* in the Soviet Union was to serve as a whipping boy; one could still argue about how Shakespeare should be done, but there was no doubt that Akimov had shown how Shakespeare should not be done. The Russian was the spiritual kinsman of such great Soviet directors as Meierkhol'd and Tairov, both of whom regarded texts of plays as mere raw material for their own ingenuity. Unlike Meierkhol'd or Tairov, however, Akimov himself was never purged; he even participated in a production of *Twelfth Night* several years later. He has had a fine career since then. When the war ended, he was made a People's Artist of the

R.S.F.S.R. Nowadays, he is the chief director of the Leningrad Comedy Theater on the Nevskii Prospekt.

The Soviet arguments about this *Hamlet* were always conducted within an attempted Marxist framework. Varying opinions were allowed—provided that they all expressed belief in Marxism. Thus, one could still argue over whether the play was optimistic, but one could not argue that Hamlet's main importance lay in his individual significance rather than in his social importance, in form rather than in content, in his psychology rather than in his relationship to Soviet Marxist philosophy with its historical materialism. The discussions connected with the play at the Communist Academy and the *Vserosskomdrama* were the first attempts at semiofficially organized Shakespeare appreciation in the Soviet Union. They were the forerunners of the annual Shakespeare conferences, which would begin in November, 1936, and last until they fell victim to the Stalin-Zhdanov policy of paranoid chauvinism in literature and other disciplines during the late 1940's.

The pattern of Soviet Shakespeare studies too began to take shape after Akimov's *Hamlet*. Instead of stressing originality, the Soviet Shakespeare critics began to stress whatever they considered "correct" in the Marxist sense. The efforts of the 1920's in this direction—especially by Friche and his Rutlandites—had by now been branded "vulgar sociology" and were therefore in the process of being discarded. No positive attitude had yet been formulated to fill the gap. "Socialist realism" was still two years away.

After all that has been said above, fairness demands the acknowledgment that Akimov did make a major contribution to Shakespeare in Soviet society—but not the one he thought he was making. His *Hamlet* was important because it brought Shakespeare back to the Soviet stage with an explosion that still reverberates through the Soviet theater. Akimov's efforts helped revive the interest of Soviet critics in Shakespeare, an interest which Rutlandism had almost destroyed. Akimov also attracted the attention of Westerners to Soviet interpretations of Shakespeare to a degree that had never been seen before and has not been duplicated since in non-Communist countries. This was his positive contribution, and its significance ought not to be forgotten merely because he accompanied it with an "antic disposition."

Emory University

NOTES

[1] Elena Zarudnaya, "Shakespeare in the Soviet Union," unpub. baccalaureate honors essay (Radcliffe, 1939), pp. 15-16.

[2] M. Iu. Lermontov, *Sobranie sochinenii*, Moskva, GIKhL, 1957-1958, IV, 416-417. I. S. Turgenev, *Sobranie sochinenii v dvenadtsati tomakh*, Moskva, 1956, XI, 191.

[3] Thomas G. Winner, "Chekhov's *Seagull* and Shakespeare's *Hamlet*," *American Slavic and East European Review* [called *The Slavic Review* since 1961], February, 1956, pp. 103-111.

[4] Akimov's total responsibility and the lectures he arranged are mentioned in Ivy Low (Mrs. Maksim Litvinov), "Mr. Shakespeare's *Hamlet*, Soviet Style," *New York Times*, June 26, 1932, Section IX, p. 1. His previous career is outlined in A. A. Bartoshevich, *Akimov*, ed. by K. N. Derzhavin, Leningrad, 1933, pp. 63-65, 103. His decision of 1931 comes from N. P. Akimov, "'Gamlet.' K postanovke v teatre im. Vakhtangova," *Sovetskii teatr*, March, 1932, p. 15. Akimov mentions Lozinskii's and Shostakovich's contributions in Akimov, "O postanovke 'Gamleta' v teatre im. Vakhtangova," *Nasha rabota nad Klassikami*, Leningrad, 1936, note, p. 264.

[5] The size of the stage is given in M. Gorelik, "The Horses of *Hamlet*," *Theatre Arts Monthly*, November, 1932, p. 883. Akimov mentions modernizing the play in his "O postanovke 'Gamleta' . . ." p. 141. The *Kabale und Liebe* data come from (Caption under picture,) *Theatre Arts Monthly*, April, 1933, p. 266. The attack on Goethe is in Akimov, "Kak teatr im. Vakhtangova stavit 'Gamleta,'" *Izvestiia*, March 26, 1932, p. 4.

[6] Comparisons show Akimov's western sources, *viz.*: Akimov, "'Gamlet.' K postanovke. . . ," p. 16, and Geoffrey H. Crump, *A Guide to the Study of Shakespeare's Plays*, London, 1925, p. 117; Akimov, "'Gamlet.' K postanovke. . . ," p. 15, and Elmer Edgar Stoll, *Hamlet: An Historical and Comparative Study*, Minneapolis, 1919, pp. 7 and 1; Akimov, "O postanovke 'Gamleta' . . . ," p. 132, and Lorenz Morsbach, *Der Weg zu Shakespeare und das Hamletdrama*, eine Umkehr, Halle, 1922, pp. 99ff. Akimov acknowledged his indebtedness to these sources in "O postanovke 'Gamleta' . . . ," pp. 134, 135, 143.

[7] For Akimov on Hamlet, see Akimov, "'Gamlet.' K postanovke . . . ," pp. 17, 15, and Akimov, "O postanovke 'Gamleta' . . . ," p. 133.

8 Quoted in I. S. Grossman-Roshchin, *"Strashnaia mest'. 'Gamlet' v teatre im. Vakhtangova,"* *Sovetskii teatr*, June, 1932, p. 8.

9 Quoted in Karl Radek, *"Po povodu postanovki 'Gamleta,'"* *Izvestiia*, July 24, 1932, p. 4. Radek himself would be purged in 1937.

10 Akimov, *"O postanovke 'Gamleta'* . . . ," p. 139; Richard Watts, "Hamlet in Harmony with the Five-Year Plan," *New York Herald Tribune*, June 26, 1932, Section IX, p. 6. The dialogue in Erasmus is "The Exorcism: Or, The Apparition." The idea of Hamlet speaking the Ghost's lines may also have been western in origin; when Norman Bel Geddes produced the play in New York during 1931, he had done the same thing.

11 Akimov and the soliloquies are discussed in Akimov, *"O postanovke 'Gamleta'* . . . ," p. 156; Grossman-Roshchin, p. 9; Gorelik, p. 886, and Watts, p. 1. The transpositions of scenes and unusual stagings are mentioned in Lotte Schwarz, *"Hamlet? Zur Aufführung im Wachtangowtheater,"* *Moskauer Rundschau*, June 12, 1932, p. 4; Akimov, *"O postanovke 'Gamleta'* . . . ," p. 127; Alexander Woollcott, *While Rome Burns*, New York, 1934, p. 240; Ernest J. Simmons, "A Russian Version of Hamlet," *Soviet Russia Today*, February, 1933, p. 8; Gorelik, p. 886, and William Henry Chamberlin, "Shakespeare and Flaubert on the Soviet Stage," *British Russian Gazette and Trade Outlook*, new series, July, 1932, No. 10, pp. 252-253.

12 Akimov, *"O postanovke 'Gamleta'* . . . ," pp. 146-147, 149.

13 Schwarz, p. 4; Radek, p. 4; Gorelik, p. 887, and Iuzuf Iuzovskii *"Perecherknutyi Gamlet,"* *Literaturnaia gazeta*, June 5, 1932, p. 3.

14 The German is W. S., *"Der rote Hamlet,"* *Vossische Zeitung*, June 5, 1932, unnumbered page overleaf from *"Unterhaltungsblatt der Vossischen Zeitung."* Simmons, p. 8; Gorelik, pp. 886-887; Watts is quoted in "Elmer Rice Praises Soviet Theater," *Moscow Daily News*, weekly edition, June 20, 1932, p. 4; Chamberlin, p. 252; Ivy Low (Mrs. Maksim Litvinov), "Hamlet 'De-Bunked,'" *Moscow Daily News*, weekly edition, May 30, 1932, p. 3; Ashley Dukes, "Old Style: Experiment and Tradition," *Theatre Arts Monthly*, April, 1933, p. 270, did not like it.

15 P. A. Markov, "'Gamlet' v postanovke N. Akimova," *Sovetskii teatr*, July/August, 1932, p. 17; Grossman-Roshchin, p. 8.

16 Iuzovskii, p. 3; Bartoshevich, p. 100.

17 S. Podol'skii, *"K voprosu o traktovke 'Gamleta' v teatre im. Vakhtangova,"* *Sovetskii teatr*, July/August, 1932, p. 14; I. A. Aksenov, *"Tragediia o Gamlete, printse datskom i kak ona byla igrana akterami teatra im. Vakhtangova,"* *Sovetskii teatr*, September, 1932, p. 20; Radek, p. 4.

18 Grossan-Roshchin, p. 7; Beskin, p. 4, and Podol'skii, p. 14.

19 S. Petropavlovskii, *"Sotsial'nye korni gamletizma. (K postanovke teatrom Vakhtangova 'Gamleta' Shekspira.),"* *Staryi bol'shevik*, January/February, 1933, p. 204; Markov, p. 16; A. S. Bulgakov, *"Shekspir na russkoi stsene,"* in anthology *Vil'iam Shekspir: Zhizn' i smert' korolia Richarda III.*, Leningrad, Leningradskii bol'shoi dramaticheskii teatr im. Maksima Gor'kogo, 1935, p. 24, and Radek, p. 4.

[20] Anon., *"Pervyi disput o 'Gamlete' v teatre im. Vakhtangova,"* *Literaturnaia gazeta,* June 3, 1932, p. 4; Anon., *"Sniata-li problema gamletizma (diskussiia o 'Gamlete' v komakademii),"* *Literaturnaia gazeta,* June 12, 1932, p. 3, and Anon., *"Dokladchik byl prav,"* *Literaturnaia gazeta,* June 12, 1932, p. 3.

[21] Anon., *"Pervyi disput . . . ,"* p. 4, and Vsevolod Vishnevskii, *"O sovremennikakh i Shekspira,"* in anthology *Dramaturgiia,* Moscow, 1933, p. 31.

[22] Podol'skii, p. 11; Iuzovskii, p. 3; Anon., *"Pervyi disput . . . ,"* p. 4, and Petropavlovskii, p. 205.

[23] Cited by Nina Gourfinkel, *"Shakespeare chez les Soviets,"* *Mercure de France,* June 1, 1936, p. 328.